PRAISE FOR
Mystic Nomad

"This beautifully written and brave spiritual memoir is a powerful exploration of the human heart and mind. It is the rare and raw account of a woman's liberation from her culture, role, and expectations into a life of purpose, meaning, and great compassion. It is a must-read for anyone on the path of awakening."

—**ROSHI JOAN HALIFAX**, abbot, Upaya Zen Center; author of *Standing at the Edge: Finding Freedom Where Fear and Courage Meet*

"Sharply intelligent, tenacious, and unsparing, this extraordinary account of Knopp's spiritual awakening proves that the willingness to confront our most menacing shadows—with open eyes and a tender heart—can ignite our greatest illumination. Her wisdom is hard-earned, grounded, and profoundly feminine in its scope and inclusivity, the testament of a thoroughly modern woman determined to penetrate life's deepest truths and unwilling to settle for easy answers. This is an indispensable book for seekers of all backgrounds, disillusioned by the spiritual marketplace, and drawn to an integrated path of self-knowledge inseparable from nature itself. A remarkable achievement."

—**MARK MATOUSEK**, author of *Sex Death Enlightenment: A True Story*

"Whether new to the spiritual path or a seasoned practitioner, you will find wisdom and allyship in these pages. *Mystic Nomad* is an essential offering to the rapidly emergent canon of breakthrough literature on feminine empowerment and spirituality in the twenty-first century. Not to be missed!"

—**SARAH DREW**, author of *Gaia Codex*

"Impossible to put down, *Mystic Nomad* is a riveting page-turner. Knopp skillfully weaves her hard-earned wisdom about healing from trauma into this brave and honest tale of profound spiritual awakening. In this quintessential tale of one woman's struggles to bridge the transcendent and the everyday, she illuminates the path to wholeness and a free heart for all of us."

—**TRUDY GOODMAN, PHD**, founder of InsightLA

"As you read this remarkably honest and luminous book, you will embark upon the heroine's journey in its depth, darkness, light, and continuing liberation. A true tale of the feminine descent to ultimately retrieve and know the ultimate spiritual wisdom of living on and with this Earth in all of its beauty and horror."

—**MEGHAN DON**, author of *Feminine Courage*

"*Mystic Nomad* masterfully weaves the author's inner and outer journeys together. As Knopp traverses the globe—encountering teachers, guides, sages, and companions—inspiration and disappointment take turns guiding her path. Though often self-critical, she gradually discovers self-love and the call to serve others. A beautifully written and riveting spiritual travelogue that kept me captivated from beginning to end."

—**DAVID NICHTERN**, author of *Awakening from the Daydream*; founder of Dharma Moon Inc. and Strawberry Moons Media

"*Mystic Nomad* is the tale of a seeker who has found her way home, and generously illuminates the path for kindred spirits to follow. It does so with honesty and emotional depth, facing deep grief, violence, and systemic injustice with the same candor with which it celebrates intimacy, love, and transcendence. Most importantly, it embraces the paradox at the heart of humanity: that we can at once be luminously whole in our essence, and so exquisitely vulnerable. An important contribution for those wanting to traverse spiritual life with their eyes and hearts wide open."

—**FABIANA FONDEVILA**, author of *Where Wonder Lives: Cultivating the Sacred in Your Daily Life*

"In this tender, personal read, Knopp has given us a gift. Within *Mystic Nomad*, you will find an intimate invitation—like a conversation with a close friend, you are called to sit with your innermost self. Not only does she courageously lean into the struggles of this human life, she provides a powerful tether to a sense of meaning that coexists with the complexities of this human experience."

—**ARIELLE SCHWARTZ**, author of *The Post-Traumatic Growth Guidebook* and *The Complex PTSD Workbook*

"An open and honest look at the life of a true spiritual seeker. Wondrously detailed and inspiring. I recommend it to anyone looking for a deep connection with a fellow soul on her journey to awakening."

—**MELISSA MYŌZEN BLACKER, RŌSHI**, guiding teacher, Boundless Way Zen Temple

"*Mystic Nomad* invites us to open to the deep nature of who we truly are. On the surface, we are shaped by the experiences with our parents, our teachers, our culture—and this compelling memoir reveals those forces at work in an unforgettable personal journey of discovery, healing and liberation. But Annette Knopp takes us beneath these common cultural clinging lessons of an illusion of separation and certainty, ones that tell us we are noun-like entities, and into the truth and freedom to live fully present with the verb-like emergence of our deeply interwoven identity, part of a larger whole of all of nature. The personal becomes the universal in these wise and poetic reflections on an awakened life. What a gift for us all."

—**DANIEL J. SIEGEL, MD**, founder, Mindsight Institute; *New York Times* bestselling author of *Mindsight*

"...a nuanced exploration of diverse spiritual paths and a riveting narrative of a seeker's fraught efforts to find peace."

—***PUBLISHERS WEEKLY***

"...an eloquent examination of the timeless search for meaning amid the inevitable pains and joys of life."

—***KIRKUS REVIEWS***

mystic nomad

A WOMAN'S WILD JOURNEY
TO TRUE CONNECTION

Annette Knopp

BOOK PUBLISHING COMPANY
RHINEBECK, NEW YORK

This memoir is a truthful recollection of actual events in the author's life. But in order to maintain the anonymity of friends, family, teachers, and past acquaintances, in some instances the author has changed the names of people and places, as well as some identifying characteristics and details such as physical properties, occupations, and places of residence.

Content warning: This book deals with rape and sexual assault. The author has taken great lengths to ensure the subject matter is dealt with in a compassionate and respectful manner, but it may still be troubling for some readers. Discretion is advised.

Paperback ISBN 9781958972977
eBook ISBN 9781958972984

Library of Congress Cataloging-in-Publication Data

Names: Knopp, Annette author
Title: Mystic nomad : a woman's wild journey to true connection / Annette Knopp.
Description: Rhinebeck, New York : Monkfish Book Publishing Company, [2025] | Includes bibliographical references.
Identifiers: LCCN 2025022766 (print) | LCCN 2025022767 (ebook) | ISBN 9781958972977 paperback | ISBN 9781958972984 ebook
Subjects: LCSH: Knopp, Annette | Spiritual biography--Costa Rica | LCGFT: Autobiographies
Classification: LCC BL73.K645 A3 2025 (print) | LCC BL73.K645 (ebook) | DDC 204/.22092 [B]--dc23/eng/20250625
LC record available at https://lccn.loc.gov/2025022766
LC ebook record available at https://lccn.loc.gov/2025022767

Cover painting: "Neither Day nor Night" by Jane Martin
Book and cover design by Colin Rolfe

Monkfish Book Publishing Company
22 East Market Street, Suite 304
Rhinebeck, New York 12572
(876) 876-4861
monkfishpublishing.com

To Stephan
For walking by my side

Acknowledgments

This book wouldn't have come into existence without my ancestors and parents, who gifted me with this life in form. Deep gratitude as well to the formless life that didn't allow me to give up on myself in the darkest of times.

Immense appreciation for my husband Stephan, who never faltered in his love and support while reading my countless (first, second, third ... I lost counting!) shitty drafts and for enriching my life in the last twenty-plus years.

A deep bow of gratitude for the priceless teachings and practices I have been able to absorb through the wisdom and generosity of Sri Ramana Maharshi, Tenzin Wangyal Rinpoche, Tsoknyi Rinpoche, and the Q'ero elders.

So much love for my ever-steadfast soul sisters in this life; Lydia, Gisela, Catrin, Suma—for keeping it tender and fierce, beautiful and real. Much gratitude for my first mentor Ilse, my big sis Claudia, deep friend Jane and the many other dharma sisters and brothers, colleagues and clients whose names may not appear here but whose presence have profoundly shaped both this work and my path.

To Mother Nature, all her sacred forces, and my sweet furry companions who continue to nourish my heart with beauty.

While writing is an act of precious solitude, my writing voice wouldn't have blossomed without the exquisite guidance of my editor Alice Peck (working with you felt like a match made in heaven) and the enthusiastic encouragement of Mark Matousek.

I am forever grateful to the amazing team at Monkfish Publishing: the founder Paul Cohen for being a true Mensch and supporter of seekers, and my wise editor Jon M. Sweeney for his heartfelt and collaborative spirit.

And to you, the reader—this book is for all the brave souls thirsty for finding freedom in limitation and living from a deeper love and understanding.

Contents

PART THREE
RETURN

PART FOUR
WHOLE

The spiritual teacher Ram Dass once said, "I am explicitly making my life a teaching by expressing the lessons I've learned so it becomes a map for other people. Everybody's life can be like that if they choose to make it so, choosing to reflect on what they've been through and share it with others."

In that sense, my humble wish is that the insights, trials, and tribulations of my quest for true connection offered in the following pages may contribute in some ways to your own awakening, remembrance, and repair.

Each of us is needed. We all affect each other. Everything is interrelated.

Preface

Since death is certain, but the time of death is uncertain, what is the most important thing?
PEMA CHÖDRÖN

FROM A distance, it looked quite innocent—five little German girls with braids and ponytails, dressed in play clothes and rubber boots, waiting, skipping, lurking as children do.

We had been in front of the closed gate for a couple of hours when the shiny black hearse arrived. It stopped quietly, the driver's door opened, and a cleanshaven man in an impeccable dark suit emerged from the vehicle and walked toward the back entrance of the cemetery. Behind the gate ran a smooth paved road framed on both sides by neat plots with gravestones, shrubs, and flowers drawing a direct line to the chapel where the memorial services were held.

"And what are you little girls up to today?" the driver inquired, smiling, without slowing his steps.

My sisters, two cousins, and I exchanged a glance and then two of us uttered simultaneously: "We are here to see the dead!"

He stopped as a stunned expression crossed his face. Pivoting on his heel to half-turn, he glanced at his colleague still in the passenger seat of the hearse and then turned toward us again. He cleared his throat, then shook his head. "No, I am afraid that is not possible."

We had expected an answer like this and took it as the signal to ramp our request up a notch. Jumping up and down on the spot to underline our demand, we started hollering in unison, "We want to see the dead! We want to see the dead!"

The driver looked understandably aghast. Who would expect a group of little girls between the ages of five and nine to express so unapologetically this rather morbid wish? For us, it seemed natural, though, since none of us had ever seen a human corpse, not on TV or in real life. I cannot say with certainty if it was one of my cousins, the oldest of us, or if it was me, seven at the time, who had come up with the idea to ambush a hearse.

The man got back into the car and after what seemed a long discussion with his colleague, both men emerged, progressed to the back, and opened the panel. The driver gave us a serious look: "But this needs to remain a secret between us, you understand? None about this to your parents!"

With wordless, eager nods we sealed the pact, and craning our necks, moved closer.

The men pulled out a light-brown wooden casket, opened the hinged lid and revealed a peaceful looking man in his seventies or eighties dressed in a starched white button-down shirt and fine black cardigan. His hands were clasped, resting on his belly as if in silent prayer. I am pretty sure some of our mouths fell wide open as my curiosity was satisfied.

Back then the image of the lifeless but tranquil body seemed to confirm what I had hoped to believe about death. From the priests in mass and my father I had heard a lot about hell and heaven, and the mere mention of a realm where "bad souls" were purged in an eternal fire stoked by the devil terrified me. But whenever I had given it further thought it hadn't made much sense that "*der liebe Gott*," the dear Lord, to whom I prayed every

Sunday in church, at meals and bedtime, and with whom I maintained lengthy daily conversations in my head, could be so mean or unforgiving. Even though I tended to believe my dad without reservation, one glance at the figure with the serene face in the casket seemed to confirm that dying was nothing to fear. *It looks like falling asleep!*

As a girl and even a young woman, I had no clue what it meant to feel safe in my body. I believe this compelled my psyche from early on to look for some kind of haven, a way out of pain and confusion; I was born with a seeker's heart and mind. For as long as I can remember, I had an unshakable, nagging urge to pierce through the layers of the known and familiar to realize the underlying truth of existence. In cultures with predominantly materialistic views of reality, seekers tend to become the unwilling misfits, the odd ones out, the loners, or outcasts who, as Swami Satchinanda put it, need to swim against the stream to reach the source. The fact is, whenever strangers ask me how I got to do or be where I am today, I hear myself answering, "An equal portion of hefty suffering and incessant yearning to understand who I am and what this life is all about."

My first brush with physical mortality happened around the age of nine. On a hot-humid summer afternoon my friend Anneliese dragged me to a *Freibad,* one of Germany's many public open-air pools. The penetrant smell of sun lotion hung heavy in the air, and the sprawling lawn around the water was crowded with noisy teenagers, mothers and crying infants, retirees playing boccia or dozing off in the shade under the trees. I remember how awkward and exposed I felt, clad in my bathing suit, but laying face downward allowed me at least to bury my face in my towel.

Anneliese on the other hand, flaunting a little bikini, was giddy about drawing the attention of older boys.

"Come on, Annette, let's go and take a dip. I'm hot!"

"No, go by yourself. I want to stay here," I mumbled without lifting my head.

"Don't be a spoilsport! Why did you even come if you don't want to swim?"

My body stiffened. I knew it was useless to remind Anneliese of how she had threatened me with ending our friendship if I had not accompanied her that afternoon. The reality was, I loved to swim and float in water, just not with all that racket and so many people around.

"Okay," I groaned. I pushed myself up and, dragging my feet, followed her.

A narrow concrete walkway divided the pool into two basins: one barely a foot deep filled with toddlers wearing inflated sleeves splashing around, and a much larger, deeper part for adolescents and grown-ups to frolic and cool off or practice breaststroke and crawl in two separate cordoned-off lanes. Enthroned high above, surveilling the jam-packed scene was a handsome young lifeguard in matching white shorts, polo shirt, and cap.

Anneliese steered us straight toward the concrete pad between the basins where packs of pubescents were wiggling skin-to-skin or jumping into the water. I am not sure why Anneliese felt she needed us to be in the midst of it all, and I had opened my mouth to ask, when another body pushed full force into mine from behind; I lost my footing. It happened so abruptly; I couldn't exercise any control over the trajectory of my fall. I only heard a loud "thong" as my skull collided with the poolside, sensed for a split second a sharp pain in my head, and then an almost blissful oblivion overtaking me, blurring the images and sounds of the last air bubbles escaping my mouth and nose as I sank gently as a stone downward into an all-enveloping, softening darkness.

I have no clue how long I was unconscious or underwater. Upon opening my eyes again, I couldn't piece together what had happened or why the lifeguard's face was hovering so close to mine. He smiled, relieved, mumbling "Just got you out in time," while I felt defenseless and embarrassed about laying so hapless on the ground surrounded by a crowd of staring strangers. Yet, even later, I wasn't happy or grateful about having been saved, but rather deflated by being brought back into this world.

DEATH KEPT close, and the wider tentacles of impermanence drew me in exactly on my sixteenth birthday. By this time, I had gained more of a sense of self-agency and a natural zest for experience. I was standing in my family's backyard, immersed in the buzz of humming bees and the scent of freshly mowed grass as I waited with impatience for my mother to drive me into town to connect with friends. Out of the blue, it struck me that my life was moving fast toward an eventual yet unavoidable ending. Worse than coming to grips with my mortality was the realization that everything around me—the vibrant beauty, all the things I loved—would sooner or later perish and disappear. *This can't be—God must have made a terrible mistake.*

Fear and helplessness churned my stomach, and the pain of all the potential losses edged into my heart. Right there I vowed: *I will do everything in my power to live to the fullest. I will not settle for a mediocre contentment, let alone for the unhappiness I witnessed at home. I want to devour and know the world before I die.*

Equipped with that potent mix of grandiosity and naiveté which perhaps only teenagers can conjure, I believed by gulping down life in heaps and chunks I could avert the dread of impermanence. As unrealistic as this was, it served as a compelling reminder to not waste my time. That urgency brought with it an often unhelpful attitude of impatience, but it also fueled a disposition of staying open and curious, paired with the willingness to bear with the fears and failures which become natural companions when taking what mythologist Joseph Campbell called "the left-hand path."

We heed an inaudible call while moved by an ineffable moment-to-moment flow that makes no sense to the formulas of conventional society or scripts in our conceptual mind. This principle, which Campbell described as following "your bliss," is often grossly misunderstood as a life of pleasure or instant gratification—but it's not that simple. Instead, it's a way of living with little security and many risks, more focused on inner rewards than outer recognition.

I BELIEVE having death sitting on my shoulder was one of the key factors in dropping my studies of piano and voice at twenty-one. My favorite pianist had always been the Polish-born American Arthur Rubinstein, whose two-volume autobiography I had devoured in my teens. In it, Rubinstein not only recounted his musical beginnings and decades-long career in global concert halls, but also portrayed his extraordinary appetite for life. I admired his fluency in eight languages and his elation in mingling among cosmopolitan social spheres and artists of his time, relishing every invitation to sophisticated culinary feasts during his travels.

Disillusioned by what I judged to be a stuffy, nerd-like, and close-minded atmosphere at the conservatory in my hometown, and feeling I was being trained to become a mere instrumentalist instead of a musician, compounded my belief I was heading in the wrong direction. Trying numerous times to discuss the issue with my parents, my suggestion I'd be better suited to studying to become a film or theater director fell on deaf ears. The idea of me quitting the conservatory was unthinkable to my mother. Not out of care for my musical journey, but because she would lose the opportunity to tell her social circle that her daughter is "studying to become a pianist"—a phrase that seemed to elevate her own status. Already the odd one out at home and feeling trapped in a box that was not mine, I bolted. Without my family's knowing, I quit the conservatory and began working three jobs at once—in a shoe factory and copy shop, as well as waitressing late nights—to save money. The plan was no longer to leave my studies, but my country and the mainstream culture altogether.

Shortly after my twenty-first birthday, accompanied by a girlfriend who had long wanted to ditch her assistant job at a medical clinic, I boarded a four-and-a half-hour flight from Frankfurt to the Canary Island of Lanzarote in Spain, eighty miles off the coast of North Africa. I had only basic Spanish language skills, a two-week holiday rental apartment, and the intention to find—despite lacking a residence or work permit—a job and an inexpensive place to live before I ran out of money.

Despite my mother's loud protests and my father's heartbreaking threat—*If you leave now, you don't ever have to come back*—I took my first step onto the left-hand path.

PART ONE
The Unwalked Path

Too many dare not explore
to draw closer and quest for what
lies beyond our mere bones and flesh

and, civilized society does its utmost
to numb our urge to feel what it takes
to come alive and surf the edge

it's not worth the venture
God forbid, you could get lost
play it safe, don't look over the hedge

truth be told—sticking out our neck
to enter the woods at the darkest place
where none have yet been

is unnerving and frightening at best
it's the unwalked path that doesn't reveal
where it may lead or what to expect

still—the wide-open road, the horizon without end
unravel our mind's knots and delusions
unveiling our own beauty and depth

without daring to question and inquire
nor meeting and melting into the fire
of our griefs and fears, we'll never know true love

and worse, missing aliveness and spirit itself
our burial may likely be shallow
and death will find us full of regrets

chapter 1

Stripping the Layers

We have allowed ourselves very little space for not-knowing.
Very seldom do we have the wisdom not-to-know,
to lay the mind open to deeper understanding.
STEPHEN LEVINE

EIGHT YEARS later in India, I stared into the dark-brown eyes of a young Asian woman who sat cross-legged on her black cushion opposite me. We had never met before, but neither of us uttered a word. No "What's your name? Where are you from? What brought you here?"

Pearls of sweat coalesced into tiny trails that ran down the back of my neck and India's humid heat made my skin itch in ever-changing spots, yet I didn't dare scratch. The sound of a gong reverberated through the stark white walls of the loft-like meditation hall on the top floor of the two-story pyramid-shaped building. There was a last ruffling of our maroon robes—the ashram's obligatory clothing—then the straightening of backs, adjusting of legs. The gong signaled the start of a new round of an inquiry process that consisted of repeatedly asking and answering the same question: Who is in?

We were all participants in the ashram's "enlightenment-intensive" program, and we had been uttering this question back and forth with our ever-changing partners for two days now. From five-thirty in the morning until ten at night we kept at it, with only silent meals, bathroom breaks, and a few hours of sleep offering reprieve. By now I felt reduced to an insignificant dot, a tiny island in a sea of fifty participants, erect or slumping on black zafus, engrossed in their process of quizzing or responding to the stranger facing them.

In the beginning, my words had bubbled and fizzed. "I am from Germany, but I don't miss my country at all; I haven't even talked to my mother in months. I feel emotionally more connected with Spain, where I lived for the last eight years," or "I dropped out of the Conservatory of Music but studied in Madrid and worked as a simultaneous translator and interpreter for lawyers and economists," and "I am twenty-nine, and just broke up with my Spanish boyfriend Sergio. I have no clue what my future holds..." After over twenty iterations of this inquiry process, I circled down to more sensitive layers, like disclosing how I often felt sad for inexplicable reasons.

In the afternoon of our second day, I allowed the question to sink into me, waiting and listening for what wanted to come up. "Who is in? Well, actually...I don't really know!" I countered. "I guess I no longer understand the question." *Is there an answer that can resolve this and bring the inquiry to an end?*

I sighed, exasperated, then gazed intently into my partner's eyes, as if I could find the solution there, but she followed our group leader's instructions to the letter: "No matter what your partner says or does, remain an empty mirror." I couldn't detect any trace of emotions in her face, yet behind her dispassionate expression I sensed a steely determination. *Maybe she would show some reaction if I tickled or punched her?* The thought amused me for a moment.

"Who is in?" she pressed again, unfazed. For the first time in two days, I sat mute. Peeling the layers of my familiar self-narrative was grueling, but I felt an intuitive resonance with this process; something beyond words signaled to me that this inquiry was the sustenance my heart craved.

"Who is in?" was geared toward stripping the participants in this "enlightenment intensive" of all the components that comprised our habitual self-identity. We were neither our thoughts or feelings, nor the diverse relative roles that we assumed in daily life—sister, daughter, father, or friend. Nor were we the work we did or the professional titles of nurse, mail carrier, or therapist. We were not memories of a distant past or fantasies about the future. Although we inadvertently attached a permanent sense of self to our transitory thoughts, feelings, and bodily sensations, we would come to see they were not our essence. It was the first time someone had handed me real guidance: "Look into yourself. Contemplate. Don't just believe your thoughts or what you have been told; don't accumulate book knowledge, titles, or trophies; don't believe who you think you are—go deeper than the surface reality."

These instructions conflicted with everything my early environment had inculcated in me as a roadmap to a good life. Even so, I couldn't avoid getting highjacked by intense feelings of guilt for having abandoned my good and secure career or Sergio, my perfectly reliable fiancé, to go to India with no itinerary or plans to return. I had followed my bliss. Was I crazy?

Two weeks earlier on a sweltering afternoon in March, I had arrived at the tall wooden gates of the Osho ashram in Pune, in the western Indian state of Maharashtra. Located in a well-to-do residential neighborhood with lush greenery and parks, the ashram was far away from the busier streets of the city. In my backpack I carried forty pounds of my belongings—a significant downgrade from my wardrobe in Spain that included thirty-plus pairs of shoes. Satya, my yoga teacher, had recommended I come here. Osho was Satya's guru, and during our weekly classes she often quoted his words and read passages from his books.

India hadn't been my first choice, nor did I feel much connection with this Osho who had passed away five years earlier. For one, I found the whole concept of following a guru puzzling. Why would anyone want or need to worship another human being?

Satya's late guru seemed particularly controversial. Born in India in 1931, Osho Rajneesh spent the 1960s traveling the country advocating for free thought, meditation, creativity, and a more open attitude toward human sexuality. I had a faint memory from my teenage years of reading a headline "der Sex-Guru" emblazoned on the cover of a German magazine. At the time I didn't know what "guru" meant, but I was unnerved yet captivated by the accompanying photograph depicting a crowd of people clothed in unadorned red tunics or half-naked, their eyes lost in ecstasy while dancing wildly.

During Satya's yoga classes, I connected more of the dots when a young man who had spent time in a different ashram in India challenged Satya's account of her master by asking, "Why in the world does a holy man need ninety Rolls-Royces?" Satya mostly laughed-off his question, arguing that no one could really understand an enlightened being's motivation or actions. She claimed Osho used the over-accumulation of wealth as a provocation and invitation to question our sense of reality.

Her reply sounded unconvincing, even disappointing, but I cared little for discussions about this or that guru. I attended Satya's classes not for Osho, but for myself. I felt at home with the practices of yoga and was grateful to have found someone who could teach me further. Satya also offered something that was like breathing fresh air: after each class, she invited us to sit on the big plush pillows on the floor in her living room with an unobstructed view of the swirling dark-blue waters of the Atlantic. After brewing a big pot of tea, she encouraged everyone to share their experiences during the yoga practices—whether they were positive or negative. Especially when one of us reported a lot of anger or sadness arising, Satya offered non-judgmental curiosity, even courage and acceptance. It felt radical—not needing to censor my feelings; all my human confusion and complexity were welcomed.

TRAVELING TO India wasn't the first time I shed my old self for a new one.

I had moved to Spain to find a warmer, more heart-based culture, hoping it would help relax my Germanic genes of cerebral seriousness. Born in the mid-sixties, like so many of my generation, I'd grown up in the thick ancestral soup of unprocessed guilt, war trauma, and moral injury that our country had inflicted on itself by perpetrating the most bone-chilling crimes against humanity—the Holocaust and World War II.

My hometown Dortmund, in West Germany's Ruhr region and at the time one of the most industrialized areas in Europe, also exuded bleakness. As a teenager, I rationalized this phenomenon with the fact that nearly all the historical and more ornate buildings in the region's cities had been destroyed by massive bomb raids during the final years of the war, and the unadorned architecture of the hasty post-war rebuilding efforts made for a gray-grim urban landscape. Also, many of the Ruhr region's residents were Gastarbeiter or "guestworkers" from Italy, Turkey, Greece, or Portugal who had uprooted themselves from their homelands to find work in the area's coal mines and steel mills. They had not come for natural beauty but rather needed to feed their families. Whether I could sense their lack of belonging or projected my own onto them, from early on I had an impulse to get as far away as possible.

In Spain, I felt I could breathe with more ease, drop into a leisurely pace, and spend quality time with friends. This made it even more difficult to offer any satisfactory explanation as to why I had such a pressing need to, once again, leave everything behind for India—nothing that could have appeased the incredulous reactions. Viewed from the outside, my life was idyllic: my family saw Sergio—a successful architect and my partner of eight years—as the perfect future son-in-law and his family had always been affectionate and loving toward me.

To the people in our life, it had been a question of when I would finally give in to Sergio's numerous proposals to marry and have children. But the rift between us had begun several years before I left Spain, upon my initial discovery of yoga and tai chi. It was in these small classes where I had been given a life raft, at least temporarily, from my mind's constant turmoil, my suicidal fantasies and bouts of depression. By then, I had already grown accustomed to the black cloud of eternal doom enveloping me as I awoke each morning. As much as I tried bracing myself with good intentions, the murky heaviness was always larger, pulling me into a bottomless sea of hopelessness. Nothing helped, and I didn't dare confide in anyone. I felt ashamed, even guilty for carrying so much darkness within, which stood in stark contrast with the privileged circumstances of my life. So, I had pretended to have it all together, maintaining a façade of competence, cheer, and contentedness while struggling to hide the secret of how flawed and broken I really was.

I sought answers or cures from psychics and tarot card readers. However, their allusions to the grim forces surrounding me and suggestion I buy expensive charms to ward off this evil compounded my fear of never being able to be well or happy. Eventually I found my way to the office of a Freudian analyst. It was interesting to spend an hour every week with a neutral but friendly stranger. She listened attentively to what I carefully chose to share. But I remained guarded and suspicious of the process. I did not mention my thoughts of death, as part of me was resolute about staying in control over what she could unearth from my psyche. After six months of answering her prodding questions about the painfully complicated dynamics of my childhood home—my overpowering sense of despair hadn't lifted a bit. A few months after I stopped seeing her, I began to practice yoga and tai chi in earnest, and as I did the storm clouds of my mind dissipated enough to allow the preoccupation with ending my life to ease, yet the urgency to discover the real meaning of existence and who I really was—experiencing true connection—grew more intense.

Sergio, however, considered these ideas and classes a silly little hobby. It wasn't that he was shallow; he was content with his vision of building a comfortable family life, while I burned to understand more about my emotions and my mind and to have real conversations. The painful but inevitable moment when I told him I was leaving remains sharply etched into my memory.

"So, what exactly are you looking for?" Sergio's voice sounded as incensed as it was despairing. "We left Madrid two years ago to return to a better life here on Lanzarote, and I thought you were happy with that. I don't get it!" He vehemently shook his head. "Why do you want to throw everything we have away—to go to India?" He spat the country's name with contempt.

Indeed, two years earlier, we'd agreed to move back to the Canary Islands and leave the urban urgency of Madrid behind. We'd had enough of buying into society's twisted version of success and the capital's hedonist consumption excesses where our professions had demanded that we spend half of our salaries on being fashionably clothed. Life by the sea was simpler. *Well, what am I looking for, for God's sake?*

I did not want to cause Sergio unnecessary pain—his pleading eyes propelled a wave of guilt within me. I didn't have the courage to tell him that witnessing a passing ship on the horizon a few weeks earlier had sealed our fate. It had sparked this epiphany, this sudden clarity that if I stayed in my current circumstances, I would miss my opportunity—like the ship slowly disappearing over the horizon—to discover something utterly essential to my life.

On the third day of "Who is in?" I requested dokusan—a private meeting available to retreat participants who need guidance—with our group leader Jayagata. Osho's disciples had shed their birth names and replaced them with Sanskrit or Indian ones they received from their guru. Jayagata (which means "victorious") was a beautiful gray-haired Canadian. I met with her behind Japanese folding screens that separated us from the rest of the group. On the other side, I heard the murmuring of participants continuing to grapple with Who is in?—someone deliriously laughing, another sobbing. The emotional outbursts didn't surprise me: taking part in this exercise for over thirty hours stirred immense, elemental emotions.

"So, what is going on, Annette? How can I assist you?"

I was mesmerized by her unusual air of centeredness. Clad in a black tunic with a white belt around the waist—like all the ashram's group leaders and therapists—she held her body elegantly erect. Jayagata's dignified serenity felt genuine and inspiring, and provided a refreshing contrast to the general atmosphere that encouraged everyone to let loose and express each fleeting passion and surge of emotion. Her presence was a calm, cooling breeze to my body and being.

"I keep being distracted," I confessed.

She smiled softly, her warm eyes meeting mine.

I blurted out without any pauses or self-censorship, "There is this guy in the group with long brown hair. I haven't even partnered with him yet, but I keep trying to figure out where he is in the room while at the same time I'm trying to answer, 'Who is in?' I guess I am attracted to him, but what should I do about that?"

This captivation had come as a bit of a surprise, as I was still grappling with my separation from Sergio.

"Stay with yourself." Jayagata's voice was gentle but uncompromising. She continued to smile as, with an energy clean like a honed sword, she severed the threads of fantasy my mind had been spinning. I bowed and thanked her.

I understood what she asked me to do, but I also loved the vibrancy and sweet ache of desire. It was one thing to intend to be single-pointed in my inner exploration, and another to remain steady amid the tantalizing rush of infatuation.

Until this moment, I had never examined the dynamics of romantic attraction—why should I, when it seemed so perfectly normal to pursue this kind of love? The culture in which I had been raised only intensified the allure of passion and the affairs of the heart through movies, music, and marketing—intimate relationship was offered as the ultimate answer to the human quest for happiness. Although my experiences or fantasies about the magical other had brought me more heartbreak and dissatisfaction than fulfillment, a part of me still believed romantic love was the antidote to the sadness, pain, fear, and confusion of the world.

During the remaining days of the retreat, I wanted to heed Jayagata's advice and vowed to not let myself be hijacked by the swarm of butterflies in my belly. But my well-worn habit of looking outside for satisfaction and salvation kept me only half focused on "Who is really in here?" Over and over, my attention strayed. I felt like an inexperienced swimmer who struggled to reach the shore but couldn't help being sucked away by the undercurrent.

Many years later, I would recognize these exuberant feelings and sensations had little to do with the attractive stranger whom I believed to be the source of my rapture. Yes, the unknown man had activated these exciting feelings, but he wasn't their source—they originated within me. Undeniably, he had perked my interest, but I couldn't yet see that the rollercoaster ride was of my making. It was all my creation: indulging, heightening, and dramatizing the familiar hide-and-seek, wanting-and-not-having, aching and projecting pleasurable feelings and wonderful outcomes onto someone I hadn't even talked to!

Little did I grasp the immensity of my longing for love and safe connection. I couldn't see that addictive fantasies were not only a product of my culture's exaggerated myth of romance but also a natural consequence of complex childhood trauma. I wasn't yet able to recognize that to a large degree my search stemmed from desperate attempts to bypass the messy, dark, painful pieces of life—the energetic imprints and innocent misunderstandings—lurking in the underbelly of daily experiences. Unbeknown to me, side by side with aspirations for true understanding or freedom lay the old, encapsulated child-states and unprocessed trauma from when I had felt most separate from love, safety, and wholeness.

I left Spain nursing the genuine belief that the essence of life was a grand place to be found outside and separate from me. By leaving the familiar behind, I believed I had freed myself from everything standing in the way and had become untethered from the time-consuming conventions of modern society. But fleeing my "old life" for India's scenery, sadhus, and seekers had not lightened my load—I still lugged invisible and significant baggage within.

chapter 2

Fractured Connections

Life will break you. Nobody can protect you from that, and living alone won't either, for solitude will also break you with its yearning. You have to love. You have to feel.

It is the reason you are here on earth. You are here to risk your heart. You are here to be swallowed up. And when it happens that you are broken, or betrayed, or left, or hurt, or death brushes near, let yourself sit by an apple tree and listen to the apples falling all around you in heaps, wasting their sweetness. Tell yourself you tasted as many as you could.

LOUISE ERDRICH, *The Painted Drum*

I WAS fifteen when it dawned on me that my people at home were different from others. I spent three weeks with a family in northern France as part of a school student-exchange program, and I was baffled by how affectionate my host parents were, not just with me, but also with each other, their daughter Marie who was my age, and their younger son Jules. At mealtimes, they enjoyed conversations about everyone's experiences of the day or shared lively, even controversial discussions about what was happening in the world. At first, their unusual behavior made me hold my breath, squint, and frown, but as I realized they weren't putting on a special show for my benefit and seemed to interact naturally, I felt shame about my family's different reality.

After a few days, as I let my guard down and the knots in my stomach softened, I allowed myself to briefly dip into the warm, cozy atmosphere of my hosts' relationships. Most stunning was how, every morning, the mother came to wake me up by pressing a gentle kiss on my cheek. Two glowing eyes looked into mine: "*Bonjour*, Annette!"

As soon as I sat up, she reached for my pillow and adjusted it to cushion the space between the headboard and my back. Then she handed me a steaming café au lait and slipped a sugar cube into my mouth: "This is to sweeten your start into the new day!" As the granules melted into syrup on my tongue, she was already sweeping out of my room. I asked her once if she did the same for Marie.

"*Bien sûr!*" She erupted in laughter. *Of course!*

Conversely, mornings at my home began with a big jolt as my mother stormed like a field marshal into the bedroom I shared with my two sisters, bellowing "Get up! Get up! You have school!"

MY EARLIEST childhood memory—I must have been three years old—is of standing in the kitchen screaming for my mother to hold me while she was down on all fours feverishly scrubbing the floor. The more she yelled to shut up and go away, the more my panic grew, and the more urgent my cries became.

The last time I openly reached out to her for physical affection was when I was four or five. It was evening and she had asked me to sit on her lap: "We need to trim your fingernails before you go to bed." When she finished, she pushed me to get off. I lingered for a moment; feeling her so close to me, I wanted to take advantage of our proximity and leaned into her warm breasts to cuddle. In a split second she had yanked my body off her lap and smacked me in the face with the back of her hand, snarling, "Don't ever do this again!"

I believe I didn't even cry.

The pain of my longing for connection and closeness with her was epitomized by a recurring childhood nightmare. In my dream, I am wearing my best dress, white lace knee-high socks, and black patent-leather shoes as I walk twenty yards behind my mother and great-aunt Erna. We climb a painfully steep road as I try to catch up with them, yet each step is as arduous as if my feet were made of lead. Sometimes I must climb over confusing train tracks or duck under quickly closing crossing barriers. I keep calling out for my mother, crying, and screaming her name in vain. She is too engrossed in her conversation with my great-aunt to hear me. And then, every time I finally manage to shorten the distance between us, out of nowhere a huge giraffe grabs me by the neck from above, lifts me and places me fifty steps back. My mom is a little dot disappearing into the distance as I wake up in panic and tears.

Overall, our family's emotional vocabulary was minute, but we were well-practiced in blowing up at each other or sulking and withdrawing. My sisters and I—Christiane who was a year older and Britta who was two years younger than me—often played together, but we also fought quite regularly and at times even had fist fights until our noses bled. I never saw my parents offering or receiving repair and only rarely witnessed them sharing affectionate words or gestures. While my dad mostly guarded his feelings and often remained silent while sighing in frustration, my mother was unbridled in her unapologetic outspokenness and rage; her sharp tongue and red-hot energies could suck all the air out of the room.

It was only during the holy days of Easter and Christmas that she inexplicably pulled herself together to become cheerful, my father became solemn, and for a brief respite, our family atmosphere felt almost lighthearted and harmonious.

Looking back, I understand how my mother felt imprisoned by her role; she would seethe about being "just a mother and housewife," her voice dripping with bitterness as she lashed out about how she never should have had children and "wasted her life" on us. Whether she'd been determined to save her daughters from the same fate or felt in competition with me, she was quick to extinguish any signs of my emerging femininity. Small, innocent desires like wanting to dress up as a princess for my kindergarten's carnival festivities seemed to personally affront her, as if my joy was stealing something from her. She pronounced it more "emancipated" for me to dress up in the baggy, all-black costume of a chimney cleaner. At age five, I knew nothing of emancipation. Stuck in my muted outfit, I felt shamed and wrong for who I wanted to be while my girlfriends were all sparkles and smiles in their silky dresses and tiaras. My unrestrained excitement about wanting to take ballet classes like other girls seemed to particularly provoke her, as if my innocent desires were a betrayal of her own thwarted dreams. One day she delivered her final verdict: "I will make sure that you are not going to become another one of those stupid little circus poodles!"

Her deep resentment, I later understood, emerged whenever my happiness threatened to overshadow her unhappiness—though as a child, I simply believed I was the sole reason for her misery.

The gaping hole of motherly affection and protection led me to overly fixate on my dad for connection and guidance. He spent long hours at the office and, after work, mostly preferred to withdraw into reading his history books, but on weekends he would play board games and cards with my sisters and me or take us for long walks in the woods. On Sunday mornings, I reveled in a more exclusive closeness when I joined him in the living room to listen to his favorite Beethoven, Sibelius, or Mozart symphonies. He'd lean back into his dark-brown leather armchair, eyes shut, while I sprawled on the carpet as close to him as possible. At times, the late morning sun would illuminate the spot where I lay adding to the waves of pleasurable warmth spreading through my body as we enjoyed the shared emotions or lyrical atmospheres evoked by the haunting themes and melodies. On late summer evenings, we derived a similar joy from sitting on the terrace together during thunderstorms, watching the heavens crack open with powerful lightning while the downpour drenched the parched lawn. Particularly when I was younger and my father still allowed me the rare joy of sitting on his lap, the faint scent of his Old Spice aftershave mixed with the fresh moisture saturating the air could instantly smooth the frowns on my forehead and soothe whatever worries and pains my little mind already carried.

I equally felt united with him in our shared love of God—the fact that he never rejected my incessant curiosity about all matters related to the Bearded Man up in the sky, fed my heart in an essential and otherworldly way. As a devout Catholic, he must have been relieved that at least one in our family of five showed genuine interest in his faith.

He had inherited a strong devotion from his parents, who each followed the rules of Christianity in different ways. While my paternal grandmother had been utterly affectionate with her eight children, and the potent love she imprinted on my father was palpable in the care of his own daughters—my grandfather resembled the stern Old Testament God. Informed by the prevalent German zeitgeist that promoted breaking a child's spirit "for their own good," his regular severe corporal punishment instilled unerring obedience in my father and his siblings.

As an adult, my father never processed his own emotional injuries or dissolved the callouses around them. Despite telling his daughters how hard this cruel treatment had been, his unattended wounding led him to compulsively replicate the same drastic educational measures with us.

While our mother could explode in unexpected fits of rage and strike us with the carpet beater or her wooden cooking spoons, he was more measured and methodical. When we played too loudly or disobeyed his orders, we knew what was coming: the humiliation of being asked to bare our naked skin to be spanked. At least once a week, my father had us strip our butts and then struck us forcefully until we howled. Our tears didn't stop him—the opposite—our cries fueled him to go on. With time, I learned to keep all sound and tears in, to hold onto my dignity and not give him an inch more of myself than my bare skin. I learned to numb my body against the shock and pain.

Despite this, he was my primary source of childhood emotional bonding. I learned to hold out and wait for crumbs of affection. Whether eagerly bringing him his slippers when he arrived from work or tying his shoestrings before leaving in the morning, I wanted to make sure he knew how much I adored him, feverishly hoping he would reciprocate my gestures of love. I hungered for his attention and approval even when he seemed repelled by my overt need.

In hindsight, I understand how I was merely following my developing brain's innate drive to connect and bond. And, how the yearning and need for feeling seen, sensed, soothed, and held, compelled me to reflexively fawn over my dad—hoping he could undo the red thread of pain weaving itself through my heart. My parents, like all of us, were only able to be open to or pass on what they had received or healed in their lives—their own history of parent-infant-bonding, emotional injuries, or undischarged trauma as well as the legacy of growing up during the complex years of war and post-war Germany.

chapter 3

Unexpected Romance and Revelations

When someone violates you sexually, it does not simply haunt and aggrieve you; it alters the very shape of your soul.
CICELY TYSON

THE WATER was iridescent, the color of midnight, and resembled a deep, calm, forest pond. The lush trees surrounding the ashram's swimming pool reinforced that natural sense of ease and tranquility. I dangled my legs in the silky cool water, only faintly aware of the other visitors who sprawled on lounge chairs and chatted nearby. I took a deep inhale, pushed my body off the edge, and slid below the water's surface. Holding my breath, I propelled myself with long, slow strokes through the soundless waterscape. Against the backdrop of the luminous sky above me, the velvet dark of the world below offered an almost deafening absence of sound and movement. I stayed submerged for as long as my lungs would allow, dissolving in the peace of the bottomless stillness.

The "Who is in?" intensive program had ended the day before, and I'd come to the pool to digest my insights. Piercing through the layers and labels defining I, me, or mine had given glimpses into a limitless quiet underneath all words and movement, and I wished to continue in that concentrated intensity. This quiet was elusive and only visited briefly before the chatter of my mind drowned it out again, but submerging below the water's surface acted like an external, almost metaphorical entryway into this inner depth.

The "Who is in?" process had interrupted the automatic stream of my discursive mind. By becoming more conscious of and naming the different components that I usually attached a permanent idea of self to—thoughts, feelings, perceptions, or sensations—I inadvertently shifted my sense of identity for a moment and took a stand as a quieter cognizant presence that was not bound by these changing phenomena. The tight-knit narratives around my familiar identity—who I *thought* or *felt* I was—were beginning to loosen. I wanted more of this quietude, but I wasn't clear on how to make that happen.

When I could no longer hold my breath, I emerged, swam back to the edge of the pool, and lifted my body out of the water. I lay on a towel, the sunlit warmth of the stones seeping through the fabric. The underwater peace lingered for a few more moments before my hypervigilant mind took charge again. I sighed and closed my eyes, hoping that withdrawing my senses from the world would help me find a way back to stillness.

"There you are! I have been looking for you."

I squinted upward to see if the unfamiliar voice was addressing me or someone else. I blinked to make sure—but it was true—there he stood, the mysterious stranger from my group! I propped myself up and shielded my face with one hand as if to avert the sunlight, but in truth, I was trying to hide my blushing face. He looked down at me with sparkly, deep-brown eyes and a bemused smile.

"Would it be okay if I sat next to you?"

I kept blushing but managed to utter: "Oh, hi. Yes, sit."

"We did the 'Who is in?' program together, remember?"

As if I forgot. He unfolded his towel and joined me.

"Yes, I remember you," I said, trying to sound neutral.

"Well, I'm relieved you recognize me. My name is Ariel," he said with a teasing smile, which provoked me to laugh and release a bit of self-consciousness.

"I am Annette," I finally replied.

"Nice to meet you. So, Annette, what was your experience of the 'Who is in?' and how did you get into Osho?" Ariel looked Mediterranean with his tanned skin, brown hair, and sun-bleached blonde streaks, but he spoke English with an unfamiliar accent that I couldn't place. His cheeks and chin showed a light stubble that contrasted with the otherwise fine features of his face.

"I cannot really say that I am *into* Osho," I said slowly, "I mean, I connect with some parts of his teachings, and I got a lot out of our group, I really loved it, but there are many things here that I don't like."

"Oh yeah? Tell me." Ariel looked genuinely interested.

"I have a problem with this guru thing. You know, these evening video recordings of Osho when we have to show up dressed in white robes and then shout Osho's name aloud and throw our arms up when his image appears on the screen—it makes me uncomfortable. When I see leaders whipping their audience into that type of emotional frenzy, it reminds me of Hitler or Goebbels blinding and manipulating the masses into feeling part of something big and important."

"Are you German?"

"Yes, I was born there," and as if excusing myself for my nationality, I added "but I haven't lived there for the last eight years. I moved to Spain when I was twenty-one. And you, where are you from?"

Ariel smiled. "I am from Israel."

I had never met an Israeli or a Jew before. An inadvertent sense of discomfort and shame about my country's legacy smoldered in me. I tried to read Ariel's face, but I couldn't detect any negative reaction.

"So, you're not into gurus. What else is bothering you here?" he queried, eyes twinkling.

I was relieved he didn't seem to care as much as I did about my origins.

"Well, I read the other day that Osho tried to talk a man out of being gay.[1] He told him that his sexual orientation was unnatural and dangerous. I find this horrible! I just can't agree with that. I mean, I have friends who are gay and to them it doesn't feel like they had a choice, nor would they want to be different! Isn't a spiritual teacher supposed to be more understanding? And then the other thing—" Ariel opened the floodgates within me, as I blurted— "I don't really get the free love thing here. I mean, I appreciate that Osho doesn't exclude intimate relationships from his teachings, but honestly, I don't see what having sex with everyone has to do with love? Some men here in the ashram keep approaching me in creepy ways. They don't know my name but tell me that they feel 'so much love for me.' Why do they say that when they just want to have sex?"

Unwittingly I had talked myself into a frenzy and, without stopping, I pointed to a man at the other end of the pool. He was well into his sixties—over thirty years older than I—and talking to two other women twenty feet away. "You see that tall guy with the white-grayish hair?"

"Yeah, what about him?"

"He doesn't even say hello to me anymore, just because I didn't want to have a 'date' with him. And you know what a 'date' here means, right? It's having dinner first and then automatically sex. Can you believe that?"

Ariel laughed and shook his head. "Well, good for you, that

[1] In public discourses, Osho held contradictory stances towards homosexuality. https://globalindiannetwork.com/osho-on-homosexuality/.

you didn't go with him. Don't insult yourself with someone like that."

The humor in his response calmed me. I felt validated: until now, I hadn't admitted to anyone how much I had been stirred up by the scene. I had derived security from a more conventional relationship with Sergio, and being single in the uninhibited "free love" scene of the ashram made me feel like prey fleeing predators.

There had been another upsetting incident with a man at the ashram, although I didn't tell Ariel about it. He and I had been chatting leisurely over a cup of tea when he commented, "You know, you feel really tight to me—I think you just need a good fuck." "Oh, yeah? And I bet you're offering to help with that!" I snapped. But I kept this story to myself because I was afraid there was a kernel of truth in the man's revolting remark, a fear that made the memory only more shameful. Obviously, I didn't agree with his suggested remedy, but I sensed my own adept armor and defensiveness.

The overt promiscuous scene had brought up unbidden blurry memories of sexual abuses by older men during my childhood and teenage years. I watched these images from my past as if from a distance, randomly floating through blank space disconnected from sound, feeling, or sensation—as if they belonged to someone else's body, someone else's life, and I didn't have the slightest inkling what to do about these fragments of memory. I was around seven or eight when an older man first violated my sexual boundaries. Dr. Mahl, a retired neighbor, invited me to come to his house with the promise I could hold his newborn kittens. Of course, I went. He was a highly educated and distinguished man, esteemed in our neighborhood. I liked him; he spoke to me as if I were an adult, giving me oatmeal cookies from an expensive health food store where my mother never shopped and serving me Earl Grey tea with cream in his best porcelain. That kind of attention was not easy to come by in my home, where I competed with two sisters for our parents' erratic affection. I happily gobbled it all up—until the day when he pulled my underwear down to fondle my genitalia. A few weeks later when my mom and I were walking past his house, Dr. Mahl was standing in his driveway. He asked my mother if she would allow me to stay overnight at his place someday soon. In my panic, I hastily gripped my mother's hand, hoping she understood my urgent squeeze as a signal to refuse his request. Luckily, she laughed him off, but never asked why I had acted so strangely, and her breezy response to his suspiciously fishy invitation didn't make me feel much safer.

A few years later, when I was twelve, a friend's father used any opportunity to touch my butt and barely growing breasts. When I visited their home, he hid behind doors and groped me when I passed. I was so startled that I froze, unable to protest, my scream stuck in my throat. After the third or fourth time, I was too distressed to return to my friend's home. I couldn't tell her why, because I was ashamed on her behalf for her father's inappropriate behavior. My friend had lost her mother a few months earlier to cancer and often wept in my presence. Her father wouldn't allow her to come over to our house, so I made up all sorts of excuses to stop seeing her. I hoped that if I kept quiet, the whole issue would disappear, but it didn't. My mother called me a "coldhearted bitch" for dropping my playmate without any obvious reasons—a stinging remark that, together with the pain of being falsely accused, haunted me for years. And because my dad and my friend's father played often cards together, I was terrified about the possible disruption and negative attention that my revelation could cause. *Even if I dare to speak—will I be heard?* My shame for having been repeatedly touched sexually without consent made me believe I was somehow causing this to happen, that I was the one at fault.

A more severe violation happened when I was sixteen and another friend's stepfather tried to rape me in plain daylight at their home. My body must have unleashed all its power—I screamed, struggled, and kicked hard enough to fight him off.

Once I had escaped his grip, I ran at lightning speed all the way back to our house. When my mother opened the door, she must have sensed something unusual, as her tone was laced with suspicion. "Why are you so out of breath?"

"Oh, I wanted to see how fast I could run." I did my best to sound as neutral as possible. Our relationship was already too broken and overshadowed by emotional disconnect for me to trust her enough to disclose what had transpired. I had learned from an early age to fend for myself, so I headed upstairs up to my room, locked the door, put loud music on, and drowned my terror and humiliation in deafening oblivion.

These destructive and debilitating incidents would continue to affect my life. Like most survivors of childhood sexual abuse, I had been left stuck with the disowned shame of my abusers' actions and an internalized belief that I was the one who was filthy. The near-certainty of their impunity—given how few cases are ever reported, let alone prosecuted—only deepened this toxic burden of misplaced shame. Age-inappropriately "sexed up," many childhood survivors feel unconsciously compelled to act out that charge by becoming highly promiscuous or overtly sexual. Others, like me, go the other way, becoming numb to their bodies' sensations and shutting down their sensual aliveness. While most of my teenage friends were enjoying innocent erotic explorations, for me, the first kiss at fourteen from a boy on whom I had a serious crush provoked such an attack of panic that I immediately ended our budding romance.

As Ariel sat next to me at the pool, I didn't detect any of that aggressive, covetous sexuality. I exhaled. He felt like a friend, not an invader. His ease and comfort in his own skin rubbed off on me.

Even though the "Who is in?" process deemphasized the

conventional ways of defining ourselves, I couldn't help but feel curious about what a man like him did for a living. "Ariel, what kind of work do you do in Israel?"

"Oh, I don't spend much time there. Just a couple months each year."

"Where do you live then and what do you do?"

"Nowhere—I am at home wherever I choose to be." He smiled. "I have been traveling around the world for the last eight years."

"Really?" My mouth gaped. I had never heard of anyone living in that way!

"I buy merchandise in Asia and sell it mostly in Europe. I have been doing relatively well and I love my life that way. At least for now," he said.

My mind unhinged itself from a familiar but restricted view, like the sky opening after a long, overcast period of gray clouds: *There are no real rules about how anyone is supposed to live. It's all made up!* While I'd always secretly hoped that a more adventurous, free-flowing existence was possible, I hadn't been able to figure out how it would look.

Something deep in my chest unlocked, and I gasped, "Wow!" So, it was possible to drift for a while, to let myself loose in the world without dropping anchor or having a clear plan about what was supposed to happen next.

Ariel interrupted my reverie: "I'd love to talk more. Would you like to meet for dinner? I have a scooter, so we could ride into town for some real Indian food and help you escape the obscene ashram scene here." He winked.

"Yes, I'd love that!" I said, regretting how eager I sounded. I was drawn to Ariel, but openly owning my desire made me feel tawdry and exposed. I didn't want to come across as "needy." But he didn't seem to notice—and our evening plan was made.

Even though becoming intimate with another man so shortly after separating from Sergio was the last thing on my mind, a couple days later Ariel and I became closer. While we both enjoyed our sensual attraction, I most cherished spending hours talking about our inner explorations. From the start, I was comfortable disclosing uncensored feelings, doubts, and desires. Ariel was also into meditation and exploring his inner landscape, something I had missed sharing with Sergio. Most intimate relationships I had been in or witnessed had unfolded in a somewhat charged atmosphere. That underlying friction worked as a fuel that kept attraction running, but once the honeymoon phase ended, the air grew hazy with negotiations about unmet needs or diverging interests, and the longer phases of discontent seemed to betray the feelings of "love" that one professed for the other. It had been disillusioning to not only see that in my parents' marriage, but painful and frustrating to go through these constant ups and downs with Sergio.

As Ariel and I spent time together, it helped that, for the first time, I didn't make someone or something outside of myself my priority. I didn't expect him to be a knight galloping in to make me feel complete or fill an inner emptiness. Instead of looking to our relationship to provide absolute happiness or meaning, my priority had shifted to what I called "my inner journey."

During the weeks after concluding the "Who is in?" program, I settled into a daily routine. I found a room to rent in the household of an old Osho disciple who lived in Pune. His flat was in a three-story apartment complex in a gated community ten minutes from the ashram. The complex had a security guard at the front gate, a center courtyard with a garden, and was mostly populated by upper-middle-class Indian families. Next to the gate was an empty lot filled with little huts made of corrugated metal, random wood pieces, and plastic tarps. From my bedroom window on the second floor, I saw dark-skinned men and women brushing their teeth outside their huts and joyful children playing with old tires in the dirt. Through the foliage of trees beyond the shacks, I glimpsed the brown waters of the Mula-Mutha River.

Days began when my alarm clock rang shortly after five. I showered, threw on a maroon robe, and walked down to the apartment's parking lot to get my bike. Pedaling to the ashram early in the morning was usually a quiet affair. Later in the day, streets grew crowded with vendors of fresh coconuts or deep-fried snacks, Indian women in colorful sarees, uniformed schoolkids, motorized rickshaws, beeping scooters, and bicycles. The first meditation began at 6 a.m. in the Buddha Hall. The open-air structure had a white marble floor, a huge roof of white floating tarps, and mosquito netting wrapped around the sides to keep insects and other critters out. Hundreds of early morning risers gathered, all of us ready for "dynamic meditation." Osho created this and other more active meditations especially for his western disciples. His philosophy had been that busy-minded modern people needed to unload through emoting before being ready to sit still and discover a deeper inner silence.

Dynamic meditation was sixty minutes long and consisted of phases of heavy breathing evolving into screaming, chaotic physical movements, and then jumping up and down incessantly until a recorded voice shouted "Stop!"—the signal to freeze and remain motionless in whatever position their body happened to be. The final stage featured recorded music and participants were invited to dance in a state of celebration. Although others raved about their valuable emotional catharsis, the process to me felt forced and contrived. I hated every bit of those sixty minutes; I only felt celebratory when leaving at the end. However, instead of honoring that this process didn't work for me, I convinced myself I shouldn't criticize something without thoroughly trying it out, so

I followed the ashram's recommendation to practice the dynamic meditation for at least twenty-one days. But then I was more than relieved to let it go for good.

I did feel drawn to the ashram's daily silent sitting meditations. These lasted either twenty or forty-five minutes and I never missed one. Like many beginners, I started on the wrong foot—unaware of my underlying aggressive agenda to "get it right." My "doing mind" turned meditation into something that needed to be accomplished. And being physically still while my frantic mind rattled with cacophony was arduous. My body didn't seem to cooperate either: my neck stiffened, scalp itched, stomach tightened, lower back ached, and my crossed legs often fell asleep. The serene Buddha statues in the ashram's garden looked nothing like my experiences of meditation. However, just as with "Who is in?" I chose to show up and sit in the fire of it all instead of doing my usual thing—distracting myself from myself.

Unfortunately, there were no detailed instructions given for these silent meditation sessions—only the sound of a gong at the beginning and end. Without any real guidance on how to disengage from my busy and chaotic thinking-mind as it barked orders like a soldier, I had no clue: I simply endured the timed practice sessions. On my own, I eventually added contemplative movement like Sufi whirling and Gurdjieff's sacred dances. The rest of my time, I volunteered in the ashram's kitchen and hung out with Ariel and other new friends.

The obnoxious sexual advances from other men dissipated. Ariel's presence at my side made it clear that I was "off the market." Juniper, a new ashram friend and journalist from San Francisco who had researched the ashram's late founder and former times, shocked me one day by saying, "Look, I get how the 'free love' scene here pushes your buttons. I am not into it either, but this is rather tame compared to the really wild times when Osho was alive! I also read that he didn't just want people to free themselves of sexual repression or conventional ideas of relationship, but to find a deeper love, you know, the *real* thing in the undercurrent of our being. That's what interests me the most here," she laughed, "but some of the guys conveniently stay stuck in the free-fucking phase of it all!"

I couldn't help admiring how unfazed Juniper was compared to me. And I still felt far away from understanding what Osho meant by "real love" when I came across this quote from his book *Love, Freedom, and Aloneness*: "Unless meditation is achieved, love remains a misery. Once you have learned how to live alone, once you have learned how to enjoy your simple existence, for no reason at all, then there is a possibility of solving the second, more complicated problem of two persons being together. Only two meditators can live in love—and then love will not be a koan. But then it will not be a relationship, either, in the sense that you understand it. It will be simply a state of love, not a state of relationship."

I was starting, though, to glimpse that different kind of relating. Six weeks later, when Ariel's visa expired, our impending goodbye brought sadness, yet it also felt surprisingly free of my usual emotional drama. In the backseat of a motor rickshaw on our way to Pune's train station, Ariel held me in his arms. The station overflowed with travelers, mostly Indian along with a few foreigners, porters carrying big loads of luggage, and vendors shouting to sell hot chai in little clay cups, while an array of confusing arrival and departure announcements in Hindi blasted through crackling loudspeakers. Ariel and I laughed about the hassle and effort it took to merely find the right track for his train to Bombay. When we finally did, the last passengers were already boarding. We hugged and joked until there was not a single second left for him to jump into the car.

As the train rolled out of the station, he leaned out from the open door, waving, smiling, and throwing kisses into the air. Only when the train shrank into an ever-smaller dot in the distance did

I allow myself to feel blue. My lover, my friend, my fellow pilgrim had left; I was on my own again.

In the next days and weeks, I missed his presence next to me during the early morning audio lectures and wished we could talk at lunch about meditation or make plans to hang out in the afternoon. It felt so easy, so natural, to be with him and whenever my Germanic seriousness had taken hold it was Ariel's humor that snapped me right out of it. We had promised to stay in touch via mail, the usual way to remain connected in 1995. After a month, a much-awaited first letter arrived at the ashram's post office. Reading Ariel's love-filled lines made me happy while rekindling my longing; yet for the first time in my life, I could call myself back more easily from spinning endless fantasies about happily-ever-after scenarios. My heart opened, I felt my longing, and let go of Ariel as a necessary fixture in life. While we hadn't had the time to go further into our relationship, he had been a crucial steppingstone on my path. I realized that I no longer wanted to place mere romantic feelings or sensual attraction at the center of my intimate relationships; any future connection with a man would need to be sourced from something deeper.

chapter 4

Confronting Family Truths

The truth will set you free, but not until it is finished with you.
DAVID FOSTER WALLACE

After Ariel left, there was still always a lot going on in the ashram: Sufi Whirling, Kundalini meditation, and silent sittings, and then the more exclusive week-long intensive programs. Yet for most people, the essential event in the ashram was the daily "Osho White Robe Brotherhood." During this evening gathering, videos—mostly recorded during Osho's last years—were projected onto a big screen. Many were peppered with Osho telling silly or sexual jokes, and it all contributed to my conflicting mix of feelings. My inability or unwillingness to relate to Osho or anyone being my "guru" set me at odds with many of the ashram's disciples who loved to use terms like "my master" or "Bhagwan" (a Hindu term for God or Lord).

I was torn between wanting to belong and my inability to ignore the things that provoked strong aversion. *Is this the story of my life: longing to belong, but feeling separate and never really fitting in?*

Nevertheless, my time in Pune offered me something I hadn't found anywhere else. Having just broken away from my familiar life and feeling bereft of certainty or clarity, I was comforted by the fact that in the ashram I was not alone. The multitude and sheer diversity of seekers from all over the world amazed me: graphic designers, psychotherapists, bodyworkers, homemakers, entrepreneurs, students, artists, or schoolteachers from the U.S., Israel, Japan, Korea, Germany, Australia, Brazil, Italy, Russia, or Sweden—and of course India. They had all ventured beyond their culture's status quo to find a deeper truth, inner happiness, or at least a reprieve from suffering.

As the months progressed, I felt more like a part of the community. I celebrated my thirtieth birthday dressed in a saree with my Indian and international ashram friends and signed up for another intensive program, a three-week-long primal healing group. I wondered if the program's location in a soundproof chamber resembling a bunker on an underground floor should give me pause. I couldn't help wondering how it would compare to my six-month stint in conventional talk therapy during my mid-twenties in Madrid.

The primal healing program was led by a long-term Osho disciple, a German-born therapist called Bhavat. Together with several assistants, he kept our group of fifty participants fully engaged from early morning to late at night. During the program we were instructed not to interact socially with anyone outside our group and to remain in silence during meals or when going home at night. Some participants found this emotionally complex, but for me, the permission to "mind my own business" felt blissful. I had never noticed how overwhelmed and frazzled interacting with others could make me feel.

The content of the program, however, was arduous. A substantial chunk of time was spent on encounter-style processes like loud emoting and holotropic breathwork sessions and, to my lament, the obligatory participation in the daily dynamic meditation that I disliked so much. These forceful energetic approaches worked wonders for many, but not me. My body only armored up more; often, I watched myself as if from a distance going through the motions. Even as I followed the instructions, holding the image of one of my parents in my head and screaming "I hate you" repeatedly while pounding my fists into the spongy cushion, my mind kept saying: *This is so bloody silly!* Other than gasping for air from the physical exertion, and feeling like a fake, I didn't get much out of this. For Bhavat and his assistants, I must have been a pretty tough cookie to deal with—but they were hell-bent and dedicated to unearthing our buried feelings and unconscious defenses.

One afternoon, after Bhavat had delivered his favorite tenet, "Family is a completely neurotic structure in which everyone fights and rivals for love and attention," I snapped.

"Really? Something seems awfully amiss in your message! I mean, isn't love supposed to be a given? Sure, my home wasn't exactly warm and cozy, but I will not give up on my mom until she finally shows me more love and affection."

Without missing a beat Bhavat replied, "She is not going to give it to you. Let it go."

"Yes, she will." I held my ground.

"No, she won't."

"Yes!"

"Okay, let's take a closer look. Are you open to trying something new?"

I nodded.

"I want you to show me your family. The way we'll do this is by you choosing a woman and a man from our group who will represent your mother and father. Any siblings?"

"Yes, two sisters. *I* am the one in the middle." Unwittingly, my words were spoken with a slight tinge of pride, as if being in the middle automatically meant inhabiting the central position, a more valuable role, in our family.

As Bhavat suggested, I began looking around for my family members, and to my amazement, even though my real parents or sisters bore no significant physical resemblance to the people in my group, each of them stood out to me. I chose a man from Chile to be my dad, a German woman to be my mom, a Brazilian woman to play my younger sister Britta, and a Dutch woman to stand in as Christiane.

"Come to the center and arrange each of your family members in an order that feels true to you," Bhavat guided. "Feel how close or distant your father or mother should be standing from you. Also, notice if they should look toward or turn their face and body away from you. And then I'd like you to do the same with your sisters."

I had never done any type of psychodrama or constellation work, yet found this therapeutic intervention required neither practice nor intellectualization. I felt an uncanny visceral certainty about the energetic placements of my family members in relationship to myself. I positioned my Chilean "father" five feet away, with his body and face slightly turned toward me. Then, placing myself in the central position, I asked the German woman representing my mother to stand on the other side, but at a much greater distance from me than my father, and to not look toward me at all.

I glanced at the Dutch woman playing my older sister. We were strangers, but through her presence I felt the safe bond I'd always experienced with Christiane, even though we had quite different temperaments. She had been the proverbial older sister I admired. Then, without giving it further thought, I asked the Dutch woman to position herself next to my mum and for the Brazilian woman to stand with my dad. As I saw Christiane and my mother staged that close together, I was flabbergasted by how much sense it made. As "the neat and responsible one," Christiane had been heralded as "the good daughter" who had ironed and folded our entire family's weekly laundry for years until she left home for university.

"Look how helpful your big sister is," my mother had often hissed. "You, instead, are just a mess, a real *Schmarotzer*!"—which meant parasite in German.

It was true that I had a tough time sitting still or concentrating for too long. I tended to be overactive, restless, and high-spirited—the proverbial wild child. Whether it was due to Christiane's quieter character or her strategy of navigating the emotional desert at home by "functioning well," she usually didn't create much of a fuss for my parents; she was a diligent student and found solace in quietly reading books in her room. While she mostly withdrew into herself, my main coping strategy had been to forge ahead by being boisterous or outwardly cheerful as well as escaping the unhappy scene altogether by playing outside as much as possible, rain or shine. Christiane had found some reassurance and safe space in her intellect, while I experienced solace in nature and my devotion to God.

In the bunker, I looked at the people I had chosen to represent my family. I was aghast: *Shouldn't I be the one closest to my dad? Why am I so far away from everybody?* Bhavat understood. "So, tell me, how does it feel to be the one in the middle?" I couldn't speak; I was overwhelmed by a painful lump forming in my throat and a harrowing sense of isolation.

"You look pretty alone," he added gently.

As if feeling so forlorn and separate wasn't enough, unprompted, my "father" began to affectionately stroke "Britta's" hair. She responded by leaning into him while sending a victorious smile in my direction. In a split-second, hot-coiled pangs of jealousy—even hatred—ripped through my body. As a kid, I'd always felt Britta was cuter than me—she was the baby of the family—and I'd desperately wanted to be the little one again. Unbidden, a memory arose from when I was four. I repeatedly squeezed my feet into Britta's tiny *Pantoffeln*, her red felt house slippers, which must have been at least two sizes smaller than my feet. For weeks, I tried to literally walk in her shoes—and eventually gave up, exasperated by the blisters on my toes.

As I stood in the middle of the bunker, my raw emotional pain and jealousy arranged around me, I finally opened to what

I hadn't been able to face and feel as a child. It hurt like hell, but a sense of relief and rightness about making the unconscious conscious bloomed in my chest. My carefully crafted narratives of being the center of my family—and most importantly, my dad's favorite—crumbled around me in real-time. My aching sense of unlovability and isolation throbbed, exposed, as tears streamed down my face.

As I left the ashram for the night, I was stunned by the painful truths uncovered by the family constellation exercise. *How have I duped myself into believing I was my father's favorite, or that I occupied a central role in our family?* It was clear that the spinning of my alternative narrative had allowed me to protect myself against the hurt and helplessness that had felt too unbearable as a little child. *However, where else in my childhood—or even now—was I living in self-constructed parallel realities?*

On one of the last days of the program, after a grueling afternoon and evening of emotional processing, Bhavat told our group to grab some crayons and spontaneously draw pictures of our parents. I wanted to draw my dad in bright yellow and golden orange, but somehow, I couldn't. Instead, my hand reached for black, brown, and dark green crayons and I drew a gloomy scene of huge ashtrays filled with cigarette butts and my father's somber face behind a curtain of thick smoke. *Yes, my dad had been a chain-smoker, I know that.* But as I sketched lots of empty bottles around him, it dawned on me—*my hero and the center of my universe as a child was an alcoholic. How have I missed that?*

I remembered: I had not only seen my father drinking every day—as a kid, I had poured his whiskeys on demand. And on many occasions I had watched his swaying walk or heard his slurring voice. Whenever it happened, I had been overcome by a strange mixture of fear, embarrassment, and dizziness. Also, my mother's heated and at times despairing command of "Stop drinking so much!" had been a regular refrain.

I must have been around eleven when my father's and my relationship turned even more confusing. It was when he began to drunkenly vent grief and frustration about his unhappy marriage. I was torn between anguish and an anxious need to fix my father's unhappiness, yet elated and proud to be his confidante, the "favorite one." Those times were the exceptions; most often he had successfully played the part of the high-functioning family provider until his last two years of life when bankruptcy left him broken and his identity as a powerful self-made-man crumbled.

Still, I missed him and even three years after his passing was overcome by feelings of abandonment, left behind and alone on earth, ever since Britta's boyfriend Massimo called Sergio's and my apartment in Madrid on a frigid cold January evening. His voice had been calm but somber: "I am sorry, Annette. I have some sad news." He paused. "Your father was diagnosed with lung cancer and brain tumors. The doctors don't give him more than six, maybe ten months, to live."

It was typical of our family to avoid any real conversation; this was why Massimo was chosen to make the call. The news left me spinning like a planet out of orbit, and after consulting with Sergio, I made plans to fly to Germany even though the relationship with my father had remained strained. I still bore scars from his cruel reaction to my choice to move to Lanzarote, and Dad had continued to express his aggravations about my not "following his orders" and my unapologetic rebellion against his conventional and patriarchal worldviews—but none of that mattered as I traveled to Germany to be with him.

His body had fallen weak fast, and he struggled to take full breaths and find words. His medical professionals disagreed on the next steps. The hospital wanted to release him so he could spend his remaining time at home, but our old family physician was adamant we send Dad to a special lung clinic 130 miles away.

We knew what that meant: he would live out his last months in an iron lung. He had already lost much of his ability to speak due to metastases in the brain, but he was lucid enough to make it clear with gestures that he didn't want to prolong life—or his dying—encased in a machine, isolated, far from home.

A stoic patriarch himself, our family physician hollered, "No, I will have nothing of that! You don't even know what is good for you, Herr Knopp. I will make the referral today and tomorrow morning an ambulance will pick you up. Period!"

I couldn't keep myself in my chair; in an instant I jumped up and snarled, "I think it's clear what my father wants—or doesn't want. Respect his wishes, for God's sake!"

"Shut up, you stupid women's libber!" the doctor yelled back. For a moment I thought he might even slap me, but he composed himself. "At least, I will send a proper nurse who will take care of you, Herr Knopp."

Dad shook his head vehemently. Then, he pointed his finger at me. *He wants me to take care of him?* He looked, with a vulnerability that I had never seen before, as he awaited my answer. Choking on tears, I nodded unreservedly.

I had an undefined foreboding that the prognostics of his eventual passing were too optimistic and was comforted that my father wanted me close for those remaining days. It was clear I was the one best suited to take care of him, as my parents' marriage was strained and unhappy. My older sister Christiane lived four hundred miles away; she promised to come visit. Britta, who had become a physiotherapist, lived near my parents' house, and came to check in daily after leaving the clinic. However, once Dad was released from the hospital and back home, the scenario turned painful in a way I hadn't anticipated.

"Do you want more?" my mother lulled in a sing-song baby voice, as she fed her husband yogurt with a spoon. I shuddered. *Why does she need to infantilize him?* Also, she didn't await his answer. She wanted the procedure to be over with.

We'd placed Dad's bed in the living room. "Instead of being up alone in our bedroom," Mum explained, "he has more access to what is going on in the rest of the house." I suspected, though, that was only half of the truth as I saw how she avoided spending time with him.

Dad's pressed-closed lips signaled that he'd had enough yogurt; his eyes were pleading. She got up with a gruff sigh and rushed back to the kitchen. A few minutes later, I heard her slam the front door and drive off fast. She had been going to work as usual since my arrival two weeks earlier. Her boss had offered her paid vacation for as long as she needed and although Dad had gestured many times that he wanted her to stay and sit by his side, she continued to run away. I couldn't figure out if this was because of her fear of losing the man with whom she'd shared nearly thirty years of her life, dying in general, or if it was simply another symptom of an inability to be emotionally available.

Two and a half weeks after my arrival in Germany, I intuited that my father's passing was imminent, so I stayed at his side all day long, placing a big armchair next to the bed where I remained half awake and half asleep during the night. Death was a powerful catalyzer. The possibility of caring for Dad stripped us clean of mutual grievances and repaired whatever had ruptured between us.

At one point, I was awoken by his heavy convulsions, choked by intense fear. I didn't know from where the wisdom arose in me to not try and fix his feelings. Instead, I reached forward and held him in my arms while feeling the speed of my heartbeat. Gradually, as the wave of angst ebbed from both of us, we wept until, eventually emptied out, our breaths grew smooth and calm.

One night when Dad had soiled himself and I was too exhausted to lift his torso to change his diaper, I woke my mother and asked for help. She was livid. At first, I believed her fury was directed at me, but as I followed behind as she rushed down the stairs from the bedroom and stormed into the living room, I realized she was angry with him. In one forceful move, she lifted his hips to rip off the diaper and reached for a fresh one. That's when I realized she had no intention of cleaning him.

I only managed to howl: "He needs to be washed first!" She dropped my father's hips and stormed back upstairs.

A few days later, I knew in my heart and gut that Dad's time had come. Like every other morning, Mum, car keys in hand, was ready to bolt from the house, but this time I ran after and grabbed her by both arms: "You are not leaving, get a grip on yourself, your husband is dying. Stay home for God's sake!"

I was shaken, but at last, she came out of her trance, took off her coat, and sat at Dad's bedside. I called both of my sisters, asking them to come as soon as they could, but it didn't take long for his eyes to glaze over in a final breath. I was stunned by how fast a life and spirit can slip away. The wrinkles and traces of suffering vanished and his expression became serene and peaceful. A little later, his entire body felt so fully emptied of his familiar presence that I wondered if he had ever been here.

THE DEATH of my father had a bigger impact than I could fathom at first. Our family was grief illiterate. When my maternal grandmother or beloved godmother had died in my early teens, I hadn't been allowed to go to the funerals. There hadn't been any conversations with "the children" to help us grapple with the feelings of loss. Now again, as my mother was eager to "move on," my sisters and I did our best to console each other.

I returned to Madrid, pretending to get on with life, but my understanding of impermanence was no longer imaginary. Other than bottling up or masking my feelings, I had no capacity to let myself experience the pain, and so, instead reverted to my mind's intellectual questioning of existence. I had seen my dad trying his best to live a life of integrity in accordance with his Catholic faith, and even though he'd accomplished a lot of what society deemed "correct"—a family, house, stable career—I had rarely seen him happy. I didn't know for sure, but it didn't appear that he had died fulfilled or in peace when he closed his eyes at sixty-four.

As I walked out of the bunker after the final session of the three-week Primal Healing group, I felt victorious and exhilarated for having made it through the intense emotional roller-coaster ride. Unlocking important pieces from my unconscious gave me a more coherent sense of self, as if I had dropped emotional weight. Several days later, though, that euphoria waned. Some of my friends were already signing up for the next program, but it was too costly for me. Also, I doubted that spending more time in the ashram would lead me to the ultimate clarity I sought. Witnessing the relentless cathartic processing, and Osho devotees hanging onto each of their dead master's words while waiting for "enlightenment," was not for me. It also led me to wonder: *How could relentless reverence for somebody supposedly "superior" but long gone, or the constant examination of what was wrong with oneself, bring us any closer to what was already right with life?* Whatever the truth I sought was, it had to be simpler, closer. It couldn't be so contingent upon another person.

After six months in the Osho ashram in Pune I was done. I resolved to find my own way, follow my bliss. Once again, I strapped on my big travel backpack.

chapter 5

Little Lhasa Lessons

If you find no one to support you on the spiritual path, walk alone.
SHAKYAMUNI BUDDHA

I STEPPED onto the open-air gallery in front of my room at the Tashi-Deleg guesthouse in McLeod Ganj, India. It was as cold outside as in and my breath drew clouds with the atmosphere. I held onto the wooden balustrade and with eyes closed offered my face to the first rays of early morning sun. Its light and warmth relaxed my body; I yawned and sighed. I opened my eyes again to take in the majestic vista of the snow-covered peaks of the Dhauladhar Mountains of the Outer Himalayan Range. Underneath the guesthouse's gallery sat small huts and simple dwellings nestled like colorful dots on the slopes of the hill; to my left, the pine forests wove a dark green carpet framing the outskirts of the village.

McLeod Ganj was also known as Upper Dharamsala or even "Little Lhasa." It had earned its name by accommodating a large Tibetan population and for being the seat of the government in exile and official residence of His Holiness the Dalai Lama. After leaving the Osho ashram, I'd traveled throughout India, making my way toward McLeod Ganj, 1,200 miles north of Pune, with the intention of learning more about Buddhism and receiving in-depth instructions in meditation.

I stretched my arms overhead. My body ached, stiff from another miserable night. My room's freezing temperature didn't allow for relaxation or deep sleep. A thin sleeping bag, bought with warm Indian nights in mind, was the wrong equipment for the higher mountain regions and the winter season. My budget dictated a simple guesthouse and enduring the unheated rooms and night chills.

That morning, though, I intended to give myself a treat—for ten rupees extra (roughly twenty cents), one could order a bucket of hot water to be delivered to the shower room, a walled-off ten-square-foot space with no ceiling. A thin metal tube stuck out from one of the uneven red brick walls, serving as showerhead. Once the steaming bucket had arrived, I undressed as fast as I could. Instead of using the ice-cold water from the metal pipe, I submerged a plastic cup into the bucket and poured the hot water over my back. A loud sigh of pleasure escaped my lips, and I shuddered under the wave of bliss. I closed my eyes to savor the warmth that melted not only my physical contractions, but those in my mind as well. There was that immediacy again—for a moment, my thoughts stopped grasping and gave way to an ecstatic sense of pure aliveness. I chuckled. I couldn't remember ever having felt such rapture while taking a shower! *I want to feel like this forever.* At last, I took the half-empty bucket in both hands and let the remaining water spill over my head. I rubbed my body and hair semi-dry and donned several layers of thick clothing.

It was around seven o'clock when I stepped onto the unpaved streets where a few maroon-and-yellow-robed Tibetan monks and nuns were already out and about. The elation lingering from my shower was heightened by their friendly greetings of "*Tashi Deleg!*" After the overt sexual energies in the Osho ashram and Indian men groping me on overnight bus journeys, or undressing me with lecherous stares during travels through other parts of the country, I felt more at ease, and even an inexplicable kinship among the mostly Tibetan population in McLeod Ganj.

Walking a hundred yards, I entered a café with a rooftop terrace. At one of the six metal tables sat two Europeans drinking steaming chai from glass cups. We nodded wordless smiles to each other. My day had started so nicely, so I amped it up by ordering my favorite breakfast: fresh mint tea and pancakes topped with slices of banana and honey. The sun illumined the glistening snow-covered mountains. On the roofs of nearby houses, monkeys bickered and groomed each other, and apart from the sound of a rooster nearby and a distant dog's bark, all was quiet.

The waiter arrived with my order and, after uttering a little prayer, I dove into my honey-dripping pancake. After two or three glorious bites, I put my fork down to close my eyes; as with my delicious shower, I wanted to prolong pleasure by savoring my food more consciously. It felt a bit contrived, to force myself to slow my habitually hasty chewing, but I was set on cultivating more cheer and joy.

My body suffused with a glow of satisfaction when suddenly, a loud *PANG!* jolted me from the chair. I heard the monkeys' high-pitched screams and, following the sound, spotted one of them high on the roof wolfing down the rest of my breakfast while also aggressively guarding his plunder from his brood. Two young guys at a table next to mine erupted in roaring laughter. I blushed, feeling terribly self-conscious. My bliss was gone! But dumbfounded by the swiftness of the pancake thief, I sat down again. *I should at least stay on the terrace to enjoy my tea in the warming sun.* And returning to my habit of distraction from uncomfortable feelings, I reached into my bag for the little book on Buddhist philosophy I'd found in a secondhand bookstore. I opened to a random page and stared straight at the Buddha's words: "Life is suffering." *What does that mean?* I heaved an exasperated sigh and reached for my cup, as if the tea would wash away all irritation.

The Buddha's words—also known as the First Noble

Truth—seemed to point in the opposite direction of what I longed for. The part of me that still hoped to find a magical shortcut, an easy escape from life's pain and challenges, couldn't grasp the connection between this statement and my aspiration for deeper freedom. Like many moderns, I unconsciously assumed I could bend reality to my favor and find happiness if I pressed hard enough and pursued what I wanted. Suffering was simply too big a word, reserved for those enduring war, torture, genocide, or famine. I couldn't bring myself to call my mental-emotional roller coaster rides—the anxiety, worry, and self-doubts gripping and tossing me about day in and day out—"suffering." *I am not helpless. I don't suffer*. I pushed the idea away; a large part of me was scared that if I acknowledged the most obvious and common of all human truths, a looming sense of darkness would swallow me up.

Years later, I would understand the statement "Life is suffering" didn't mean I *shouldn't* enjoy beauty or good fortune when it presented itself, nor that I should resign passively to unfavorable circumstances. It pointed out that cultivating my likes and dislikes and trying to feel good all the time was keeping me mired in constant conflict with reality. I didn't recognize that my clinging to the pleasant (within or without)—the continuous seeking, scheming, strategizing, and struggling to make the right stuff happen and hoping it would last—was fraught with failure. After all, a little monkey had been able to steal my bliss in a split second. Generally, I had trouble allowing my experiences to just be what they were. I was an expert in automatically rejecting and bracing against painful emotions and natural vulnerabilities. Even momentary feelings of sadness or insecurity felt so threatening that my mind would churn and spin endlessly: *Why is this happening? What is wrong with me? What do I need to do to feel differently?*

If I'd continued to read a bit further in my Buddhist booklet that morning, I might have gleaned that suffering was not a matter of *what* was happening, but *how* I related to experiences.

Buddhist teachings offer a poignant analogy for my typical yet unnecessary self-created suffering: we are all eventually struck by arrows of pain, fear, loss, and adversity. It is mostly unavoidable, but we have a choice when it comes to shooting a second arrow: our knee-jerk reactions to what is happening, the resisting and complaining, the trying to escape our discomfort or suppress our pain, the instant fault-finding of who is to blame, or berating ourselves for feeling the way we do. I could have gathered that there was a more liberating way to relate to all my experiences—pleasant, unpleasant, or neutral ones—but instead I stuffed the book back into my bag and abruptly stood up to pay for breakfast.

The street was more crowded now. Apart from the Tibetan monks and nuns, Indian laypeople had opened their stores and a few foreigners wandered the stalls. I still felt too out of sorts to return to the inn. Instead, I chose to hike up to Tushita, the Buddhist meditation center nestled in the forested hills two miles above McLeod Ganj. I intended to register for their two-week-long meditation retreat. Then, suddenly, I heard someone call my name.

I turned around and recognized a man I had chatted with in the bookstore. "Oh, hey—it's Lars, right?"

"Yes, Lars it is." He grinned. "I'm on my way to the office of the Tibetan government in exile and I believe you might want to come with me."

"Why is that?"

"Well, do you have your passport with you?"

"Yes..."

"Great, come on, we'll be getting our permit to attend the public audience with the Dalai Lama tomorrow morning."

"What? We're going to see the Dalai Lama in person?" In a split second, my bad mood had lifted.

The next morning, I was among the first foreigners to arrive at the square between his Holiness's official residence and the Tsuglagkhang temple, but there were already around 200 Tibetans patiently sitting on the stone ground. Most of them uttered prayers or mantras while swiftly moving mala beads through their fingers. A Tibetan organizer appeared and gently led me to a spot where five other foreigners were sitting on the ground on this chilly but otherwise glorious sunny morning. We greeted each other with a friendly nod, content to wait for the Dalai Lama's appearance.

Thirty minutes passed as the sun shone down. I began to feel sweaty and scratchy in my woolen sweater and took off my thick jacket. I looked at the Tibetans around me who didn't seem to mind the waiting or the rising temperature. Ninety minutes later, with the Dalai Lama still nowhere in sight, the gathering had increased to around twenty foreigners and more than 300 Tibetans. Total ease and calm permeated the crowd of seated Tibetans while some of the other westerners and I shifted uncomfortably from one butt cheek to the other. I berated myself for my lack of patience. My self-judgment amplified when it dawned that each Tibetan present must have risked their life fleeing Tibet after the Chinese occupation, embarking on a week-long journey by foot under the harshest conditions. Not only were they refugees, but they lived with the knowledge that their relatives still in Tibet were enduring grave dangers, imprisonment, and even torture for proclaiming devotion to the Dalai Lama. *That qualifies as suffering!* My all-too-familiar mental cacophony grew louder and instead of feeling shared humanity with the refugees and acknowledging that we were all trying to overcome anguish or hardship in one way or another, self-judgmental thoughts isolated and shamed me even further.

A sudden wave of murmuring erupted in the square. The Dalai Lama and a small entourage of monks emerged from his residence and the leader of the Tibetan people in exile positioned himself in front of a microphone. I was all attention! I never dreamed of seeing him in person or this close, and while I didn't know much about Buddhism, I was impressed by how humble this great spiritual leader appeared. I'd once read that he saw himself as "nothing more than a simple monk" and that his religion was kindness.

The microphone gave a little shriek of feedback, then the Dalai Lama addressed his audience in his native language. The longer he spoke, the more I realized that no matter how much I was eager to understand what he was saying, there would be no translation into English. His motive today was to address his compatriots. From the beaming faces of the Tibetans around me, I felt the importance of his presence and speech, and was happy for them.

After speaking for over an hour, the Dalai Lama concluded, and the organizers motioned the audience to stand. They asked us foreigners to organize ourselves in a line next to each other, separate from the Tibetans. His Holiness stepped down from his little podium and approached with his entourage. When he finally progressed toward our group, excitement and nervousness took hold of me. He moved swiftly along the line, speaking a few words to each person, and then the monk next to him handed out a little red thread that had been blessed as a protection against negative influences. When it was my turn, his dark sparkly eyes beamed into mine. I didn't register what he said—his presence combined with my nervousness and awe completely tied my tongue. All I knew was my sense of urgency to support his cause. Only long after he had walked on did I come out of my haze. I too received the little red string and, copying Lars, eagerly tied it around my left wrist.

With a sense of elation, I climbed the hilly path toward Tushita that afternoon, my mind replaying scenes from the morning audience; the soothing serenity of the surrounding woods and the pristine mountain air barely registered. Instead of taking a leisurely stroll, I scampered with hasty eagerness to sign up for the meditation retreat.

Once I reached my destination, I caught my breath—the meditation center looked eerily quiet. I stepped closer and found the entrance doors securely locked. *How can that be?* Just yesterday I'd checked the opening times down in the village and saw a small note pinned on a board next to the entrance: "All courses and retreats are suspended until further notice due to the unusual cold temperatures." My heart sank. *I only have a few more weeks left before I'm supposed to meet my German girlfriend in Kathmandu for hiking in Nepal.* Our travel dates were unchangeable, so even if Tushita opened eventually, I wouldn't be able to attend a full retreat. My mind clouded with heavy disappointment.

As I made my way back down the mountain, deflated, I wondered if the meditation instructions I might have received there would have changed my life in a lasting way, maybe even helping me to no longer be a prisoner of the constant ups and downs of my mind. I had no choice but to wait and see where life would take me next.

chapter 6

Fall in San Francisco

When your desire for wisdom is as great as your desire to breathe, you will find wisdom.
SOCRATES

PRESSING TWO heavy grocery bags against my chest, I closed the apartment door behind me with my foot. A cacophony of voices from the kitchen said that my landlord and roommate, David, had guests. During the last weeks I had come to appreciate David as a hip and amiable guy and I liked meeting his friends, but today I was in the mood for some alone time. Instead of heading toward the kitchen, I took the groceries to my room.

After a year and a half in India, Nepal, and Thailand, and (inspired by Ariel's example) a brief stint in Germany where I'd replenished my bank account by selling precious stones, Asian silver, and gold jewelry bought with that plan in mind, I'd made my way to California. I continued my daily, mostly grueling, meditation practice, but my main intention was to explore creative inclinations in San Francisco, because, after my time in the Pune ashram, I'd come to judge my earlier career choice of interpreter as too cerebral.

Quite miraculously, everything I hoped to find in San Francisco came to fruition rather quickly. Within a few weeks, I found a beautiful room to rent close to the Haight Ashbury district, signed up for sculpture classes at a Mission District art school, and against all odds, had beaten other, better suited candidates to become an unpaid intern at the MOMA rental gallery at Fort Mason. As I explored the city's colorful neighborhoods, trendy galleries, and great museums, or splurged on cappuccinos and cranberry scones for breakfast in hip cafes, my life felt on track to become "picture perfect."

Sunlight flooded the large windows of my bedroom; its lofty ceilings with ornate stucco and white walls made the morning light feel extra luminous. My chest swelled with gratitude for this surprisingly affordable room in one of San Francisco's iconic Victorian houses.

I was walking toward my writing desk to put the grocery bags down when out of the blue, what felt like a lightning bolt shot through my body—my vision went white, the grocery bags fell to the floor, and I tumbled. For a split second, my mind tried to figure out what was happening, but my senses were flooded in a brilliance so profound I could no longer hold onto thoughts. Currents of light pulsed through me, drenching and softening mind and body until I felt weightless, suspended in an otherworldly radiance—and love. Something deep within unlocked and I sobbed tears of relief and gratitude for feeling held in my entirety by this benevolent field—a love that asked for nothing in return—I was loved, just as I was. Long-clenched constrictions opened, and I wept in wonder. I lay motionless on the floor until the benevolent luminosity gradually subsided and I found myself stunned by a mesmerizing infinite silent openness. I chuckled in delight.

Diving deep into the swimming pool in Pune had offered a moment of otherworldly peace, but this experience revealed an all-pervasive field stretching endlessly in content-less stillness.

Fascinated, I stared into the absence of anything, but surprisingly, it didn't feel lacking. Instead, it was complete. I lingered in this boundlessness, free of any notion of time, until a gentle impulse to move again arose.

I rolled onto my side and softly lifted onto my hands and knees, then my feet. *How long have I been on the floor?* I couldn't tell, but I didn't need an answer; the silent openness was much more potent and intriguing than my thoughts. A gentle inner nudge moved me, though, toward the desk to grab paper and pen to capture this unusual experience. I spontaneously jotted down the lines:

Thick sweetness
Gladly I surrender at your feet
One step
...and I dive
Gliding into luminous gray
Following the weightlessness
Where time slowly runs out
World without outlines
Soundless vastness
At the bottom of the Ocean is only the inner echo
Being without Being
Unfathomable Peace
Tears are shedding the veils from my eyes

I couldn't remember ever having known such a pervasive contentment, not even in my childhood moments listening to Sibelius with my father. How could something so undefinable be so fulfilling? I had long sought *something*—a palpable solution, a concrete answer—yet this wordless openness wasn't any*thing* in particular. I had believed that the bolder colors of life, the exalted moods, and ecstatic highs, were key defining qualities of happiness, yet this silent expanse, absent of any phenomenal features was the closest I had ever come to real happiness. Strangely, if pressed to describe its utter neutrality, I would have to call it a "peaceful gray." It struck me I had tried so hard to achieve a shred of calm in all my meditations; meanwhile, silent openness was *already* calm and peaceful in an absolute way that required no doing, no addition or subtraction—in fact, the invitation was to let everything simply *be.*

During the following days and weeks after my "fall," I shied away from unnecessary distractions and retreated whenever possible into my bedroom. So often in my life I'd craved the presence of others to make me feel complete. Not until the three-week Primal Healing group in Pune did I discover how soothing it was to disengage from social interactions. Now I felt even more sacredness in solitude and a sense of privilege for being in my own company. No longer driven to look for novel experiences or external fulfillment, I felt myself arriving, again and again, in the calm contentment and suchness of what was already here.

WHILE I had been gifted with a significant spiritual opening, my uncovering of a silent, infinite substratum hadn't yet translated into a more thorough understanding of reality. Eckhart Tolle's *The Power of Now* had not been published yet, and terms like stillness, presence, or mindfulness had not reached the mainstream. Like many people—spiritual seekers or not—who experience glimpses of silent openness when discursive thinking falls to the side, I still believed the wordless vastness existed as something *other* than myself, that I was somebody separate experiencing or witnessing silent openness. This subtle sense of separation between me on one side and silent infinite on the other perpetuated the illusion that this wide-open presence was a powerful and utterly pleasant experience that "I" could visit, instead of the very material out of which my being and all of existence was made. Even though the sense of being a confined, separate entity dissolved whenever I dropped into silent openness, I didn't yet fully grasp its scope and ultimate meaning. With a little help from a knowledgeable guide or skillful teacher, I probably could have examined the habitual view of my identity in this context more closely. I could have discovered that the separate me as the looker, experiencer, or visitor to silent openness was neither as real nor as solid as it appeared to be. However, for the time being, my sense or seat of identity remained mostly as the Annette who lived in a world that appeared as concrete and solid as herself. In other words, I was still half-dreaming the dream of separation.

After my "fall," my goals and pursuits felt trivial—they paled in comparison to the causeless contentment of silent openness. With this in mind, I decided to end my nomadic travels and settle in San Francisco. I sent a letter to the U.S. immigration services applying for an extension of my visitor's visa. Two months passed with no response. Uncertainty gnawed at me. My bohemian lifestyle had eaten a considerable hole in my savings and with a tourist visa's expiration date looming, it became more difficult to not be highjacked and flooded by the mind's constant chatter. In fact, my mind's old, hardwired worrying-mode returned with a vengeance: *What if my visa's extension was declined? When would I need to prepare myself for a possible departure? Do I have enough money left to start all over again in a new place, a new country? And most important—where should I go?*

As the days clicked by, my formal meditation practice did nothing to help me calm. More than ever, I felt trapped on the rollercoaster ride of frantic thoughts and free-floating anxiety. The taste of that peace of silent openness only magnified and exacerbated my sense of becoming more unhinged. In some moments, my body was so electric with fear that it didn't stop trembling, and when I sat down to find that peace and calm, a few seconds later I had already jumped up and out of my seat, pacing relentlessly back and forth between the walls of my room.

At last, the much-awaited letter from immigration arrived. I tore the envelope open, but the news pulled the rug out from under my feet: the extension request had been denied—I had to leave the U.S. in two weeks. The short-term notice left me rattled and rudderless, but at least I knew what to do. I settled the bill with my landlord, drastically reduced my belongings again to fit into my backpack and said goodbye to my few friends.

There was one problem: I couldn't figure out where to go! I had no concrete ideas for a new destination, let alone a clear vision for the next chapter of my life. San Francisco had offered me what I had been searching for—an inner contentment and peace independent of external conditions, but also an inspiring and vibrant multi-cultural city atmosphere. I wished I could make it my permanent home, but this was not a possibility. *Maybe one day I can plan my return more carefully with the right visa?*

Looking back at those last days in California, I never considered returning to Europe where, at least, I could have recreated a stable home for myself. The "old me" was irrevocably gone; returning to the familiar held no appeal. Something deep within had been unleashed since I'd left Sergio and Spain. As I packed to leave San Francisco, I realized a different sense of expansion had arrived: the thrill of letting myself drift and discover where life was leading in the absence of having a perfect plan.

To say that leaping across the groundless space of the unknown once again felt distressing and disturbing was a serious understatement, but it also appeared strangely right. No, I wasn't ready to drop my anchor in Europe. I was thirty-one—had no partner, kids, or mortgage—the world was mine! *Why shouldn't I make good use of my extraordinary freedom for a bit longer?* As I stood in a travel agency and perused possible flights from San Francisco to other countries, the travel agent told me of a special discount Air New Zealand had announced—an inexpensive around-the-world ticket. I smiled: *The Heavens are clearly supporting my idea!* The left-hand path beckoned me onward.

chapter 7

Down Under Wanderings

I would love to live
Like a river flows,
Carried by the surprise
Of its own unfolding.
JOHN O'DONOHUE, "Fluent"

AFTER A couple weeks on Canada's west coast and the Fiji Islands, I was eager to arrive in what the Māori called the "land of the long white cloud." My travel funds were nearly depleted, and I couldn't afford any further idleness or vacations. I spent a few days in Auckland on the North Island, then following an intuitive hunch, traveled further south to find some way to make money. Apple picking season was about to begin and I intended to lodge at a backpacker's hostel in Nelson on the northern tip of the South Island. The so-called Nelson Tasman region was famous for its endless variety of hiking trails with stunning coastal views and gold-sanded beaches.

As I pulled out my German passport to check-in, the owner of the hostel asked how many languages I spoke.

"Four."

My answer prompted him to offer me a job on the spot to

help him at reception. Surprised, grateful, and utterly relieved, I accepted. *So much better than apple-picking!*

I spent two and a half happy months working in the hostel, where I met travelers from all over the world. I shared a tiny apartment on the property with a British woman who also helped out there, and in my free time I explored the breathtaking landscape around Nelson. One time, I swapped several of my working shifts with a colleague to get three free days in a row to explore the Golden Bay area. From Nelson, I hitched a few rides in direction toward Takaka, which lay sixty miles away, but when my first ride dropped me somewhere halfway and I stood waiting to get picked up on the side of the road for a longer while, I let go of my planned destination on the spot and instead ventured off through pastures and fields. I ambled for hours without seeing another soul, collecting feathers and stones that spoke to me. In the late afternoon, I arrived at a small empty bay with a white sanded beach. *What luck!* I wandered down from the dunes and set up my tent at a safe distance from the shore before the dark set in. When I awoke the next morning and unzipped my tent, I spotted a small seal emerging from the water, rolling onto the beach to doze off unencumbered in the sun. I was happy to stay in my sleeping bag gazing at this free creature and the horizon beyond, while munching on some apples and nuts for breakfast.

As the seal slipped back into the sea, I finally got up. The waves felt too chilly and rough to swim, so I hiked through the surrounding hills. When I got hungry again, I warmed up some beans on my little gas stove for late lunch, and after making myself some tea, pulled my sleeping bag out onto the sand to nestle down with some crackers under the afternoon sun and read a book while gusts of wind tussled my hair. From time to time, I looked up, relishing my solitude and the unfettered wilderness. The next morning, though, any euphoria about my private little paradise waned quickly as I detected a male silhouette in the distance high up on the dunes overlooking the bay. I believed the man had noticed my presence or at least seen my tent. He stood motionless for a minute and then disappeared over the dunes. My body tensed and my mind spun anxious thoughts: *Would he come back? What if he had bad intentions, seeing a woman on her own in the middle of nowhere? If I were a man, I wouldn't need to put up with this shit of needing to run for safety!* I didn't wait. I scrambled to pack my belongings while staying alert, and once I had my backpack strapped on, I strode for several hours toward the road and headed back, a day earlier than intended, to Nelson.

When my three-month tourist visa neared its end, I quit my position at the hostel to explore more of the South Island's stunning nature with a friend. There was so much to see: ancient glaciers and majestic peaks, windswept rugged beaches and pristine glacially fed lakes, rolling farmlands and vast open plains.

For my last three days in New Zealand, I booked into a solitary retreat cabin at a Tibetan Buddhist center in the mountains. I felt called to draw inward again, sitting longer in meditation, and digesting my travel experiences before heading to Australia, the final stop on my around-the-world-ticket.

ON THE second morning at the retreat center, I descended from my small cabin to the stupa, a white painted hemispherical shrine of sacred relics, and passed the meditation hall. Seeing it empty, I felt a pull to enter and practice there. The peace and quiet was tangible, and I remained standing with eyes closed for some time. When I opened them, my gaze fell on a curtain on one of the side walls. Curious, I stepped closer to peek behind it and was surprised to discover a small niche housing an elevated platform with a meditation cushion to one side and a mesmerizing tapestry on the opposite wall.

The artwork was a Buddhist thangka depicting a pale, luminous female figure. She sat in full lotus position with the soles of her feet pointing upward. Each sole featured an eye in its center, and so did each palm. Above her two human eyes was a seventh eye in the center of her forehead. Her left hand held a lotus flower and her right, extended down to her knee, formed a mudra. I had no idea who she was, but as I continued to take in this stunning presence, an all-encompassing benevolence and compassion enveloped me as tears trickled down my cheeks. I was inadvertently reminded of the vast, impersonal love I had felt in my "fall" in San Francisco. I was awestruck by the power of love emanating from this luminous feminine being. I realized that for my entire childhood, I'd believed God to be male without question! Yes, we had prayed to Mother Mary, but women were nothing more than a sideshow in the Church, sometimes even completely absent and shunned from any relevant positions. The "real deal"—the men—were always center stage.

Upon discovering silent openness in San Francisco, my childhood fixations of a male God-figure had morphed into a more universal, even impersonal, presence. This had left me with a dilemma: I had no longer been able to pray or direct my devotion toward a particular form. But in this niche, in the powerful presence of this luminous being, I grasped that there was a feminine face to Spirit. I could relate to her. Feeling her so intimately within my heart and being made me sob. My devotion had found a place to abide.

Once emptied of tears, I noticed a scroll of paper nearby; it featured the following lines: *I take refuge in wisdom, I take refuge in compassion, I take refuge in non-clinging awareness. May I develop the six perfections and speedily awaken for the sake of all sentient beings.*

The full meaning of these words—non-clinging awareness, awakening, or six perfections—were nebulous to me, yet they felt viscerally so right. I learned the invocation by heart and vowed to recite it daily.

At the end of my stay at the Buddhist retreat center, I visited the bookstore on site. Here was where I learned more about the luminous feminine being I encountered in the thangka. She was known as White Tara and her name meant "the one who saves." In Tibetan Buddhism she is known as the Mother of Liberation, a completely enlightened being and female Buddha who had promised to always appear in the form of a female bodhisattva and goddess for the benefit of all living beings.

The six perfections on the scroll of paper were the qualities of generosity, ethical discipline, patience, enthusiastic effort, concentration, and wisdom. *Is it even possible to judge how I'm faring with all of these?* I possessed enough self-awareness to recognize that neither patience nor concentration had ever been my strong suits. Most important, though, the words "awakening for the sake of all sentient beings" struck a deep chord within me. It had never crossed my mind that my struggles or seeking could possibly benefit others.

MY TRAVELS led me onward to Australia where, after a few days of sightseeing in Sydney, I itched to get out of the city and do what I had dreamed of for quite some time: cross the 1,900 miles of the big red continent starting south in Adelaide, heading toward Darwin in the north. I first traveled by Greyhound buses but soon was offered rides in the cars of newly found friends. On my way through the "red center" (Australia's Outback), I became fascinated, almost intoxicated, by the arid open plains. Like no other place in nature, the vast desert landscapes evoked a silent openness that felt palpable. So far, I had mostly stayed in inexpensive lodges, but in the Outback I couldn't resist the temptation to pitch a tent in the bush off the road. Camping wild in the sheer expanse of nature made my body and heart spasm with joyful rapture while the immense canopy of stars and velvety darkness of the night sheltering me swallowed any concerns about my physical safety.

Since leaving San Francisco, a quieter presence had woven itself more prominently throughout my days. When it emerged into the foreground of my experience, I let inner and outer activities drop away to rest without distraction in the natural expanse. At other times, I experienced a neutral, unassuming presence, a peaceful backdrop to the movements in the foreground of my life. I was determined to stay where I was!

One day, I met a woman, a fellow backpack traveler, who gave me the phone number of a man named Doug, the boss of one of the opal mines in Coober Pedy, who sometimes offered temporary work to travelers passing through. I called him and we came to an agreement.

Coober Pedy was known as the "opal capital of the world," but capital was a big word for this little town of 2,000 souls that sat halfway between Adelaide and Alice Springs. With over seventy opal fields, Coober Pedy's mines supplied the world with the largest quantity of gem-quality opals. It was late in the evening and dark when I arrived on a Greyhound bus.

While the idea of working in an opal mine had sounded like an interesting adventure on the phone, as I descended from the bus a murky feeling swirled in the pit of my stomach. *Other than another woman's assurance of Doug being all right, I don't really know this man. What have I gotten myself into?* As I retrieved my pack, I nervously tried to spot another woman at the bus stand or at least a taxi in case I needed to change my plan; there were neither. Doug had said I should look for him next to his red pickup truck. I could only make out three older men—none appearing particularly friendly—and then what looked like an Aboriginal man of undefinable age and a teenage boy, both dressed in western clothing.

At last, I spotted someone waving. My mind raced as I ambled toward Doug. He was in his mid-forties, with a stocky body, furrowed face, shock of what in the dark looked like reddish-blond hair, and an unkempt beard. He was as rough-looking as I'd imagined a man who lived most of his life in a desert mining town. As Doug stepped toward me, his face cracked into a broad, warm-hearted smile. "Howdy! How was your trip?" He shook my hand, reached for my backpack, and flung it without effort into the bed of his pickup truck. "You must be hungry! I already ate, but I still have some dinner for you. Let's go."

The woman traveler's words replayed in my mind: *He is really nice. You don't need to feel unsafe with him at all...if you know what I mean.* My alertness settled a bit.

Doug took me for a quick drive through town, which consisted mostly of poorly illuminated streets, a row of stores, funky looking opal galleries, an open-air cinema in a dusty parking lot and, overall, remarkably few buildings.

"This town is much smaller than I expected," I commented.

"Yes, it seems that way at first sight, but it's because most of us live underground," Dave chuckled. "You'll see, when we get home!"

Like most of the Coober Pedy's inhabitants, Doug lived in a dugout—a residence either built below the earth's surface or bored like a cave in a hillside. These dwellings were the only way to escape the scorching daytime temperatures, which in summer months could run between 100°F and 120°F. Doug's dugout looked surprisingly cozy. While it featured only one window next to the entrance, it didn't feel claustrophobic, as the rough stone walls of the kitchen, living space, and each of the three bedrooms were well-illuminated and painted in a warm white.

"Here is where my traveling workers sleep." He opened the door to one of the bedrooms. It was neat and friendly with a woven carpet in front of the bed, a small closet, a little wooden desk, and chair. "Maybe you want to eat something before unpacking? And then, I leave you here by yourself. I need to go to the claim. You can start work tomorrow night."

"The claim" was Doug's mining field, and the following evening, we drove out together in his truck. I learned that no one worked on their claims in the desert during the day. With the sun blazing hot eleven hours a day, temperatures during the night could cool down to sixty degrees Fahrenheit, offering needed reprieve. My job was to sit in a little metal shed above the ground which had a conveyer-belt coming in to one side and leaving on the other. The shed was completely dark except for a small lamp that spotlighted the part of the belt right in front of me. I was tasked with sifting and looking for pieces of opals among all the dirt and stones that Doug and his worker Bob extricated with an excavator from the desert's ground. I was exhilarated when I found my first pieces of opal, but they were not substantial compared to what could be found, so my income remained rather minimal. We agreed that my pay was to live rent-free with all meals included, plus a small percentage of all the gemstones that I fished from the conveyer-belt.

Doug was always good-natured, and we had many enjoyable conversations at dinner which we traded off cooking for each other. His slightly younger worker Bob, on the other hand, was unsympathetic. He existed mostly in a bad mood, always had a can of beer in hand, and hardly ever talked, except for one evening when he dropped by at dinnertime to ask if we wanted to join him and some others to go out shooting kangaroos.

"Is he serious?" I looked at Doug, waiting for both men to laugh out loud for pulling my leg, but Doug nodded. I was horrified—I was a vegetarian, after all.

I got another reality check about life in the Outback when on my night off I told Doug I planned to walk into town to watch a movie at the outdoor cinema. He jumped off his couch, alarmed. "Let me drive you! Maybe I'll even stay and watch the movie with you."

"What? No, that's not necessary..." But he was already pulling his truck keys off the nail by the door.

"Oh, believe me, you don't want to walk around at night alone. Over the years, girls and women have disappeared here.

With all the empty mining shafts, you see, there are a thousand places where you can hide a dead body."

I swallowed, my mouth suddenly dry, and accepted his offer without further protest.

THE FANCY outfits I'd worn as an interpreter in Spain seemed 10,000 miles away from my daily wardrobe in Coober Pedy: jeans or shorts, t-shirt, sweater, and my *blunnies*—the quintessential Australian worker boots. At night, when I took a break and left the shed to stretch my legs, or sat under that endless, silent dark night sky, I dropped into a simple but profound delight of being alive.

After three weeks working on the claim, I had made hardly any money and wondered if it wouldn't be smarter to soon move on. Australia was the last stop on my round-the-world-ticket, and if I wanted to continue north toward Darwin and arrive in Europe in time for my younger sister's wedding, I needed to make enough money to buy an out-bound plane ticket. Flying "home" to Germany after my Australia adventure seemed like a natural bookend to my free-roaming life and putting down roots somewhere.

Whether Doug felt sorry for me or just wanted me to stay longer, I don't know, but when I told him of my intention to leave, he offered: "Look, let's make a deal. Whatever pieces you find on your shift tonight, fifty percent of the gains will be yours!"

Lo and behold—I couldn't believe my luck—that night I found a big piece of opal and, honoring his word, even though I could sense a whiff of reluctance, Doug paid me a considerable amount for it.

As I lay in bed after my night shift, I realized my lucky strike was one of the many synchronistic incidents that had continued to happen since I had entrusted myself to the heavens. During the last two years, I had exposed myself to the most diverse circumstances, setting up temporary homes in diverse cultures, and had replenished my funds as I went along. While it had often been nerve-racking to be so untethered, I noticed now how it had spurred my mind to surrender its relished certainty and control and allow my relationship to life's inherent unpredictability to blossom. I marveled at how I had begun to experience a deepening sense of fluidity in which my previously held notion of having a specific, fixed personality loosened. A visceral knowing had settled in that—like life itself—I too was a constantly changing, living process and that there was so much more to me than I ever could have imagined. Naturally, there were those unchangeable characteristics like my ethnicity or the color of my eyes; however, most of what I believed to be me were mere images and thoughts *about* me in my mind—plus a bunch of habits of feeling and behavior, but these too could change! As some old assumptions and emotional rigidities softened, my usual sense of identity and boundaries stretched and even the world at large no longer felt so overpowering or disconnected from my self. With it all, a new confidence had begun to throb within: *If I keep listening and trusting the natural flow of life, I should do okay—I'll be in good hands.*

INDEED, THE flow soon carried me back to Europe, propelled by my sister Britta's upcoming nuptials. I accepted the journey home to Germany as a natural closure to my free-roaming existence which had started in India more than two years earlier. I told myself, *"It's about time to put my head straight back on again,"* and resolved to pour energy into a career change: something in the humanistic, therapeutic field, like becoming a shiatsu practitioner.

But after my sister's wedding and then living and working for three months in Berlin, the contrast between open-ended explorations and the confines of conventional, structured German life made me uneasy. In my native country one planned far ahead, something most people didn't mind, but I chafed against. *Why do I have so much trouble with what is so appreciated by most people?* I had felt more at home in the largeness of the world, and yet in my own country the walls closed in and I struggled; I could feel the onset of depression.

Soon, I connected with two women I'd met in India, and after hatching a plan to travel together to Japan, I bought my ticket and pulled my trusted backpack out of the closet again.

chapter 8

Skeletons in Tokyo

The attempt to satisfy greed is like drinking salty water when thirsty. When lost in greed we look outward rather than inward for satisfaction, never finding enough to fill the emptiness we wish to escape. The real hunger we feel is for knowledge of our true nature.

TENZIN WANGYAL RINPOCHE, *The Tibetan Yogas of Dream and Sleep*

In my eagerness to get ready, dress up, and dash out to meet Julie at a trendy dance club in Roppongi, I wolfed down the last bits of my late dinner. I sat the empty bowl down, still picking out the last grains of rice with my finger and putting them into my mouth while looking around with satisfaction: my new home was tiny, but I loved it! It measured only seventy-five square feet, with a floor covered in tatami—yellow-golden rice straw mats with edging around the borders. The few pieces of furniture—little fridge, gas stove, and folding table—were all low to the ground. I soon got used to following the Japanese habit of moving around my room on my knees, or sitting in *seiza*—shins on the floor, legs together, buttocks resting on the ankles, and back straight. At night, I folded the small table and stored it in a niche in the wall to make space for a thin futon sleeping mat. The toilet and wash sink, to be shared with other tenants, were down the corridor. However, I was fond of visiting the *sento*, one of the old, traditional public bathhouses still in use throughout modern Japan. Copying the other mostly older women, I first soaped and scrubbed my body vigorously clean, and then joined them to soak in the steaming hot water as they chatted about the neighborhood news.

Even in the face of Japan's stock market crash and its economy deteriorating into crisis in the late fall of 1997, Tokyo was extravagantly expensive, but I knew by now how to scrape by. After a few bumpy weeks, I'd found my affordable room to rent and was managing to make a decent income with odd but well-paid translating jobs, teaching German at a language academy and to private students, and working a few weeknights behind the counter of a bar in Akasaka where my job duties were to make light conversations with Japanese customers and "smile a lot." It was where I learned the most about Japanese culture in exchanges with patrons. There was the professor for Hispanic language studies from Tokyo University who came regularly to talk in Spanish and share his unfiltered views on Japanese society or high-ranking businesspeople who made at times archaic and incomprehensible comments like: "*I love my wife. She is truly amazing, because I never know how she really feels.*" During free time, my private German students (most of them well-situated homemakers) invited me to taste *Kaiseki Ryori*, the traditional Japanese multi-course haute cuisine, and visit Shinto shrines or the Buddhist Zen temple in the seaside town of Kamakura. With expat friends, I often ventured out on weekends to relax at an *Onsen Ryokan* (a natural hot springs hotel) near Mount Fuji.

After forging a close friendship with Julie, an Australian who had taken a year off from Asian studies in Australia to improve her Japanese in Tokyo, my exotic lifestyle had become ever more exhilarating as we roamed the nightclub culture in the Shibuya or Roppongi neighborhoods, open for business twenty-four hours a day, seven days a week. My lingering questions about my life's true purpose and the haunting, existential ache I had felt so starkly when returning to Germany a few months earlier had faded into the background as I bustled through a new life in Japan.

AT FIRST, Roppongi appeared as usual: the midnight scenery on Gaien Higashi Dori Road was as busy as ever. The flashing neon lights from hundreds of billboards competed with the bright facades of bars, restaurants, and dance and Karaoke clubs. The night air was cool and dry, and I was one step away from crossing the threshold of a club I already had visited many times before. From inside emanated the usual muffled cheers and throbbing beats. The bouncer nodded with a knowing smile and signaled for me to enter. As he opened the door, I caught a glimpse of the scene inside and gasped, stopping in my tracks. *Is this for real?* My ears rang, my pulse pounded in my temples, and I couldn't move. The bouncer motioned again, but feeling all my energy drain, I politely declined with a quick hand gesture. He nodded and closed the door again.

Dizzy nausea spun my head as the scene inside the club replayed. With weak knees, I hunched with my hands on my thighs, letting my gaze drop toward the ground. The usual partying crowd had filled the club—only this time I hadn't seen people, but instead...skeletons. Human bones without flesh or blood: dancing and laughing, drinking, and smoking in the dark, illuminated by the eerie disco lights. I was stone-cold sober; I never took recreational drugs and had no trace of alcohol in my system; my vision felt as acute and real as the pavement in front of me. What was happening?

"Hey! So cool, you could make it," a woman's voice called.

Julie's strong Australian accent gave her away in an instant. Shaking, I lifted my torso up and my friend pressed a kiss on my right cheek, her breath minty from chewing gum. "Am I late?" she grinned, ruffling her bleached blonde pixie cut.

"No," I rasped.

"What's going on? Are you waiting for a special invitation to go in?"

I swallowed with my mouth dry, and still feeling my legs floppy, I bent over again.

"Are you okay, sweetie?" Julie's cheery sing-song voice tilted into worry.

She told her companions, two handsome Japanese hipsters with long hair, to go ahead without us. She took my arm and lowered her face to meet mine, trying to decipher what on earth was happening.

"It's okay—just give me a moment," I mumbled, trying to regain my bearings.

By focusing on the ground, I hoped to make the seen unseen. And yet, in some corner of my mind, I was lucid enough to intuit that the skeletons were only visible to me. There was no way I could explain this to Julie. The vision was probably gone by now, and if I wanted, I could simply follow her inside for another night of wild partying.

"Are you feeling sick?" she insisted.

And then, it hit me: *Are the morbid skeletons a warning sign, a wake-up call to stop squandering my life?*

The last months had brought me much rapture and release—it had been so cathartic, almost therapeutic to unleash my wild side amid Tokyo's night scene. I relished outgrowing the hapless girl who still had felt so insecure in the ashram in India as I unapologetically explored my sensuality here with different men. I knew there was nothing wrong with pleasure or having fun—and yet, if I was honest, these sexual encounters heightened an underlying longing for *true* connection. In fact, none of my larger-than-life-experiences freed me from a harrowing sense of hollowness. And, instead of practicing my formal sitting meditation, I'd been running to the gym in the mornings, having grown obsessed with giving my naturally slender frame an athletic look by sculpting my arms and abs with weights, and sweating profusely on the treadmill.

Unwittingly, I fell victim again to my mind's grasping for *more or better.* I was certain: having or fulfilling one's desires wasn't the problem—but it didn't seem to be the answer either. The skeleton vision sliced through me like a surgical incision, dividing everything before from what lay ahead—the next minutes, hours, days, months, or even years to come. The future wasn't here yet, but it would depend upon what I did or didn't do next. *I needed to put an end to this mindless pursuit of self-gratification and fast-lived pleasure.*

I lifted my head to meet Julie's eyes saying, "I need to go. Sorry!" And without waiting for her reply, I ran, leaving my perplexed friend behind.

Fifteen minutes later, I slowed down, catching my breath in Shibuya's biggest traffic crossing. There, mega TV screens streamed video day and night from surrounding buildings. As the lights turned green, I crossed, weaving through crowds of people toward the subway station. I hastily bought my ticket at one of the countless vending machines, passed the ticket barriers and bounded two steps at a time up to the platform of the Inokashira line. The train arrived immediately; the doors slid open. As I collapsed onto the bench and the doors closed, I felt like I had narrowly escaped the peril of wasting my precious life. *Maybe I've gone mad?*

I intuited that if I'd crossed the threshold into the club for another night of partying until daylight, I would have become a skeleton myself—a hungry ghost, always wanting, always looking, but never finding fulfillment or coming to rest.

It was long after midnight when my train rolled into Eifukucho station in western Tokyo. Compared with the relentless buzz and business in most neighborhoods of the metropolis of twelve million people, this residential area was quiet. All the shops and grocery stores on the main street were closed, except for the twenty-four-hour 7-Eleven at the corner. After five minutes, I turned right into a smaller side street. The single-family houses on both sides were dark; the entire neighborhood seemed fast asleep. I stopped in front of an old wooden gate and opened it as quietly as I could, but it gave off its usual squeak. I followed the little stone garden path toward the main entrance of the large two-story residence.

My landlord, who lived with his French wife and young children on the ground floor, told me the house had been owned by his family for many generations. In fact, the unusual large size of this old, traditional building was the main reason it had been spared from destruction during the bombing raids of World War II—the Allies assumed it was a hospital. I entered through the heavy main door, slipped off my shoes in the dark and climbed the broad wooden stairs to the second floor where different tenants, like me, occupied various studios and rooms. I was close to two people on my floor: Mikkel, a Danish man who had come to Tokyo years ago with his dance company, fallen in love with a Japanese woman, Yasuko, and never left. Both lived non-traditional lives like I did and often invited me for tea in their much more spacious place.

In my room I switched on the light, took off my jacket, kneeled in front of the small gas stove, and poured water into a pot to make tea. I moved onto my sitting cushion under the sliding windows. While waiting for the water to boil, I contemplated the strange skeleton vision. I shuddered but felt lucidly awake. What kept me pushing on? Was it more freedom, more fun, and deeper reasons to be alive? Hadn't I looked everywhere—music, books, career, the eyes of my lovers, different countries, adventure, ashrams, even discotheques? When was it ever going to be enough?

The memory of my sixteenth birthday resurfaced: my first conscious recognition of the unrelenting fact of impermanence. I sighed. *Perhaps I've fulfilled that sixteen-years-old's vow to live to the fullest, but I will never outrun death.*

THE NEXT morning, following an urge to ritualize my renewed commitment to my search, I visited a hairdresser in Harajuku where I had my long curly mane cut short above my chin. Continuing with a much lighter head, I walked straight to nearby Yoyogi Park. With over 130 acres of sprawling lawns, ponds, forested areas, and wide tree-lined paths, it was one of Tokyo's largest green zones and my favorite hang-out space in the city. On Sundays, it filled with jugglers, musicians, hip-hop dancers, martial arts practitioners, romantic couples, and families picnicking; but on this weekday morning the park exuded an air of serene dignity.

I was drawn to Meiji Jingu, the large Shinto shrine which, with its several courtyards and ceremonial halls, many considered to be the true heart of the park. In Japan, the ancient Indigenous faith of Shintoism co-exists peacefully with the practice of Buddhism. The Shinto philosophy resonated with me, as it isn't about the worship of one supreme God, but more about the fundamental goodness inherent to all beings; it also sees sacred spirits residing all around us—in rivers, trees, mountains, the stars, even the wind.

I loved following the shrine etiquette for paying respect to the sacred spirits. Upon entering through the *Tori* (a forty-foot-tall, massive wooden archway) I bowed and then proceeded to the *Temizuya*, a fountain with cleansing waters. There I dipped a bamboo ladle into the water to rinse my left hand, then my right, then poured more water into my left hand to cleanse my mouth, one more time to clean the left hand, and at last I rinsed the handle of the bamboo ladle. I positioned myself in front of the main shrine where I placed some coins into an offering box, bowed two times, and then loudly clapped my hands twice. Now ready to address the spirits, I solemnly vowed to no longer let myself become distracted. I asked the ones who could hear me to please help me find what still seemed amiss. Knowing that I had been extremely lucky until now, I concluded with a final bow, giving thanks for the good fortune of my life.

THREE WEEKS later, feeling forlorn amid the high-towering modern structures of gray cement, stainless steel, and shiny facades of Shinjuku, Tokyo's business and commercial district, I wrapped my arms around my torso in an attempt to ward off the cold autumn air. Ever since the skeleton vision, I had felt disoriented and out of sorts, my robust bounce and usual capacity to function dissipated. I'd lost access to my reliable inner compass and my days were barely held together by a routine of work, study of *Sai Tai* (an ancient Japanese form of bodywork), grocery shopping, and gym visits. Additionally, several sources of income had recently dwindled, so paying my bills was tricky.

An endless stream of neatly groomed office workers, impeccably dressed businessmen, and secretaries with designer handbags passed without noticing me. I stopped for a moment to catch my silhouette in a store window. The reflection looked neat and presentable, but inside I was a total mess. I'd lost my way to a job interview at a new language academy, and on top of it, couldn't call them for help because my cellphone's battery had run empty.

Amid the street bustle, out of the corner of my eye I glimpsed a still presence. Ten yards further on the pavement, undisturbed by the frenzy sat an old monk in clean, unassuming robes. I looked around: *Does anyone else see him? How did he get here?* I forgot my shivering body and stepped closer.

In front of the monk on the ground lay a colorful display of ancient-looking images. He was selling pictures of Buddhist statues, mandalas, and calendars adorned with mystical landscapes. He looked straight at me and smiled. The naked warmth in his eyes made me smile back and we held each other's gaze for a moment. I followed his gesture inviting me to take a better look at what he was selling and kneeled on the cold stone. My elemental Japanese was no match for the monk's complex words; he seemed to be explaining the different symbols. Whether it was his clear, peaceful presence or the exotic renderings that drew me in, the world around me vanished and a great calm took hold. The monk picked up one of the calendars and waved it, inviting me to support his cause.

"*Sumimasen*," I said, bowing slightly to underline my apology. Speaking in the most rudimentary Japanese, I told him that I loved what I saw, but my pockets were truly empty.

The monk kept smiling as he pushed one of his calendars into my hands. I didn't want to be disrespectful, but as he didn't seem to understand that I couldn't afford it, I got up and stepped away. Something in his voice, though, was adamant. He continued waving the calendar and it finally dawned on me that it was a gift. Teary, I bowed down a couple of times to thank him.

I gave up on the interview. Back home, still with my coat on, I took some scissors and carefully separated the images from the calendar and plastered all twelve on the walls of my tiny room. Later, when I lay down upon my thin futon mat to sleep, I didn't want to draw the curtains as usual. The moon shone its beautiful silvery light inside my room, illuminating the images of Buddha and mandalas on the walls around me. I couldn't stop looking at them, as if waiting for an answer to the question: *What does the monk know about happiness that I don't?*

When I awoke the next morning, something was different. The windows framed the grayish November sky as I lay on my futon on the floor. Strangely, though, it felt as if the sky was not above me or *out there*. I tried to shake off this unfamiliar experience, but it didn't fade. I noticed I could sense my body, but "I" no longer experienced being located behind my eyes. Rather, I was nowhere in particular. Dumbfounded, I closed my eyes again and stopped any further attempts to get rid of this peculiar notion. As I let myself *be,* my mental bewilderment relaxed, and I recognized the familiar wordless openness expanding endlessly. *There is something different now.*

I opened my eyes, and it hit me: there was no longer any boundary between inside and outside. Any sense of separation had collapsed, everything was infused with a strange insubstantiality. *How can this be?* Yet, this ineffable groundlessness felt more real and true than anything I had known. Even more startling: *I* could no longer find...*myself*...at the center of it all. *This doesn't make sense!* My thinking mind raced like a computer scouring its data to search for a matching piece of information which could explain my experience. But no concept fit this alien perspective, nothing that could sort it into some familiar idea or proven theory about reality. Any movements of grasping for an accustomed sense of orientation felt futile. My familiar perspective and distinct self were gone.

Prickly sensations arose, a surge of heat—physical sensations which *I* could feel but at the same time didn't belong to *me*. Unsettled, I pushed myself up into a seated position and looked around. Nothing else had changed in the room. My eyes fell on the wall mirror close to the door. Pushing the blankets aside, I hastily stood but then hesitated before looking into the mirror. *What if I don't have a reflection—like vampires in movies?* I took a breath, bracing for the possibility of further shock—but, of course there it was—my face in the mirror produced relief, yet as I continued to stare, I couldn't shake off the strange knowing that the image or what it seemingly pointed to was rather...the absence of *me*.

In the following days and weeks, anything I had previously identified as me or believed to be objectively solid and real, appeared as a mere illusion. The memories of being Annette growing up in Germany, Annette working as an interpreter in Spain, Annette the adventurous world traveler, Annette the meditator, or Annette enjoying pleasurable abandon in Tokyo's night clubs felt as transparent as gossamer garments that I had slipped in and out of—only I couldn't find the me who had been wearing them. I had no cognitive framework to help navigate this unfamiliar territory. A knowledgeable spiritual guide could have reassured me I wasn't going mad, but rather, gaining increasing clarity and insight into the truth of reality. I didn't understand yet that the familiar identity of a separate me located in an apparently solid body was nothing more than an idea—a construct of the dualistic thinking mind—which was continuously backed up and kept alive by my culture's predominant worldview of separation. And yet, this direct, non-conceptual experience conveyed there was no *me* standing apart from the seamless symphony of images, sounds, or sensations. My mind continued to struggle as it looked for familiar markers and reference points of *me,* but there were none. The openness I had experienced back in San Francisco as benign and accommodating now felt radically earth-shattering and groundless. I assumed I still existed in some undefinable, way—but *how* and *where* were unsolvable riddles. *If I am not Annette—the actor or director of my life—who am I? And, if I am not in this body, where?*

I WAS overcome by the terror of ceasing to exist once before. One hot summer night at eight or nine, I was unable to sleep, tossing and turning until, unexpectedly, I became aware of an endless stream of words in my head. I observed for the first time my thoughts as separate and unfused from "me."

Accustomed as I had been to entertain ongoing dialogues with my beloved "God" high up in the sky, I simply asked, "God, where do all the words come from?"

The reply was immediate, yet beyond language: I was staring into a black shimmering vastness. Initially, I was mesmerized, but as I gazed, the expanse became an abyss swallowing me up. Feelings of wonder twisted into horror and a silent, frightened scream: *I don't want to disappear!* I opened my eyes to shake off this threat and prayed feverishly, "Please, God, please—never again allow the words to stop!"

I would feel the same angst a few months later, when my father enthusiastically showed me pictures of our galaxy and Milky Way in his new astronomy book. One look at the image of the shimmering black expanse was enough to remind me of the night when I feared dissolving forever into untethered no-thingness. It evoked too-familiar feelings of isolation and insignificance—my ache of not really belonging in this world. I told my startled father I didn't want to know about his galaxies.

Many decades later I came to understand how, for the egoic mind structure, there is nothing more terrifying than confronting the void-like, unborn ground of existence: the ego is threatened with annihilation. Hearing about the possibility of "no-self" or the Buddhist term "emptiness" can easily be misinterpreted as nihilistic: a depressing loss of all meaning. To the egoic mind—the very center of its own constructed universe—reality *is* its self-importance or illusion of control, stemming from the ingrained belief of everybody being an island onto themselves. This assumption bears a mighty weight—it shapes how most modern human beings think, act, and feel about love, life, and death.

Seeing through our mind's construct of a separate solid self can feel like actual death. Some spiritual traditions speak of it as "dying before we die." Yet funnily, in some way we all die and let go of our skin-enveloped self-identity every time we are released into a deep dreamless sleep. The world, our body, and our mind's construct of being a separate someone fall away, and yet no one is ever afraid of a good night's sleep. Instead, we cherish it, precisely because we are resting back into the vast openness of not being anybody or anything in particular, and thus are freed from the *somebody* who struggles to be happy and avoids suffering at all costs.

This was still unclear to me in Tokyo. Living without a separate self at the center of experience was serene and spacious as long as my conceptual mind didn't wrestle with this unusual perspective and as a result become hysterical and unglued. Before the discovery of "my own absence," the familiar identity of an Annette who seemed in control had rendered the smug certainty that surely, sooner or later, my search for a bigger truth, meaning, and fulfillment would be rewarded with success. The downside of the Annette who grabbed life like a bull by its horns was her minute tolerance for feeling powerless or vulnerable as well as her self-protection against feelings of fragility which armored her with a boisterous, stubborn pride. Now, the last specks of feeling in charge had vanished. Trying to sustain a sense of normalcy, I painstakingly held on to my daily routines: going to work, doing the laundry, shopping for groceries, cooking meals. To avoid in-depth conversations, I made excuses for not meeting with friends. I was scared to speak to anyone about my experience, panicky that their incredulity would multiply my brain's perplexity and further confirm my assumption of having gone mad. *How can I even begin to explain the radical groundlessness of this no-self?*

But I could only knit myself together for so long. One night, I unraveled completely.

chapter 9

Razors and Redemption

For a seed to achieve its greatest expression, it must come completely undone. The shell cracks, its insides come out and everything changes. To someone who doesn't understand growth, it would look like complete destruction.
CYNTHIA OCCELLI, *Resurrecting Venus*

I WAS teaching until late evening at the language academy. During class, I sensed the spacious insubstantiality chewing at my edges, but the familiar teacher-student interactions and everyone responding to me as per usual tethered me to a comforting degree of normalcy.

Later, standing among the anonymous mass of commuters on the station's platform waiting for my train home, the lurking notion of no-self haunted me. With its habitual punctuality, the train arrived, doors opened, and passengers poured out and in without disorder. I dropped onto one of the last empty seats, and we sped out of the station. I looked around, taking in the familiar scene of passengers sitting with eyes closed. The Japanese worked extremely long days and used what could be several hours of commuting to nap, but also to create a bubble of privacy for themselves and others within the overcrowded spaces and ongoing stimuli of metropolitan life. I had appreciated and adapted to the social agreement of avoiding eye contact with strangers... until tonight.

I was flooded by an urge for another human being's eyes to meet mine, as if this small act could restore a sense of solidity and relieve my increasing panic. Yet, no matter how much I tried to catch another passenger's glance, nobody met my gaze, and this pulled me over the edge. I began to drown in a sea of despair; my lungs felt like they were filling with water—I could hardly breathe.

Thick snowflakes fell as I exited at Eifukucho station. It had been snowing nonstop for the last few days, and fluffy white layers blanketed the streets, swallowing the sound of my steps and eerily illuminating the semi-darkness. Instead of inducing peace within as before, the winter scenery intensified my desolation. I stepped through the squeaky old gate into our front garden. Light shone at the entrance of the house, but otherwise I detected no proof of human presence or activity. I left my boots inside the door and quietly climbed to the second floor.

Heading to my room, I passed Mikkel and Yasuko's apartment door. I hesitated: I could knock, apologize for the late intrusion, and tell them I needed help. They might offer some tea, be open to listening—but then what? *What could I say that would make any sense or difference at this point?*

My room was ice cold as I entered. Hanging my heavy coat on a hook, I slipped into some thick socks and an oversized sweater. Too restless to sleep and despite not being hungry, I heated some miso soup on the stove. As I sat with my bowl, stirring strands of *wakame* into my broth, my mind gnawed: *Where have I gone wrong on my journey? Yes, I had defied the conventional ideas of how one ought to lead a sensible life, but that was the point: to adhere to my own rules and follow this inaudible calling—so, Christ's sake, when exactly should I have made a different turn? Or have I entrusted myself too naively to the Heavens?* As much as I examined my past actions and decisions, I couldn't find the moment where I'd veered in a wrong direction.

Yet, I hadn't found any final happiness or liberating truth—and now I am paying the price for my recklessness: I've lost my mind.

Besieged by my somber examination, I noticed a bottle of sake on the shelf above the stove, an unopened token of appreciation from one of my private language students. The frosted glass bottle imbued me with a strange comfort and gave me the idea that these depressing thoughts about rudderless, wasted life might loosen their sharp contours if I drank a bit—or a lot—of it. Perhaps, I could let myself drift away into an endless sleep.

In that moment it seemed that the most natural idea in the world would be to end my life. There was no point in going further or returning to what once was, like "going home" to Europe or trying to find answers in some ashram or spiritual book. Realizing a way out of my hopeless situation gave me relief, even a strange sense of control. *I don't need to suffer any longer—I need to get some razors.*

I looked at my watch: 2 a.m. The 7-Eleven was open. Eerily calm, I grabbed my winter coat from its hook. Images of my mother and sisters appeared in my mind. *I will cause them so much suffering.* And my friends here or even my landlord who probably would be the one to find my corpse—what about them? I wavered.

I was exhausted. I believed I had tried everything, given it my all in my search for understanding—and in the process, I had gone irrevocably mad. Was I supposed to live like this? *No.* I was finished.

I silently stepped downstairs through the dark, slipped back into my damp boots, and left the house as quietly as I'd entered. Buffered by clouds of numb blankness exuding a strange comfort, I no longer felt the cold night air. The convenience store was empty except for a small-statured clerk with metal-rimmed eyeglasses. For a few long minutes I roamed the aisles in search of razors before I asked for help. *What is the damn word for "razor" in Japanese?* I tried sign language while the young man looked at me quizzically. As I pretended to shave off my non-existent facial hair, I heard a phone ringing. The clerk nodded with a half-smile, and I nodded back until I realized the sound was coming from my coat pocket. *Who is calling me at 2 a.m.?* I didn't want to talk to anyone, but the clerk kept smiling with utmost politeness, waiting for me to take the call.

Pressing the green key on my cell, I answered, "*Moshi, Moshi?*" The alive and strident sound of my voice surprised me, so far was I into my plan of leaving this life.

"I am sorry, really sorry," a male voice declared. "This is clearly not the time to call anyone, and I swear I usually wouldn't, but—"

"Who is this? What do you want?" I angrily bit into his apology.

"It's Brett, Annette. Brett—remember? We had coffee... um...six weeks ago. Remember, on Sunday morning at a café on Omotesando Road?"

"*Brett?* Oh...yes," I stuttered, irritated. I'd met Brett a couple times. He was an acquaintance, a warm-hearted man from New Zealand, who lived in Tokyo. *Why is he calling me now?*

"Again, I am so sorry to wake you, but I...how do I say this? Look, I just woke up and I felt this urgency that I should phone you right away. I can't explain this, and—"

"What?"

"Annette, what's going on? You sound terrible. I don't think you are well. Tell me, do you need help?"

My hand fell away from my face, taking the phone with it. I looked incredulously at the shop clerk who had stepped away busying himself with shuffling papers behind the counter. I looked back at the phone in my hand. *How does someone I barely know wake up in the middle of the night with an urge to call me—tonight, of all nights?* My mind spun as Brett's voice echoed from my phone, "Annette! Annette, speak to me!"

My determination to complete my plan dwindled and the adrenaline drained from my body. My knees trembled. I returned the phone to my ear and intoned: "I guess you are right. I am... not well."

"Okay, listen to me! I want you to get into a taxi right now and come straight to my house."

"I don't...I don't even know where you live."

"You are coming right now," his voice was firm. "Call a taxi and when it arrives, I'll give the driver directions. Do it now!"

At this point my life force was so weak I barely felt able to spell my name, much less follow Brett's simple orders. "I am at a 7-Eleven," I mumbled. Numbly, I handed the confused clerk my phone. He listened attentively.

"Hai, wakarimashita," he said a couple of times. *Yes, I understand.* He nodded while processing Brett's instructions, then hung up and returned my phone with another nod. I stood still, staring into space, not saying a word. Five minutes later, a taxi pulled up outside the store. The snow had stopped and the street felt almost dreamlike as the driver opened the back door for me. I sank wordlessly into the seat. As the car moved, I felt as if carried by something vast and benevolent. I closed my eyes as we glided through the night.

When the taxi slowed, I opened my eyes again as we passed through a tall gate opening onto a broad driveway. We came to a halt in front of an elegant apartment complex. I had never seen so much space around a residential building in Tokyo; this must be an affluent neighborhood. Brett stepped from inside the foyer and opened an umbrella, even though the relentless snowfall had ceased. He paid the driver and led me gently by the arm into the marbled entry. In silence, we stepped into the elevator which lifted us swiftly to the third floor.

The atmosphere of Brett's apartment surprised me—it was spacious, warm, and refined. Soft cream-colored carpet covered the floor, and delicate flower arrangements decorated the few exquisite pieces of furniture. The living area featured large windows with sweeping views of the Tokyo skyline—the apartment even had a shrine room. I realized how frugal and barebones my life had been in my tiny, cold tatami room for all these months—actually, I reflected, in almost every place I had inhabited since leaving Spain two and a half years earlier.

Snippets of Brett's and my conversation in the café came back to me. He was working for an investment firm in Tokyo; I had been surprised to hear he hated living in Japan, especially since he spoke perfect Japanese. He moved here while working for the New Zealand embassy and decided to boost his retirement account by taking a well-paid job in the private sector. I estimated him to be in his early fifties; he said he couldn't wait to get back to New Zealand, but still had to work more years to be able to permanently retire. We marveled at each other's reasons for liking and disliking our lives in Japan: he hated the fact that as a foreigner or *gaijin*—meaning "alien" in Japanese—he would never fit in, no matter how hard he tried, while I appreciated that as a gaijin I was free to live by my own rules because no one here expected me to fit in.

Brett's sophisticated masculinity made me feel safe for the first time in a long while. Maybe it was the combination of his warm, outdoorsy presence and elegant home that allowed me to finally break down and sob. Without uttering a word, he put his arm around me and held me as I wept. "I don't know who I am any longer," I said, and then broke into sobs again.

"Come on, come on...it will all be okay."

"No, you don't understand," I shook my head vigorously. "I *really* don't know who I am!"

"Well..." He cleared his throat and thought for a moment. "Look, you are Annette, I know that you were born in Germany, and you have been living here in Tokyo for a while now...and I reckon you are going through a rough time."

I didn't respond. Tears still trickling down my face, I resigned, knowing it was impossible to explain that I was *not* Annette—this time-bound form was not my true identity. *I have trouble understanding this myself!* Brett couldn't possibly comprehend...

Suddenly, it began to feel tolerable...actually, everything had become strangely okay. *If the universe manages to wake someone whom I barely know in the middle of the night to make sure I don't kill myself, then it will, in all likelihood, take care of the rest*. Maybe there was no need to continue the fight, to figure anything out? Like a swimmer who struggled to stay afloat, the epiphany that the ocean had the ultimate control over *my* life prompted my intellect to release its fear and fight against drowning. Wouldn't it be easier to let go, to turn onto my back, and let myself be held—carried by the vast ocean of existence? At last, my psyche's perpetual effort to comprehend drifted away, swallowing the relentless seeking to understand, the looking for something better—for more love, acceptance, relief from pain, or the quest for big truths and ultimate happiness. And with that, the last vestiges of my mind's constant preoccupation on behalf of an illusory self dissolved into the peaceful rest of the bigger unknown.

Brett invited me to stay at his place as long as I needed. While he went to work, I rested in the comfort of his home or ventured out for short walks and fresh air. Brett wasn't a meditator, but he had kept the traditional shrine room in his rental apartment with its original arrangement and furniture. I was particularly drawn to a vertical silken scroll hanging on one wall. I'd learned to read and write the two Japanese syllabic script languages, called *Hiragana* and *Katakana*, so I could better decipher restaurant menus or not get off at the wrong subway stations; but this scroll was in *Kanji*, the third and far more complicated character writing system used in Japan. "What do these Kanji mean?" I inquired.

His face lit up. He first uttered the words in Japanese, and then turning to me: "It says *I aspire to become a Buddha*."

"Ah..." I gaped.

I wanted to linger in the space these words had opened, but

Brett had other plans: "Come on, let's get some ramen. I don't think you have eaten much today..."

When I left Brett's apartment two days later, something had fundamentally shifted within. I didn't know how or what, but during the following six weeks in Japan, my days flowed in an unusual state of ease. In the absence of further seeking, attention melted into the immediacy of life presenting itself afresh from moment to moment. Apart from practical considerations about what to cook for dinner, preparing lessons for my students, or making sporadic arrangements to meet friends, my mind had few places left to go. My incessant pursuit of the ephemeral *something* lacking had vaporized: existence, as it was, was enough. I didn't understand how I had come to this different way of being, but I didn't need to grapple with it either. Anything I had ever taken to be solid or real had been refuted; I could no longer attach a permanent label to anything, and the consequential surrender into centerless openness made reality edgeless, calm, and dispassionate.

This suspension into the detached not-knowing-limbo was temporary, readying me for the next phase of my spiritual homecoming.

chapter 10

A Liberating Truth

The Universe is a dream dreamed by a single dreamer where all the dream characters dream too.

ARTHUR SCHOPENHAUER

THE SNOW on the streets in Eifukucho was mostly melted. The cold January temperatures still demanded heavy coats and winter shoes, but this morning on my way to the public laundry the sun shone so warm and bright I could sense spring around the corner. As I stuffed dirty laundry into one of the washing machines my cell phone rang. It was Julie, who had returned to Australia to continue her studies at university. It was so good to hear her cheerful sing-song voice on the phone.

"Hey...what're you up to?"

"Well, right now, washing dirty laundry." I laughed out loud.

"Listen, I can get some weeks off at the end of January and I wanted to drive up to Tahnee Point to camp. Annette, Tahnee Point is the coolest place in all of Australia! Lots of hippies, surfers, healthy food, yoga, and the best beaches in the entire world. Come with me! You don't need to do anything—just get your butt on a plane and show up at Sydney airport. I'll get all the camping gear, borrow Mom's car, pick you up, and off we go. We will have such a great time—say yes, please say yes!" Her voice bounced with excitement.

I didn't know what to say. "Let me sit with it, okay? I'll call you back in a couple days."

The name of the town—Tahnee Point—burned in my mind. Soon it would be three years since I left Spain, but I no longer had any urge or motivation to move around or be anywhere else on the planet than the place where my body seemed to find itself right now. Although my Japanese visa would expire by the end of February, my mind hadn't yet circled around the question of where to head after that. Julie's unexpected call and invitation didn't stir any feelings of opposition in my body, so a few weeks later I was boarding a flight to Sydney.

WE CRUISED along the Old Tahnee Point Country Road in Julie's mother's ancient Toyota sedan. After climbing up a hilly stretch and cresting the ridge, we came to a breathtaking vista of the dark blue Tasman Sea and the coastline of Tahnee Point. An almost mystical sense of homecoming tugged at my soul when I spotted a white lighthouse in the distance many miles below.

I'd been obsessed with lighthouses since my teenage years. During summer vacations, they captured my attention on the coasts of France and Portugal, exuding an unexplainable magic—perhaps it was their air of strength and solitude or the way they perched high on cliffs like sentinels guarding the boundary between solid ground and unknown waters. Though these tall, light-bearing structures had enchanted me, I inexplicably felt as if I had known this particular lighthouse all my life, as if its circling beam in the night was akin to God's finger, beckoning and assuring that there was indeed a cure for the aching gap in our hearts.

Tahnee Point is on Australia's East Coast, about six hundred miles north of Sydney. Historically, the whaling and lumber industries dominated the area, but after the 1960s and '70s, when the first surfers and hippies discovered the idyllic seaside town with its stunning white sand beaches, it morphed into a progressive tourist destination. By the late 1990s, the town also attracted high-end vacationers and mainstream folks and families.

Julie drove us straight to a small campground where we pitched our tents with an unobstructed view of Tahnee Point's main beach and the Tasmanian Sea. *Heaven!* In contrast with the cold Tokyo winter, here in the Southern Hemisphere it was summer, and walking barefoot, exposing my skin to the sun every day, breathing clean air, and swimming in the ocean softened and opened my body. Julie and I practiced yoga on the beach in the mornings, prepared veggie tofu stir-fry on our camping stove for lunch, ventured for cappuccinos in the afternoon, and chatted away while gazing into the starry night sky until tired enough to crawl into our tents.

On our third day, Julie returned from a grocery trip in town bubbling with exhilaration. "I just chatted with a really nice bloke who told me about these gatherings here in the evenings called *satsang*. It's with a spiritual teacher and they do meditation and chanting. It starts at seven thirty—it sounds amazing! Let's go tonight, yeah?"

"I don't know, Julie... I'm sort of done with all of that, but if you want to go by yourself, I don't mind."

I recalled from my time in India that satsang was a Sanskrit term for "association with the truth"—usually involving sitting in the presence of a guru. The prospect of another guru scene didn't call to me. In any case, ever since my egoic mind had un-lodged itself and surrendered into the centerless unknown in Brett's apartment in Tokyo, my seeking had ceased.

Julie and I skipped the event, but the following evening a strange force pulled me to the gathering—it was the experience of witnessing my body walk side by side with my friend until we arrived at a little wooden building in town. Inside, a long-haired man played guitar and sang a quiet Indian chant. Around him in concentric semi-circles were about eighty people. Julie found a couple of empty seats for us.

After the musician finished his song, he retreated into the audience and a tall, heavyset man in slacks and a hip-length white tunic walked to the front of the room and faced us. Once seated in his chair, he closed his eyes, and everyone fell silent. After a few minutes, he looked up again and smiled. He appeared to be in his mid-sixties, with piercing blue eyes and a weather-beaten face framed by strands of gray hair. He breathed heavily into the microphone. With a broad Australian accent, he said: "Good evening and welcome to satsang. For anyone new here today, my name is Brian. Feel free to ask anything or speak if you have something to share."

People then took turns asking questions as a handheld microphone was passed around. I wasn't particularly interested in the content of what people were saying and simply continued to rest in the dispassionate spaciousness that had become familiar by now. After a while, though, the spaciousness filled with a pervasive warmth and tinges of sweetness.

Then, unexpectedly, Brian said, "Excuse me. Can someone pass the microphone to the young lady over there?" He pointed his finger straight at me. I hadn't asked to speak, nor did I feel I had a question. Still, as the microphone entered my hands, unbidden from deep within arose words that I had never formulated: "I have a simple and yet complex question. What is all the suffering about?"

"Well... Are you willing to explore something?"

I nodded.

"My experience is that when people come here and they have pain or suffering, it has to do with who they think they are. So, if you can, I want you to be open for a moment and forget whatever you have read or heard. Any idea that you're a soul...or other spiritual beliefs? Okay? Just for a moment, look into your direct experience right now, and tell me, *Who are you?*"

With his last three words, the whole universe came to a full stop and ceased to exist. There was only unborn emptiness, an infinite absence of anything, without time or space...

Eventually, sound arose again: the waves of the Tasmanian Sea crashing on the beach. Only: I am these waves *and* the sound. *I am the entire ocean.* I was as much the world as all the people in the room—the chairs, even the microphone in my hand—I was *everywhere*. The notion of being a separate person confined in a body who in the Pune ashram had still been looking for "Who is in?" was long gone. Since Japan, I had no longer been able to locate my self or relate to any fixed sense of solidity—but now, here, I wasn't just a centerless infinite openness but also *form*—I was everything and everywhere—and to my utter surprise, formlessness and form were not even two!

"So, what did you find?" the teacher's voice sounded distant.

I couldn't speak. I grasped for words to express the immensity of me. My months-long limbo of not-knowing who or where I was transmuted into the liberating recognition of the everything-ness and completeness of *me.* But as quickly as these new insights arose, they opened and melted like sea foam into the undifferentiated, transparent infinity of *me*. There were no words for this.

"Hello...are you listening?" Brian's voice was faint as he tried to reach me. "Tell me, what is your experience of who you are?"

I quietly responded, "Everything and nothing."

He burst into loud laughter. "Yes, that's it. That's it! Wow, that didn't take long!" His face was now bright and animated, "Okay, so let's look again. This everything and nothing, do you have to do anything to be that?"

"No," I replied. What an utterly silly question: everything and nothing was all that existed. There was no way one could *not* be this.

"Good! So, let's go back a bit more into your story. You first spoke of suffering. Did you mean emotional or physical pain?"

I wanted to tell him about all the suffering that existed in the world and about that red thread of pain that had woven itself through my heart since childhood. However, the more I looked and tried to get hold of the suffering of the past, the less I could find. It all appeared as real as a dream...the entire Universe was the arising of thought—and *I* was its dreamer! With this realization, the final trace of identity in space-time was catapulted with a blazing luminosity outside of existence. I looked into my original face—and everything slipped into place. All queries and quandaries around the truth of reality were put to rest: *I* had never been born. *I* was beyond creation, and yet, present within and as every speck of it. Wherever *I* was, *I* was at home—and best of all, *I* had never left! The universe lit up into one big smile, and with this, a raucous laughter swelled from my belly. I laughed so hard and loud that my head fell backward, and Brian joined in.

The rest of the evening melted away and I barely knew how I returned to the campground. During the night, I stayed lucid and awake while my body was fast asleep. In the early morning, I registered the physical shift from sleeping to waking state. An urge to pee prompted me to crawl out of the tent, slip on my flip-flops, and walk, light as a feather, to the campground bathroom. As I opened the door, I came face to face with the mirror, and when I saw my reflection, I laughed uncontrollably. *This is an incredible joke! How could I ever have believed that I am something separate or confined by a body?* And again, as soon as these thoughts appeared, they burst like bubbles. Everything was fundamentally open and inseparable. *Truth* was beyond all concepts and perspectives, a groundless ground, and although this evoked an incredible sweetness and unfathomable love, even these labels were incapable of expressing the liberating ineffability of reality.

As I returned again and again to attend satsang, the ceaseless field of ecstatic wonder and profound love remained. Waking up from the dream of separation had loosened the habitual knots and fixations in my body's energetic field, revealing an infinite cosmos of bliss. I couldn't stop chuckling and chortling about the incredible lightness of being and how mistaken my view of reality had been.

One day, speeding on the back of a motorcycle with my arms wrapped around the driver, the deathless aspect of consciousness became clear and vivid. I burst into giggles: *Wow...this essence never perished or ceased! Where should it go? What if I released my arms' grip and let my body fall onto the pavement? It would probably break some of my body's bones, maybe even the skull?* These musings were quite different from my old annihilating thoughts of suicide—there was no impulse to let go this time, yet I relished the total absence of fear about losing my life.

Another insight occurred one morning when I found a bird's corpse on the beach. Upon seeing the decomposing body in the sand, the fragile bones sticking out amid rotting flesh and dull feathers, I felt the unfathomable beauty underlying all existence—even death or decay were not to be feared. All that humanity conventionally saw as scary or ugly was made of the same incredible splendor we commonly attributed to the pleasant aspects of life. Reality was inherently benign, open, and complete.

But as much as my journey up to this moment may read like a glorious adventure story, I was soon to discover that waking up wasn't the end of spiritual unfolding. We might have heard variations of tales like: "And then the monk saw the moon's reflection on the surface of the water and was enlightened!" Yet, there is not much reporting about what happened afterward. No account of whether the monk died painfully of bone cancer a year later, or if his ego co-opted his realization and he exuded the "stink of enlightenment"—a term in Zen Buddhism warning sincere practitioners against falling into the trap of believing themselves to be special, or superior to anybody else. Naturally, we prefer happily-ever-after endings! Who wouldn't want to escape all the pain, discomfort, or complexity of human existence with one strike?

Descents follow ascents: we are asked to return into our bodies and interdependence with our practical world. And unless we are cave yogis or invested in holding on to a transcendent but disembodied swoon, once the spiritual honeymoon of waking-up wanes, the marriage begins. This marriage of spirit and form is a profound alchemical process that can only unfold in the crucible of humility and honesty: we are asked to stand naked in the silence of aware openness, witnessing how "the old self"—our familiar pain identity—slips back again and again into the center stage of consciousness. This is where the compassionate mirror held by mentors or empathic feedback offered by peers become invaluable, and why some kind of formal practice, contemplation, or inquiry becomes a necessary pilgrimage. With the first light of awakening, some egoic shadows dissolve like morning mist, while others—tenacious as old gnarly roots—surrender only across the slow arc of years or decades.

Practice in this alchemical marriage remains free of any aggression or ambition of "needing to get somewhere," as it is precisely this compulsory grasping and striving inherent in the egoic perspective which clouds our innate clarity, openness, and completeness. What we are cultivating is an effortless effort—a continual recognizing and remembering not just intellectually but experientially of what we essentially already are. Yet this is easier said than done. We've learned a thousand ingenious ways to flee from what is here and now—believing freedom lies in some better future experience, some achievement just beyond reach. The invitation to do nothing sounds deceptively simple, yet requires the courage to stand fully exposed in life's wild current, feeling equally its rapture and beauty as well as its utter groundlessness and raw pain.

This mysterious unfolding follows no linear path, respects no timetable. Though it appears intensely personal, its purpose stretches beyond our individual awakening—rippling outward through the living tapestry of all sentient existence. The marriage of boundless awareness with finite form serves something vaster than our own liberation. Each moment of true presence nourishes the collective consciousness from which we're never truly separate. As Sharon Salzberg reminds us with elegant precision: "We practice not to attain Buddhahood, but to express it."

IN THE three decades since leaving Australia, I have collected an abundance of myths and misunderstandings about awakening. The late Indian sage Anandamayi Ma famously said, "Consciousness wakes up to itself in six billion ways." Borrowing the number of the world's population during her time, she used this analogy to point out that there is no single or same way in which awakening unfolds. Each journey is unique, and yet, what is uncovered in waking up is free of individuality, distinction, even birth and death. I have met seekers who can point to a particular moment when they experienced a crucial shift of identity and perceived reality as radically different; for others, the recognition of their true nature and open ground of existence slipped in through the back door without much fanfare.

I believe that apart from our individual karmic momentum, our earnest desire for a deeper understanding, or practices that can "open" the gateless gate, the circumstantial byproducts of spiritual realizations have a lot to do with our energetic propensities and makeup. If we have an energetic constitution, for example, with a lot of natural earth element, our spiritual unfolding tends to be more grounded and without many bells and whistles. Some who have more fire or air element in their constitution may have plenty of big experiences, but on the downside, often must work more diligently at integrating and translating their insights into a steady, collected way of living.

Interestingly, many of us who have experienced significant trauma often have easier access to more subtle realms of reality: on one hand, severe suffering provides us with the rocket fuel to seek *real* relief, but we also don't experience life as tethered to our earth body and gross-motoric world, as trauma forces parts of us to disconnect from the dimension of form.

Also, awakening often unfolds in various shifts. There can be a first *Aha!* when we recognize we are not our fleeting thoughts or feelings as we glimpse the stillness at the core of our being. We experience relief as our deficient self-identity is revealed to be nothing but a mirage. And our constructed view of reality becomes seriously perforated upon not only realizing the open empty nature of ourselves, but the essential insubstantiality of all appearances—our body, the world, and other people.

To me, one of the important stages is to recognize the unborn facet of our being and existence, devoid of any experiences. To grasp this non-experiential aspect is crucial because, if we don't, we'll continue to hanker for beautiful experiences or try to cling to sublime meditative states. However, in the end, all experiences come and go, appear and disappear. In other words, none of the peaks of ecstatic bliss or thrilling fireworks often accompanying our openings are "it." To the conceptual mind, though, the utter absence of experience is ungraspable, as its very function is to reify and particularize through labeling, thus "creating" separate events or objects.

In its depth and essence, awakening is forgetting all that we think we know about ourselves or spirituality. A humbling act of letting go, of stripping ourselves naked—not once, but moment to moment. Even genuine insights like *I am infinite consciousness itself*, or *I was never born,* can be corrupted and used as convenient slogans to defend against unwanted experiences and the radical groundlessness of life. This is why the first line in the Tao Te Ching by Lao Tzu states, "The Tao that can be told is not the eternal Tao."

There is a metaphor, used in the Hindu Advaita Vedanta teachings, which can sound a bit sterile but illuminates the non-experiential, non-graspable nature of the open ground of being: Let's consider for a moment we are watching a movie and we are engrossed in the unfolding plot, our full attention glued to the moving images and sounds. We are absorbed into what is happening to our main character and the other actors—and feeling either tantalized or tortured by the ensuing emotional reactions of fear or hope, pleasure or pain, elicited by the narrative. The movie we are watching is the ever-changing story of "Me, My Life, and the World." As long as we're engrossed by the seesaw of trials and triumphs of the characters on the screen, we stay entangled and encumbered by a constant reactivity about the events. If we are serious about finding relief from suffering, we must come to a pivotal realization: anything *on* the screen can supply only temporary reprieve or happiness at best.

Instead of letting our attentional system remain hooked onto the ever-changing content of My Life, we can learn to release our narrow focus and become aware of the wider, empty screen upon which all the dramatic ups and downs unfold. By letting go of the mind's chronic fixation with "what happens next?" attention can relax and find rest in the content-less context of the screen. And we discover: no matter what happens in the plot—the main character getting a promotion, falling in love, or being injured in a car accident—the space-like substratum of the screen is still unaffected. Then, we can explore further: Who is actually looking? What is cognizant of the screen? Is there a separate *me* doing the observing—or is the spacious screen itself aware and void of a separate me?

Taking this analogy further: In the strictest sense, waking up is not happening to the character on the screen, nor does it occur on the plane of ever-changing experiences. It is an unassuming but pivotal shift of perspective; instead of looking out or at events, there is a becoming aware of what is looking, a shift into the essential, undamaged openness as our true identity. Although this discovery often brings spiritual seeking to an end, it is also the beginning of an ever-evolving journey of living from true connection.

As LIBERATING as it had been to uncover the unborn dimension of reality, at that time in Tahnee Point I had no idea that walking and talking from abiding openness wasn't solely about being drunk on bliss. I still had no real comprehension of what had occurred. Traversing the initial raw and unrefined phases of awakening I naively believed that nothing "bad" could happen again; life from now on would continue to unfold in utter sweetness.

I was soon to discover the aftermath of awakening might not look or feel glorious. In fact, truth doesn't always come dipped in honey. It can resemble for many, as it would for me, a plummet from grace. We might seek the light and indeed it might open us up, but nothing can root and transform us like re-entering the dark.

PART TWO
Descent

I wish I could tell
which were my darkest hours
and how even then through the broken glass
came shining rays of light

"Those were happy times,"
you might sigh and want
to remember the colorful feathers when the burden
feels as un-lift-able as broken wings

Hold close to the center, my dear
soften into the edges and surrender
like tender meat leans into a knife
without a trace of fear

I wish I could let you know
that you are never lost
and that when you stumble,
you simply fall, fall into God

There is no other ground

chapter 11

From Honeymoon to Homelessness

To be fully alive, fully human, and completely awake is to be continually thrown out of the nest. To live fully is to be always in no-man's-land, to experience each moment as completely new and fresh. To live is to be willing to die over and over again.
PEMA CHÖDRÖN

I WAS rolling on the ground, laughing uncontrollably, still unable to get over the great cosmic joke that all the tombstones and memorial plates in Tahnee Point's cemetery had been built and erected in earnestness on behalf of fictious separate selves. I kept alternating between holding my belly and slapping my palms onto the lawn until my howling and convulsing quieted. I stayed still, flat on my back suspended in timelessness, until a thought of Brian arose: *He is my accomplice in this dream*. His gatherings were the only place I knew where the open secret of transparent insubstantiality was at the center and foreground of each interaction. I was no longer interested in anything else.

I stretched my arms over my head and sat up. *Satsang will start in two hours. It is time to have dinner with Julie at the campground.* I stood, brushed blades of dry grass off my pants and walked out of the cemetery.

Julie grinned. "Hey, look, at these fabulous veggies I got us from the market." Squatting in front of our little gas stove, she bounced the frying pan up and down over the flame, swirling the onions, peppers, and string beans through the air. "I can't believe it's already time to get back to university. Only two more days." She put the pan down and heaved a tiny sigh.

"Are you sure you want to leave me all the camping gear?"

"Of course," she exclaimed with her usual zest. "I'll just take one tent back with me, and the rest of the stuff I'll leave with you. You want to stay longer here, don't you? Camping is the cheapest way!"

"Thank you, Julie...you're such an amazing friend."

We held each other's gaze for a moment, exchanging a deep smile.

"Come on, now," she pushed herself up. "I know your satsang starts soon. Let's have dinner, all right?"

Since our arrival two weeks earlier, Julie had only come to satsang twice, and then decided that it wasn't her scene. I hadn't inquired about her reasons, nor had I told her what had transpired in Japan or been revealed since coming to Tahnee Point. I lacked words to capture this new perspective of reality, but as I continued to mostly float in a blissful swoon, there was no need to have anybody validate or corroborate my experience.

A little while later, the sun was setting as I walked into the wooden building where Brian's gatherings took place. The warm yellow lights inside were dimmed, and most of the sixty plus chairs were taken; some people had made space for their meditation cushions and backrests on the floor in the front. I scouted for an empty spot and sat down as a murmur traveled through the audience signaling Brian's arrival. He approached his chair in the front, and once seated closed his eyes for a few minutes, then opened the gathering as usual saying, "Welcome. Feel free to speak if you have any questions or want to share something."

I had been sitting with my eyes closed steeping in the general quiet and the bigger, underlying silence when the first query of the evening was raised.

"Hi, Brian. I have been coming here for the last seven days or so, and to be honest, I am still not sure what this is all about. My partner here," the speaker pointed to a radiant woman sitting next to him, "doesn't want to miss any of your satsangs...but I don't get it."

The man must have been in his early forties. Dressed in a washed-out T-shirt and surf shorts, his hair was bleached from the sun, his face earnest.

Brain remained quiet for a moment before replying, "And, what is it you want to get?"

Someone in the audience erupted into giggles. The man looked perplexed as his hand wrapped around the mic dropped down into his lap.

"No, I am serious," Brian inquired. "What is it that you are looking for in your life?"

The man's eyes narrowed into a squint, then he slowly answered, "I guess, generally speaking...having a good time?" He sounded uncertain.

"Okay, and what prevents you, generally speaking," Brian chuckled now, "from having a good time?"

"Well, a lot of stuff!" he blurted, "I mean, there is—"

"Stop right there," Brian interrupted. "Hang on, check for a moment, before you speak. Whether you wanted to tell me about your struggles around money, work, or politics—or maybe even problems with the lovely lady sitting next to you—" More people in the audience snickered but Brian continued undeterred, "Can you see that whatever you wanted to tell me about appears first as thoughts in your mind?"

The man blinked as he processed the question. He exhaled. "Okay, yes. You are right, but then—what? I mean, there are always a lot of thoughts in my head. And mostly, they are not fun...I can tell you this." His tone sounded almost defiant.

"I get that. And do you still want to explore a bit further?" Brian had deflated the tension by giving the man some space; I could see his body softening and after a moment, he nodded.

"So, you are aware of these thoughts appearing in your mind. And we could even venture to say, your mind or anybody's mind is nothing but a bunch of thoughts. But most importantly, as there is seeing of thoughts, check right now in your direct experience: are you these thoughts coming and going, or are you what is looking at them?"

The man glanced upward as if the answer was to be found behind his forehead. Then, he closed his eyes and remained quiet for a moment, before uttering in an almost inaudible voice: "... what is looking at them."

"And how is that?" Brian prodded.

"Unusual." He paused. "I mean...it's peaceful...there are no thoughts, they are all gone."

"And are you still here? Without thoughts?"

The man nodded, as his face brightened like a light bulb.

"Any problems here, in this moment?"

"No, no problems." His voice now emanated a grounded calm.

Brian smiled. "Any more questions?"

"No," he grinned. "Well, at least, for now."

"That's right," Brian countered. "And, if you find another problem, look first directly for the one who thinks he's having them. Got it?"

The man nodded, with an eager but peaceful expression.

This exchange evoked an aura of serenity in the hall, and a prolonged period of silence followed—until a faint but steady snore arose from the front of the room where people lay stretched out on pillows and blankets on the floor. We all erupted into laughter, and the snorer woke up. Brian smiled. "It's all okay. If the body is tired, it can relax so sweetly in satsang." It was this non-striving, non-judgmental atmosphere, together with my mentor's light-hearted humor which made these gatherings so welcoming.

I asked for the mic to be passed onto me. "May I share a short poem, please?" I inquired.

Brian looked around and then spotted me. "Ahh, you...of course!" I extracted a folded sheet of paper from my bag, and read aloud:

One instant
The gaze of your eyes
And Life dissolved
Sailing
And yet, no-body to glide
To surf this Inner Ocean
One instant
Sage without name
You took me on this timeless flight
To where no words ever can arrive
One twinkle of your eyes
And the whole universe
Became a smile

When I looked up again, Brian's face was glowing, his eyes gleamed. I beamed back at him. No longer encumbered by my old self-consciousness or shame, I was free and luminous. It was like the proverbial ugly duckling realizing she was a beautiful swan.

IT MUST have been around a week after Julie's departure when I first noticed my sweet rapture becoming punctuated by the occasional return of more ordinary thoughts, sensations, and perceptions. Also, practical common sense kicked back in, alerting me to the risk of running out of money if I focused only on attending satsang. I decided to share my concerns with Brian after one of his evening gatherings. It was my first time approaching him for a private conversation. "May I talk to you for a moment?"

His face lit up. "Sure, sure. What can I do for you?"

"I am so grateful to you...and for satsang, and I would like to continue to attend as much as possible, but my money is dwindling. What do you advise I do?"

Brian drew a deep breath, stayed quiet, and then replied with a mysterious undertone to his words, "Look, something brought you here to satsang, so that something will also take care of the rest. Don't worry!" He chuckled and shook his head, as if amused by a good joke.

I paused, mystified by his answer. I wanted to ask for clarification, but he had already gone to grab the donation bowl from a wooden table, making his way out of the building. His answer surprised me, but I concluded he surely could see and know things I wasn't aware of yet. I believed his spiritual wisdom extended to all areas and practicalities of life. *After all, he has a large following and I have only recently come to satsang and this new way of seeing reality.* I decided to put my worries to rest.

In the days to come, I chose to ignore my rapidly diminishing funds, setting my street smarts and hard-earned clarity aside. Whenever I paid for groceries or the campground fee, my gut squeezed a bit, my heart beat faster, but I dismissed these bodily cues, telling myself *the grace that brought me to satsang will also take care of the rest.* This was quite different from the "Trust in God and tie your camels" attitude I stuck to during my past three years of traveling. The way I relied on the heavens from the moment I left Spain must have appeared reckless to anyone living a nine-to-five life, but in all that time I never completely abandoned a reasonable outlook on practical matters—until now. Brian told me I could just trust! *And why shouldn't I? Hadn't grace brought me to realize the ultimate nature of reality through his form? My mentor knew what was best for me, as we had met on a plane devoid of separation where there was neither inside or out.*

Looking back, I see the invisible: I was unconscious of how my sincere devotion was overlaid and muddled by the unhealed parental projections from my past. The same way I'd once adored God as a child—loved, submitted to, and fawned over my dad as all-powerful or perfect in order to cope with the emotional chaos, instability, and unsafety at home—I was now blind to Brian being, behind his role of a godly messenger, yet another imperfect and mortal human. Since coming to satsang, my senses had overflowed with an openhearted innocence and profound love, prompting me to see only essential goodness in everyone and everything.

Unaware of my regression into infantile infatuation, or the guru worship I'd shied away from in Pune, I allowed my mentor to morph into an all-knowing, idealized father figure. In contrast to my late dad, though, Brian displayed no judgmental rigidities or emotional unavailability. On the contrary: whenever our eyes met, he beamed love at me without reserve. Never had I felt so seen or accepted without any conditions. And while I had gleaned some insight from Osho's early audio recordings, Brian was alive and available to answer any questions I might have, but mostly I was content to stay quiet, steep, and rest in the trust of our shared knowing of a perennial truth.

A COUPLE weeks after my private conversation on finances with Brian, I was yanked off my lofty perch. After a particularly deep gathering, he ended with an unusual announcement: "As you all know, we have two more evenings of satsang, then there won't be any for the next six months. I'll be traveling to Europe and the U.S. to teach, returning to Tahnee Point in November." Placing his hands in prayer-position, he ended with a hearty, "Namaste!"

He is leaving town. Why hasn't he mentioned this? Or maybe he has, but I didn't listen? Somehow, I never thought this could end. Sure, real satsang wasn't going to end—it was always present within us—but during the last months I had bound my devotion so tightly to the form of Brian that his announcement of imminent departure felt like being kicked out of a nest. Making matters worse, I was down to seventy Australian dollars and without an airplane ticket out of the country. The cruder level of reality struck me: if I didn't find some way to make an income, I would end up destitute. My heart raced, my stomach shriveled, panic seized my body as my mind went full force into projecting worst-case-scenarios. I had never felt fear as vivid or sharp in my life! *Has my organism become more sensitized or is the presence of openness now magnifying the intensity of everything?* There was no turning away from the unleashed thrust of my emotions, no possibility of ignoring, suppressing, or distracting myself from this agonizing rawness. Before waking up, I realized, I had lived mostly buffered by cotton clouds of my own making, but now with reality unconditionally open—there was nowhere to hide.

With Brian out of town, the regulars attending satsang dispersed within days, some returning to Europe or their homes in different Australian cities. When my money dwindled to a mere seven Australian dollars and even the campground was over my budget, I too packed up and left. I spent a long, sweltering day walking around with all my belongings, looking unsuccessfully for "help wanted" signs in store windows. I was exhausted, thirsty, and hungry.

As darkness set in, the streets around me came alive with jugglers and musicians asking for money on the curb. How I wished I had one of their skills! The tables on the open-air restaurant porches filled up with suntanned, freshly showered tourists sipping white wine and cold beers while the smell of grilled fresh fish and crispy French fries filled the air. My stomach growled as

I realized: *I have become a street bum!* What I avoided so diligently throughout my travels had become, at thirty-two, a reality: I was penniless and stranded on the other end of the world. *What am I supposed to do?* In a state of shock, I stood motionless on the curb.

Barely five minutes later, three men walked by, and a broad Ozzie voice belted, "Hey, you're alright?"

"No, I am not," I replied. I had no energy left for social graces.

"You look to me like you could do well with a drink!" declared another in a cheery tone.

"Maybe...but thank you, no, a drink wouldn't help."

"Well, what's going on? How *can* we help you?" he insisted.

The question sounded genuine. I inspected the three men more carefully. The tallest of them, a slender man in his mid-forties, with metal rimmed eyeglasses on his nose, introduced himself as Randy. His companion, roughly the same age, but more heavily built, half bald and with protruding ears, was Ben. And the third, who looked to be in his early twenties and rather shy, went by the name of George.

"In a nutshell, I am completely broke. I've been unable to find work and I don't even have enough money to pay for a bunk in the local hostel," I stated in a muted tone.

Randy and Ben exchanged glances. Randy cleared his throat, "Well, if it's that serious, why don't you come with us? You can stay for tonight. We have two tents, and you can share the one with George here," he pointed toward the youngest one, who nodded in my direction with the corners of his mouth lightly lifted.

I tried to read their faces to sort out if they were trustworthy. They didn't feel like serial killers or rapists, just decent human beings. I accepted their offer, and as we made our way to where they'd pitched their tents, they explained they were technicians from an Australian phone company who had come into Tahnee Point to install extra lines on various private properties. In fact, they had set up camp in the garden of one of their customers. As promised, George made some space to accommodate my sleeping bag and belongings in his tent, and after expressing my appreciation for their kindness, I fell asleep with great relief.

The next morning, Ben and Randy assured me I could stay until I got back on my feet, or at least until their work assignment in the area was complete. This gave me a grace period of two weeks. I thanked them profusely and after they fixed me a cup of tea and several slices of toast with butter, I headed back to the commercial streets in town in search of work. After an hour of fruitless scouting, I decided to rest. I sat down on the curb and observed the steady flow of cars through the streets, some with mothers at the wheel and children in the back seats, some driven by vacationing surfers carrying boards on their rooftops, some with local folks who were likely on their way to work. My eyes were drawn toward a young woman in a colorful hippie skirt and tie-dye T-shirt on the opposite side of the street. She was dunking a mop into a bucket and passing it over the floor tiles of a store's entrance. *That could work!* Feeling encouraged, I walked out of town toward Tahnee Point's more residential neighborhoods.

I approached the first house that looked inviting. Apprehension buzzed through my body, but I felt remarkably free of shame for not having any money. Without further ado, I walked through the front garden and rang the bell. Footsteps approached and the door opened. An older woman in her bathrobe with unkempt short gray hair and no make-up appeared. "Yes?" she squinted.

"I'm sorry to intrude on you so early, but I was wondering if you might need by any chance a housecleaner? I mean, I would love to clean your house, if you would let me."

She moved her lips into a tortured smile and curtly answered, "No, don't need any help with that" before closing the door.

Five houses and twenty minutes later—I realized I needed to be more transparent in my approach. *I am not just looking for a job—I need to eat, for heaven's sake!*

The clean-shaven, gray-haired man in his fifties who unlocked his front door probably didn't have any choice but to help me when he heard my plea: "Good morning. I know this must sound strange, but would you please let me clean your house in exchange for some food? I am totally bust!" I kept my eyes glued to his. He examined me for a few seconds and then waved me in. After showing me around, he handed me cleaning tools and I set to work right away. I felt relieved, content, and buoyed by the flow of grace. Life had sent three angels to offer me shelter, and now this stranger was giving me respite as well. After three hours, I'd finished my job and received fifteen Australian dollars as well as a bag of groceries—half a loaf of bread, some carrots, apples, and a small piece of cheese. In the following days, I found more cleaning gigs and soon I was able to afford the weekly rent for a modest room in a shared household. With immense gratitude for their no-strings-attached kindness and decency, I bid goodbye to my gracious telephone-technician saviors.

chapter 12

The Perils of Blind Trust

The path of truth is profound—and so are the obstacles and possibilities for self-deception.
CHÖGYAM TRUNGPA, *Cutting Through Spiritual Materialism*

With a roof above my head and enough money to feed myself, I was back on my feet and content to stay in Tahnee Point. It was there where I found my innermost home and now I wondered if it could also be a more permanent worldly home—at least until Brian returned in six months.

I still hadn't made any real friends among the locals, but a sense of belonging and community developed as I visited the colorful farmer's market on weekends. It was there I bumped into some of the other regulars from satsang, who were either buying their organic fruits and veggies or selling healing tinctures and jams at their own stands, offering tarot card readings, or bodywork sessions in pop-up tents. Life then grew more roots as I found a part-time job in a store selling crystals, candles, linen clothing, and New Age books. I received invitations to attend potlucks and joined the public yoga classes. Also, I forged a closer friendship with an Australian woman who had recently moved up from Sydney. Monica had also attended satsang when Brian was in town; she was a few years older than I and had just split up with her longtime fiancé. I appreciated not only her exquisite emotional sensitivity, but also her raucous sense of humor and well-grounded view on life.

Making enough of an income was still a bit of a hustle, as my daily work of cleaning houses or helping in the store rarely exceeded four or five hours. However, it allowed me to spend a good amount of undistracted time steeped in the unfathomable silence beyond thought. Even though Brian had voiced in satsang that he didn't believe in the necessity of daily practice, I followed an inner nudge to set the first thirty minutes of each morning apart to formally "sit." This was no longer the grueling affair it once had been. I'd come to know meditation as the natural ground of my being, and abiding in unencumbered openness grew simple. Throughout the rest of my day, I was often spontaneously drawn to stop, drop all inner and outer movements, and steep in silence or attune to the sweet fragrance and open lucidity while preparing my meals or walking on the beach.

When Brian finally returned, I was over the moon to be in satsang with him again. It must have been in his third or fourth gathering, though, that something shifted.

Monica, who had become a close friend, one day mustered the courage to bring up a deeply vulnerable issue for her. She had previously confided in me about suffering from severe anxiety and panic attacks due to an obsessive-compulsive disorder. She had tried without much success to find relief through medication and conventional therapy. As she candidly spoke about her fear and daily anguish, the whole room fell utterly quiet. I knew what a big deal it was to publicly disclose her struggle and shame about this condition, and many held their breath as they listened. I eagerly awaited my mentor's answer, because I often wondered what could heal or relieve Monica's suffering. *Brian will know how to help!*

His brusque response shocked me. "Fear is a total waste of time. After all, fear isn't real, you see. The letters f-e-a-r," he chuckled, "stand for False Evidence Assumed Reality." Then he moved on.

Until this moment, I had never questioned his guidance. I was perplexed by his dismissiveness. I held my breath as I stared, waiting for him to correct his course, but he didn't. As he moved on to the next questioner, I could no longer pay attention to what was going on around me. I closed my eyes. My body drew breath again, but in a constrained pattern. My head buzzed as I grappled with what I had witnessed.

As we walked home from satsang, Monica fumed. She didn't hold back in her critique of Brian's lack of compassion and belittling. I listened to her healthy indignation, but was also confused about how my "perfect" teacher was dealing with legitimate challenges from his followers. Something didn't feel right, but I couldn't discern what was true for me. My respect and loyalty toward Brian knew no limit, so questioning the guide that the heavens had sent felt like betrayal. Instead of contemplating and grappling with the mixed messages and my incongruent feelings, I chose what felt easier for the moment: trusting "my outer teacher."

Days and weeks passed, and Brian seemed as charming as ever, mostly pointing out silent awareness to his questioners while keeping his demeanor of a friendly teddy bear pouring light-heartedness over satsang. Then one day he asked if I wanted to make a little extra money. *Do I ever!* Still living on a shoestring, I welcomed any job opportunity, so two days later, I walked to his home for our pre-arranged meet-up.

I was surprised to find an elegant mansion, but even more stunned when he opened the front door fully naked, giving me an unimpeded view of his hairy chest, big belly, and penis. Raised in

Europe, I had no trouble with partial or full nudity on a beach, but being forced to see my teacher stark naked without warning unnerved me. Without excusing his nudity, he waved me in. When I reached the foyer, I caught a glimpse of his wife Maggie with her back toward me, talking on the phone in the kitchen. She was clothed. I wondered if I should let my presence be known by saying hello, as I'd had a few short but always friendly exchanges with her in satsang. Brian, however, was in a hurry and prodded me to follow him into the garden. There he pointed to an old Balinese wooden bench, handed me some sandpaper, and instructed me to call him once I had sanded off the old coat of varnish. I set to work right away. Previously, I might have thought of this task as too boring, but now I was entranced by the overall ease and joyous flow of my movements. I was "doing from being" which allowed my focus and work to feel effortless.

I was almost finished when I heard Maggie's voice in the distance, then the opening and closing of the front door, followed by the sound of a car driving off. A minute later, Brian came into the garden where I was working.

"Oh, this looks great!" He seemed pleased.

I saw with relief that he'd wrapped a sarong around his hips.

"Thank you. I think I need a bit more time to finish, and then I can start to brush the new varnish on."

"Yes, and you can also take a short break."

"Okay," I said. I rose from my kneeling position on the ground, shaking my legs and placing the sheets of sandpaper on the bench.

"Let's sit down for a minute." He pointed to the bench. "So, Annette, how is it going for you with intimate relationships? Any men in your life?"

His casual directness caught me off guard. Was this part of some teaching he wanted to give me or was he genuinely interested?

"No, there is no real relationship at the moment," I answered truthfully. "I mean, there is a man in satsang I really like, but he doesn't seem that much into me." My heart sank a bit with that last sentence. A few weeks ago, I had begun to feel romantically attracted but thus far, my feelings hadn't been reciprocated. I was surprised to be confronted with strong emotional pain around my unrequited longing.

"Ah, who is that?" Brian probed eagerly.

"Ahem, it's Greg, you know, Greg with the dark hair? He lives up the coast in Burnie."

"Oh, I see...Greg. Yes, nice guy, nice guy. Mm, I also can see how he is still a bit of a boy. You'd be much better off with a more mature man," he remarked matter-of-factly.

Stunned by his frank comment, I felt exposed and vulnerable.

"And what does that bring up for you?"

"What do you mean?" *Did Brian notice how vulnerable I felt?*

"Well, you liking him, and him not really responding to you?"

"Oh," I fumbled. I could hear how my voice had lost its strength and volume, but I pushed through. *This is my teacher; I can be frank with him.* "I feel a lot of longing and sometimes strong sadness."

"Longing?" He sounded amused.

"Yeah. I mean.... You know, longing to be loved," I replied quietly.

"Longing to be loved?" He looked at me as if I had delivered the punchline to a great joke, and cracked up into a loud laughter, his big body shaking.

I shrunk, wanting to disappear, tongue-tied by shame. I knew my answer wasn't "spiritually correct"—after all, I had seen the deeper truth of existence where absolutely everything, including Annette, was made of love! *Then why does it feel so darn real? How can I possibly experience this painful lack of love?*

Long after I left Brian's house, I felt terribly at odds with what happened—ridiculed for my experiences and confused and at a loss about how I was supposed to work with the ache and longing for human love within me. I didn't grasp yet there was no real help or clarity to be expected from my mentor. Overemphasizing the vertical axis of spirit, he had successfully settled into a convenient, "transcendent" ivory tower. By flatly refusing to acknowledge the personal and interpersonal dimensions of reality, he opted to block out the complexities of embodied and relational life.

Only much too late would I come to understand how a wholesome integration of transcendent truth required developing a finely attuned flexibility to abide as openness while staying grounded in functional reality—and how holding on too tightly to either of them, meant one was going astray.

During my time in Tahnee Point, though, I was already sliding down the slippery slope of relinquishing my authority only to realize that the messenger had unwittingly become the message. Instead of drinking the tea, I had begun to worship a cracked teapot.

chapter 13

Motherland Reflections

Pain is important: how we evade it, how we succumb to it, how we deal with it, how we transcend it.
AUDRE LORDE

A YEAR after my arrival in Tahnee Point, the last possible extension on my tourist visa had run out and I needed to leave satsang, my new friends, and the town that had become a home. My heart ached, but in this forced departure I also saw an opportunity. I could test my newfound freedom where it would be most challenging—Germany.

In the thirteen years since I had moved to Spain, I felt free to re-invent or discover who I was in all my new and often-changing surroundings. In my own country, though, I'd always felt strangely displaced and ill-fitting. My German culture's over-emphasis on intellectual prowess, productivity, order, and duty had mostly left me gasping for air to just be and—God forbid—enjoy life. I had never examined whether my ingrained aversion to all things German was true, and now, with a completely fresh perspective within, I wondered: *Will the negative narratives still hold?* I'd soon find out.

After nearly thirty hours of air travel from Australia to

Europe, I was groggy and dazed when my plane touched down in Frankfurt. It took nearly two hours to retrieve my backpack from baggage claim, pass immigration and customs, and wait in line to purchase a ticket for the three-hour train ride to Dortmund, where my mother still lived in my childhood home.

Once I was finally on the train, I collapsed, exhausted, into the window seat of a half-empty compartment. As the train pulled out of the station, I hungrily unpacked the buttered poppyseed roll I'd bought at an airport bakery. *Something the Germans get right.* I smiled. *Nowhere does bread taste as good!* After devouring the last crumbs, I spread my jacket over me to take a nap. However, both brain and body were too wired to doze, so I sat up and stared out the window, letting the changing landscapes and cities fly by.

I waited for any nostalgia of homecoming, but none arose. Instead, I reconnected with childhood memories of oppressive heaviness and melancholy. For instance, when I was ten, a national disgrace came to light that made some sense of my perception of "gloomy Germany." Our history teacher showed us a documentary about the Allied Forces liberating the surviving inmates of the concentration camps after World War II. I shuddered to learn for the first time that the country where I was born and raised had engaged in unspeakable acts of cruelty. The black-and-white images depicting large piles of skeleton-thin human corpses and harrowing gas chambers and crematoria nauseated me so intensely that I begged permission to leave the classroom.

That was in 1975, when the Berlin Wall was still intact, and few West Germans spoke openly about the country's collective guilt, even though more than a hundred Nazis were sentenced or put to death during the Nuremberg trials and the government began to pay reparations to Jewish Holocaust survivors. The proverbial "elephant in the room"—the shameful secrets and shocking legacies that families and societies are not ready to confront—had been as much part of my childhood as the wallpaper in our home. The unacknowledged density and darkness lingered and was passed on to those with more vulnerable energetic boundaries—children.

When I turned fourteen, what had mostly been kept quiet flooded into West German living rooms during prime time. Over several weeks, the national TV streamed the American series *Holocaust*. The tragic story of the main characters—members of an affluent Jewish family born and living in Berlin who were murdered in the gas chambers—was fictional but representative of the larger historic truth. At last, millions of unknown victims had human faces, fates, and feelings we could relate to and suffer with. It was the beginning of the country's grappling more openly with its horrific past.

My parents grew up during the war. My father was five when Hitler was elected to power in 1933; my mother was born in 1942, three years before the Third Reich finally surrendered to the Allied Forces. She often mentioned that her parents "didn't know what was going on," but I felt conflicted hearing this often-used phrase. My maternal grandparents had already passed away before I could ask them directly, so my questions remained unanswered: Had they witnessed or at least heard about how Jews, gay and Romani people, and communists were arrested and crammed like cattle for slaughter into trains and taken to unknown fates? I came to believe that apart from Hitler's fanatic and opportunistic followers, some truly didn't know, while too many were afraid to care. Maybe in those precarious times, I too would have resorted to shutting down and turning away or trying not to incriminate myself by knowing too much. After all, dissidents who protested or worked against the regime were persecuted, tortured, or killed.

Upon researching my mother's hometown, I gleaned that her parents had never become members of the Nazi party, but during the last years of the war my grandfather, an apothecary assistant, was recruited to serve as a paramedic in the navy. My paternal grandparents, on the other hand, pious Catholics that they were, had been convinced from early on that no true Christian could ever be of the same mind as the *Führer*. They forbade each of their eight children to attend the widely popular programs of the Hitler Youth or League of German Girls that physically trained and mentally indoctrinated "Aryan" youth with Nazi ideology. My grandfather owned a small construction company, and shortly after the Nazis came to power all commissions in town flowed to a competitor who was a prominent member of the party. I admired their forthright ethical stance, but they paid dearly for it: struggling to put food on the table long before the war even began, and my father and his siblings were shamed and ridiculed at school.

In the last years of the war, when Hitler began recruiting even young boys as cannon fodder for the front line, my father, then sixteen, was drafted. Supported by my grandfather's Christian anti-Nazi stance and beliefs, he refused to obey the order. He was unspeakably lucky—in most of Germany, boys his age were being shot for desertion, but he was sent to prison where he remained for half a year until war's end. Although Dad enthusiastically told me stories about his youth, he never spoke about his incarceration.

As the train barreled ever closer to Dortmund, I closed my eyes and focused on what had felt okay about where I grew up. We lived on the outskirts of the industrial city, in a more rural suburb, and the surrounding countryside offered me much solace and a lifeline. From my childhood bedroom window on the top floor, I could see in the distance, over rooftops of neighbors' houses, green pastures sprinkled with the white-black dots of grazing cows—and in late summer, sprawling fields of golden wheat. Beyond our backyard fence, I could lose myself and shake off my isolation in the forest populated with old oaks, smooth-barked beeches, and tall pines whose branches uttered the most mystical sounds while swaying in the wind.

At six, I made friends with Anneliese whose parents owned a little farm which became a haven: we spent almost every afternoon after school riding bareback on the ponies, fixing the barbed-wire fences, cleaning the stable, feeding the chicken and rabbits, or playing with the cats and dogs. At eleven, I was still happiest running around in dirty pants and rubber boots while many of the girls in my class had begun experimenting with wearing eyeshadow in public or kissing boys.

Images of my late father inevitably swirled up. Since his death seven years earlier, I had stopped going home for Christmas—the most important of German holidays. Both my sisters had moved away long ago. Christiane still lived and worked 400 miles away, and Britta married and gave birth to a baby girl. When Dad passed, the relationship between the three of us changed instantly. Our childhood quarrels and rivalries were put to rest. Since our mother had not been available to grieve our father's death with us, we pulled together, and the resulting warmth and supportive bond endured.

On the other hand, whenever I visited our mother, she had no idea of my impending arrival. I would call a neighbor making sure she was home. For years, I told myself I wanted to create a joyful surprise for her, but as the tracks rumbled under the train, I realized the truth. My unexpected-visit stunts had not been so much about her; they were fueled by a secret hope of eliciting a different experience between us. I wanted her surprise at seeing me to jumpstart a new, warmer way of relating. So far, the trick hadn't worked.

The scenario was almost always identical: I stood with my luggage outside the heavy oak front door. Squeezed by longing and expectation, holding my breath for a few moments, I then rang the bell. From inside, Mum's steps approached, the door swung open, she erupted into joy, grabbed me in a hasty hug—and then immediately let go, her eyes tearing up. Every time, she turned away—away from any potential emotional vulnerability. She ushered me inside, instructed me to bring my luggage upstairs into one of our old childhood bedrooms-turned-guestroom, and then, distracting herself from her feelings, rushed into the kitchen to make coffee or tea. By the time I'd come downstairs, she'd shifted back into her business-as-usual mood. I had long since grown accustomed to her lack of asking questions about what had happened in my life or how I felt. The "conversation" circled mostly around herself, and after ten or fifteen minutes she hurried back to her housework or watching TV. My thoughts, feelings, and experiences were like background noise, barely registering beneath the steady stream of her own narratives.

Nevertheless, every time, my throat would tighten into a lump; I felt paralyzed by an ache for closeness, but incapable of putting desire into words. In exact proportion to how my mother was unable to share emotional intimacy, I was stuck, frozen, unable to figure out what I could do to shift the relational space between us. Openly acknowledging and voicing my need for more connection or closeness always ended in failure.

Something within me, though, had never been willing to give up on motherly love. By the time I was six, I began to seek feminine nurturance outside of our home. My first substitute was Frau Mueller, the mother of my playmate Anneliese from the farm. Frau Mueller was what a "real" mom was supposed to be like. With five children of her own, from morning until late in the evening she cooked, baked, washed, and ironed, as well as tended the vegetable garden and farm animals. She was usually in a cheerful mood, and when I had sleepovers at Anneliese's I looked forward to Sunday morning when Frau Mueller would stand at the stove flipping pancakes for her large family—and me.

Seeing my plate empty, she'd ask dotingly, "Still hungry?"

I'd nod *yes*, even when my belly felt close to exploding. Her attention filled me even more than her pancakes, but I also felt ambiguous and ashamed for having my needs so readily met. *Am I deserving of this much attention?*

With another woman from our neighborhood, I was more up-front. At times I would wrap my arms around her hips and ask, "Can you be my mom?"

During teenage years, especially after witnessing healthier family dynamics during my exchange program in France, my feelings for my mother soured into profound resentment. Outwardly, I became rebellious and super snappy, while inwardly I filed details like a prosecutor building a solid case outlining all her shortcomings. It was a futile strategy and defense against my emotional pain. I believed that by retaliating and punishing her with my rejection and judgment I could shift the dynamic, and for a change, she would have to seek *my* love and approval.

As I grew older, I became luckier. In late teens I found and received warm mothering and guidance from other adult women. Perhaps this helped to soften my animosity in the end. Once I moved away, I reinitiated my attempts to shorten the distance between us, hoping the disconnect could be mended by talking about it. Yet she blew up at me every time I addressed our relationship. Outraged at being accused of falling short in any way, she declared, "I neither need nor want to have this kind of conversation. I am a good mother," as she stormed out of the room.

THROUGH THE train window the cities of the Ruhr Region passed by under a rainy gray sky. I looked at my watch—only thirty minutes remained until Dortmund station. I stood and stretched my legs and arms. When I sat down again, the memory of my primal healing group in Pune bubbled up. *What did the therapist say about my waiting for my mother's affection? "She won't give it to you! Let it go!"* I realized now that demanding my mother's love was ridiculous.

It never got me closer to what I wanted. My spine straightened as I returned to my seat; I was stunned by the clarity of this realization. And what had the therapist said countless times? "Family is a neurotic structure in which everyone fights and rivals for love and attention."

My memory skipped backward, and I recalled how Mum had often described Oma, my maternal grandmother, as emotionally cold and unavailable. She had sworn she wouldn't make the same mistakes with her own kids. Instead of going to work like Oma, she stayed home to care for us. I think my mother might have been much happier continuing in her career, but my dad had also been controlling and patriarchal. I compared my freedom with my mom's experience—at twenty-five she had her hands full taking care of three little children, a house, and a garden. Not only did she lack the time or resources to work through emotional injuries and issues, but back then in Germany therapy was often regarded as something for "crazy" people.

The Pune therapist's words resounded again in my mind: *She won't give it to you! Let it go.* I finally got it. As long as I leaned so heavily forward, reaching out for intimate connection or even demanding *her* love, I disconnected from experiencing love within my own being!

I hailed a taxi from the train station, and twenty minutes later, as we pulled into my family's driveway, I waited for the ache to return. It didn't. I hadn't seen my mother for over two years, and while I felt emotional, the usual grasping apprehension was absent. The familiar stark white façade of our two-story house greeted me. The flowerpots on the windowsills were empty, as February was still too cold for Mum's ever-same pink geraniums. I paid the driver, shouldered my big travel pack, and stepped toward the dark-stained oak front door. I rang the bell and listened as her steps approached. I breathed in, slowly, then out again. I heard the bolt click as she opened the door.

Everything was the same: first she was utterly surprised,

letting out a little scream, the quick embrace, her brown eyes moist for a moment until she squelched her feelings. But within me it was different. I no longer misinterpreted her short hug and turning away as a message I was unlovable or unworthy. It was the first time I dropped into the acceptance of our relationship having its obvious failures and limitations. By giving up my struggle with how reality appeared to be, my mind's insistence of needing *her* to be different—so that *I* could be happy—dropped away. From the open ground of being, I grasped that ineffable yet essential sameness in us both, a seamless field of presence expressing itself as two human beings on their topsy-turvy journeys through the complex landscape of love.

THE RETURN to my mother's home marked the first turning point in my learning to relate from a deeper ground of existence. Looking back at the thirty-two-year-old woman I was, I can see now how I merely scratched the surface of my gaping mother wound. I had yet to learn about spiritual bypassing, a term coined fifteen years earlier in 1984 by psychologist John Welwood to define the use of spiritual insights or practices to avoid addressing one's unhealed emotional trauma and defense strategies. It often surprises spiritual practitioners how even genuine and profound realizations do not automatically resolve the significant deficiencies or failures of parental love from their past.

Most of our unprocessed experiences continue to be wired throughout our psyche and soma until they are seen for what they are, allowed to be unpacked, and emptied out. It is one of the many profound paradoxes of reality: on one hand, we are the seamless ocean of consciousness—essentially unbroken and complete—and yet as human beings in our temporary waveforms, we are also subject to our organism's innate and vulnerable need for care and connection with others.

Human beings are primarily social creatures—no matter where our nervous system is on the spectrum between introvert and extrovert. Right after birth, our organism has the biological drive to attach and bond with another human being. We are defenseless and dependent upon others not just for food, shelter, or protection, but also for the brain development we require to be seen and felt, soothed, and held. How we are handled—the quality of our caregiver's touch, face-to-face cues, tone of voice, and embodied presence shape our notion of what love "should" feel like—for better or worse. Apart from coming into this life with certain genetic and epigenetic propensities or temperaments, our parent-infant bonding experiences lay down the precognitive blueprint for all our subsequent relationships: the implicit notion of who we are and what to expect from others or the world, as well as our capacity for emotional regulation in the face of adversity. Infants, having no ability yet for discernment or comparison, cannot help but absorb like sponges even the most severe neglect or abuse—but this doesn't mean they're not suffering.

In the best of all worlds, caregivers are spontaneously affectionate and emotionally available; they don't have to be perfect—no one is. Research has shown: when a parental figure is sincerely present, protective, predictable, and playful just 30 percent of the time, it is enough to build a foundation of healthy bonding patterns within a child. On the other hand, even with the best parenting available, it is hard to trust the fundamental okay-ness of our being without recognizing causeless love and the unborn ground of existence free of separation and experience *true* connection. Ultimately, it is by opening ourselves to this bigger love and deeper mother ground—combined with corrective experiences in healthy adult relationships and therapy—that over time assists us in seeing through our old pain identities and compels the traces of attachment traumas to lose their grip.

As for the relationship with my mother, I continued to show up with care and acceptance as I began to recognize my unhealthy levels of tolerance and an ingrained habit of "making do" and enduring uncaring, cruel, or contemptuous behavior. I learned to draw clear boundaries as well as stand up for myself with love and authenticity. At thirty-three, though, I was still blindsided by dissociative states and coping mechanisms—and, all the while, Brian's disembodied teachings presented "emptiness" as a cure-all.

I couldn't yet grasp how deeply the unhealed complex trauma and sexual abuses of childhood lurking in the shadows of my consciousness were still directing my life, setting the stage for an experience that would shatter my world completely. Unfortunately, unaddressed trauma often begets more trauma.

chapter 14

Experiment Gone Wrong

When you give another person the power to define you, then you also give them the power to control you.

LESLIE VERNICK, *The Emotionally Destructive Relationship*

I LAY on my back in the small tent I erected for myself in the garden of the retreat center thirty miles south of Munich, close to the famous Tegernsee, one of many picturesque lakes in the German Alps. After a few weeks with my mother, I had moved to Bavaria. Settling in southern Germany had proven to be a good choice. For the last five months, I had been working as a waitress in a vegetarian restaurant, and on days off, I often ventured into the surrounding countryside. The idyllic natural landscapes and quaint villages unexpectedly restored a sense of wholesomeness about my native country, even nurturing tender feelings of belonging.

It was still light outside when I glanced at my watch. Dinner would start in a few minutes, at 6 p.m. I wriggled out of my tent and looked around, pleased: the dense foliage of the big chestnut tree's canopy above would shade my tent from the hot July sun. The smell of dry grass—a quintessential scent of summer for me—tickled my nose, and I stretched my limbs with delight.

In the last months, I had put every penny aside to be able to attend this weeklong residential retreat with Brian. I let out a sigh of satisfaction and the swell of joyous anticipation expanded my heart even further: I couldn't wait to be in satsang again! The meal gong rang; I slipped on my sandals, zipped up my tent, and made my way to the dining hall where thirty-plus people had already lined up at the buffet, ready to fill their plates as more people trickled in.

"Hey, Annette. So good to see you!" Brian's voice boomed so loud that heads swiveled to look at him. With a big smile on his face, he steered in my direction. My heart leaped—I had missed him and our Tahnee Point satsang so much—and we hugged for a moment.

"Yes, so good to see you!" I chimed in, my eyes filling with tears. I still hadn't found an end to my gratitude for him. Satsang had changed me irrevocably: at last, my urgent quest for life's true meaning and who I really was had been answered. In fact, my old deficient sense of self had been revealed to be a case of mistaken identity and my "needing to fix and analyze everything" mind gave up more easily or swirled in the periphery as my attention relaxed and rested into the limitless silence of existence.

"Do you want to eat together? I have my table over there," he gestured toward a window at the far end of the dining hall. More heads turned toward us. As I was completely new to Brian's German sangha, I imagined people here were curious about who I was and why Brian would give me, a stranger, special attention. I couldn't help feeling flattered by the invitation.

"Sure...thank you. I'd love that."

After filling my plate at the buffet, I headed to his table.

"So, how long has it been since we last saw each other?" he asked cheerily.

"Well, I left Tahnee Point at the end of January, so it's been far too long without satsang."

I laughed and he joined in.

"And how is life in Germany?"

"It's okay. Not as magical as Tahnee Point, but I do like Munich and its surrounding countryside. I mean the lakes, the Alps, the nature here...is breathtakingly beautiful. And I have found some easy work as a waitress that's good enough money. Most of my colleagues are from all over the world, so I feel a bit more at home among all the foreigners." I giggled, a bit too loudly. I felt jittery and lightheaded and to my astonishment noticed my hand trembling slightly as I reached for my glass of water—*why is that?*

"I see," Brian stabbed three big slices of tomato with his fork and stuffed them into his mouth. "And what did you do before you came to Tahnee Point? I remember you had a career of some kind." He chewed with his mouth open, his big teeth flashing unexpectedly.

"I worked as a translator and interpreter in Spain—mainly business meetings between German and Spanish lawyers, some conferences, and also legal contracts here and there. I stopped all of that when I left to go to India, roughly four and a half years ago." My voice sounded hollow, as if someone else was speaking my words. Flattery and apprehension fluttered in my chest about having my mentor's attention all to myself. I could feel some participants watching us, but Brian inexplicably seemed zoomed in on me.

"But there's no way I would want to do that kind of work now," I continued unprompted. "I don't want something where I must churn my intellect all day along. Since satsang, I feel I need a lot of quiet time, so simpler work is perfect."

We chatted for twenty minutes more about his travels and teaching in other places around the world. Eventually, he announced he needed to call his wife Maggie, who hadn't come to the retreat, and that the first group gathering would begin at seven.

After the afternoon satsang on the second day, while grabbing my bag to head to my tent, Brian intercepted me. He waited for everyone else to leave the hall, then asked in a lowered voice, "Hey, would you have a moment after dinner to meet? My room is on the second floor, the last door at the end of the hallway on the left."

"Sure..." I replied slowly, wondering why he wanted to talk with me in his room.

After dinner, I climbed the stairs to the second floor. My heart raced as I knocked on Brian's door.

"Come in," he called. I opened the door to find him sitting in front of his laptop at a little desk.

"Give me a minute, will you?" he continued typing on the keyboard.

I looked around the room. It was cozy, with wooden floors and an ornate wooden balcony that overlooked the garden. It was furnished with two nightstands, a double bed with a traditionally carved headboard, and through the half-opened bathroom door I glimpsed the white tiles of the bathroom floor. He slapped his laptop closed and turned around on his chair, grinning.

"Why don't you sit down?" he pointed at the end of the bed, opposite his chair.

I wordlessly obeyed, and since there was no second chair in the room, I perched a bit uncomfortably on the edge of his bed.

"As you know, Maggie is not on the retreat with us this time," he started. He vacillated for a moment as if searching for his next words. "The reason...the reason is that we both wanted some time apart to sort things out between us."

"Aha." I nodded, trying to keep a neutral expression as my throat tightened. I was bewildered why he was choosing to disclose his private marital matters to me. I had recently learned that Maggie wasn't his first wife, but his fifth or maybe even sixth?

"I don't know to whom else I can talk about this. There is really no one here who is as mature as you and who has such a deep interest in truth." He looked at me intently, allowing his words to sink deeper.

I didn't reply, nor could I, even if I wanted to. Something in his way of speaking prompted my body to brace and the tightening sensations in my throat spread into my chest, stopping my breath. Beneath the constriction, I felt torn between trepidation and pride. *Among all sixty people here, he thinks of me as the most mature?* I didn't want to give away my feelings and pressed my lips together more firmly. The sudden sound of someone laughing out loud in the garden reached up to the room, but my tension didn't ease with it.

Brian went on, "To be frank, Maggie and I have had some problems for quite some time...*ahem*...sexual problems."

The word "sexual" rattled my ears and my head buzzed. *Too much information. I don't need to know this.* I didn't want to be privy to my mentor's love life. My stomach knotted and took hold of my heart. It was as if I was transported back to the smoke-filled living room in the late evening hours, where I was overwhelmed by my dad's disclosure of frustration about his unhappy marriage.

Brian, oblivious to my emotional shift, stood up and then leaned his bottom and thighs against the desk behind him, half sitting and facing me directly. The first three buttons of his shirt gaped open, revealing his hairy chest. He crossed his arms in a relaxed manner. I could smell his skin giving off an earthy, but slightly sweet scent, maybe musk or myrrh?

"Maggie and I thought it would be good to find out if our sexual difficulties are her problem or mine," he continued matter-of-factly. "And I wanted to ask if you would be open to do an experiment with me and...ahem...make love with me, to see, if things are still all okay on my side?"

I froze. I was too stunned to speak. *Is this for real?*

"Maggie *agreed* to that? I don't believe you!" I blurted.

"Yes, yes, you can call her, if you like," he assured me while shifting his body posture, now to full standing. For a moment, his eyes veered to the side.

He must be lying! My senses sharpened, and I assumed a more assertive stance. True or not—no part of me wanted to be involved with their sexual life.

"The answer is no," I replied curtly, my heart beating fast.

"Are you sure?" He seemed surprised, as if he had fully expected me to fall into bed with him.

"Yes." I stood up, clear that I wanted to get out of there. My heart was pumping blood as if readying itself for a sprint.

"Okay...well, thank you for listening." He ended our talk with a wry smile.

We simultaneously moved toward the door; he opened it for me and without further words I exited, feeling as if I were walking on stilts, my heart still pounding.

As I stepped down the stairs, my palms were sweaty but there was a visceral relief in having gotten away. My muddled feelings, though, didn't vanish as easily. My mind was racing; I was unsure what to do next. I walked as if on autopilot straight to the meditation hall and sank into one of the empty chairs.

Twenty minutes later, nearly all the seats and meditation cushions in the hall were filled. Brian entered and placed himself at the front. I felt anxious, my body shrinking deeper into the chair. *Will he punish me by giving me the cold shoulder like the old guy I turned down in Pune?* Brian scanned the audience. When he located me, a quick smile lit up his face. A silent sigh escaped my lips, my body relaxed again. *How stupid of me! He is awake—he doesn't need to punish me for saying no*. I had the urge to crack a half smile as if assuring him it was all okay from my side too. *This has ended well.* I closed my eyes to steep in stillness.

THE NEXT morning, as I was pouring granola into my bowl, Brian's breath was suddenly hot on my ear. He whispered in a tone that was surely intended to sound playful, "And...is it still 'No?'"

I stepped away, startled. He didn't move an inch, but lingered with a half-smile on his face awaiting a reply. I hadn't changed my mind, so I nodded to assert that my "no" remained firm. He chuckled and left.

Unsettled by this interaction, I walked into the garden, the half-filled bowl of cereal still in my hand. I paced around in a daze until I found an isolated spot to sit alone, behind a bush. Gobbling down several spoons of the dry granola, I was rapidly filling my belly in order to get a handle on my anxiety, as if ingesting something solid had the power to nullify my inner turmoil or help me feel the ground under my feet.

Still, after breakfast I attended the morning satsang as if nothing had happened, however I couldn't drop in. I kept looking at Brian as he taught, vigilant for any gestures or facial expressions. He seemed unfazed, the same as usual, and a part of me was eager to pretend and confirm what had transpired earlier as resolved.

He approached me a third time. A day later, after a particularly beautiful afternoon satsang during which he declared, "Satsang is a love affair with truth, and in this love, we feel so full we no longer lack anything." I was standing outside, preparing to leave the retreat center and take a walk in the woods when I bumped into him in the parking lot. He must have already spotted me because he headed quickly toward me. This time, he made his case in a more solemn voice, explaining that his intent of deciphering his marriage's problems by having sex with me was an experiment "for truth."

Those two words stopped time in its tracks: *For truth.*

It escaped me that the idea of sacrifice for a so-called higher truth had been foolishly or conveniently misconstrued for millennia. It had indeed caused such senseless suffering that the archetype of the martyr—whether virgins fed to wild beasts to bribe the gods for better harvests or jihadists being convinced their killing of infidels by suicide bombings were pleasing God—had to be elevated to a special spot in the pantheon of our collective human psyche.

Even though I had seen beyond all doubt and belief: there was no God separate from my own being who could ask me to sacrifice and go against what felt true in my heart—hearing the words "for truth" uttered by my mentor caused my common sense and earlier objections to collapse and vanish. Forgotten was my hunch of Maggie likely being in the dark, ignored was my previous clarity of inappropriateness, and disregarded was the absence of sexual attraction toward this man who until now had been a wise father figure. With my psyche's still unhealed need for self-validation, Brian requesting my service for truth spun me into a dizzying elation. The combination of my long history of shattered boundaries and his relentless pursuit unraveled the last threads of my capacity to hold onto myself. Everything I instinctively knew to be right or true—my better knowing, heart's integrity, and gut's wisdom—was vanished in this instant.

At around eleven that night I slipped up the stairs in the dark, following Brian's instructions to wait until all lights were out and everyone was supposedly asleep. I felt trepidation about the prospect of being naked and intimate with my mentor, but the idea of being special and a chosen servant of truth had taken hold of me. My heart pounded in my throat as I quietly knocked on his door.

He opened it at once, urging me to come inside and speak in a low voice so we didn't wake anyone nearby. He smiled broadly. "So nice of you to have come."

I think I half-smiled back, although it was hard to feel much sensation in my body. A huge part of me seemed to hover somewhere above it all, close to the wooden beams of the ceiling. From there, it all went fast—between prodding me to undress, lying down on his bed, him getting on top of me and asking, "Is it okay like this?" And after I nodded, his humping up and down until he had satisfied his sexual urgency—all told, a mere five minutes passed. Buffered by a cloud of frozen blankness, I felt eerily evacuated, disconnected from myself.

When he climbed off, I was left stunned. *Is this how a spiritual teacher makes love?* During, he had offered no gesture or interest in emotional connection. Even my uncommitted sexual encounters with men during my "wild" time in Tokyo had been more intimate, kind, and generous.

He thanked me, declared that it had been wonderful for him, and we said goodbye. As clandestinely as I'd arrived in his room, I returned to the garden like a specter, a hollow version of myself. I was bewildered, my mind blank about what had happened, but once back in my tent, a teenage-like giddiness about sharing a naughty secret with my teacher, of being special and significant to him, arose in me.

chapter 15

Paralyzing Betrayal

It's one thing to deconstruct and analyze and condemn the institutions of patriarchy and their flaws. It's another one to feel their bruises on your skin, and their grasping hands pulling your hair and covering your mouth as you scream.

ALICE MINIUM

THE NEXT morning, I awoke in my tent with a distinct feeling that something cataclysmic had happened. I was shaken by the irrevocable sense a line had been crossed, it was not going to disappear and could never be undone.

Half an hour later I ran into Brian in the dining hall. Encountering him in public and plain daylight after the night's secrecy was perplexing. I felt eerily absent and embarrassed, and tried my best to appear unaffected. He seemed unruffled, in a jolly mood, and eager to see me. "Could I talk to you for a quick moment?" A slight urgency underpinned his voice.

"Sure," I replied, looking around for a table where we could sit down.

"No, not now—later! Just come up to my room before satsang, okay?"

My body braced as he looked at his watch. "Shall we say in twenty minutes?"

Overriding my physical reaction, making myself sound as nonchalant as possible, I obeyed: "Okay." He nodded and left.

Part of me tried to feign that there was nothing unusual in his request, but I couldn't stop wondering what was so urgent. Bolstered by my new role as his mature confidante and servant of truth, though, twenty minutes later, I shoved aside my muddled feelings and climbed the stairs to his room. "Come in, come in," he encouraged. "How are you doing?" his voice sounded sweet but tinged with urgency.

"I am okay." In reality, I was too numb to decipher my feelings.

"Well...ahem...I just wanted you to know that last night was really wonderful for me, and..." he paused for a moment with a short giggle, "ahem, as we still have a bit time left before satsang," he glanced at his watch, "I thought we just should do it again. What do you think?"

His mouth opened to smirk, but the insistent energy behind his words and facial expression rang an alarm in me. My "no" boiled up and spilled out. "No, I don't want to..."

Trampling my clarity, he chimed in, "Come on! It's just a little fun..." And then he stepped closer. My rapid heartbeat scared me. It was suddenly all so clear—his proposal had nothing to do with an "experiment in truth" or needing certainty about his marital problems. Brian was plain horny and driven by lust.

"No, I really don't want to, Brian," I declared more vehemently. Hearing my voice's fervor only increased my impending sense of danger. *I need to get out of here—now!*

I turned around, but before I could even reach the door, Brian grabbed me from behind and flipped me around to face him again.

"No! Leave me alone, please." My voice cracked, gripped by panic.

"Come one, come on, just a few minutes!" He laughed it off, while firmly holding onto my arms.

I was overcome by a profound shame for being in this situation—ashamed for needing to repeatedly verbalize my "No" that he hadn't heard the first time, ashamed for needing to reject this man, my beloved mentor who until this moment I'd trusted with all my heart—as I still all the while attempted to struggle free.

He had no intention of letting me go. My bodily resistance spiked into urgency, fighting to shift and turn myself into a different angle to break free until, unexpectedly, with one fast and abrupt movement, Brian took a step back, pulling my body with him as I lost my footing.

My feelings of shame turned into shock and horror as he dragged me toward the open door next to his bed. In two quick steps he had hauled me into the bathroom, shut the door with his shoulder—or was it his foot? Gripping my wrists with one of his hands, he slammed the toilet lid down with the other, plummeted himself onto the seat, and lifted my skirt enough to tear my underwear away. This last act shocked and short-circuited my brain into its last possible survival response: in an instant all strength drained out of me, legs and arms became limp, and my hapless body collapsed. Brian pulled me down onto him and in a frenzy began jerking up and down inside of me from the toilet seat. Only after he had finished, did he loosen his grip.

chapter 16

Trauma Bonds

With dissociation, the sense of self is profoundly assaulted. Dissociation itself becomes traumatizing. Because if you can't rely on your own experiences, then your own sense of self is itself a cause of being overwhelmed by things.

DAN SIEGEL, MD, *The Neurobiology of Trauma*

I DON'T remember how quickly or even *how* my physical form was able to regain enough control again to stand, step away while pulling up my underwear, and walk wordlessly out of his room. I don't remember whether I met anyone in the corridor or not, nor how after all that had happened, I still went straight into the meditation hall.

The mixture of overwhelming horror, helplessness, and shame catalyzed my brain into a profound state of dissociation through which any sounds, sensations, or images related to the monstrous incident disappeared from my conscious recollection for nearly sixteen years. And in the meantime, until the day when my organism finally sensed it was now safe enough to remember, I would only recall how naïve I had been for having given my consent to the inappropriate "experiment for truth." After the rape, the remaining time of the retreat disappeared into an undefinable blur, registering as uneventful, and yet, accompanied by a faint sense of something not being quite right.

Contrary to what many of us assume, trauma is not so much what *happened*, but what continues to *happen* in our bodies and brains as a result of sudden, overwhelming events. When neuro-biological stimuli are coming at us too fast or too soon and our brain is incapable of coping with the onslaught, our survival physiology will prompt a split from too much helplessness, terror, or pain. With the connections between parts of our brain becoming impaired, we experience ourselves and the world only within restrictive psycho-physiological patterns. Like a submarine prevented from completely sinking by closing off the leaking compartments in its hulk, we continue to function and live on, yet parts of us stay locked in a time long gone, trapped in a painful past. Or we become so encapsulated that we become utterly unconscious of what lies in the dark. Dissociation satisfies our organism's immediate concern for survival, but the long-term impacts can bear a heavy weight, especially as our nervous system remains in highly dysregulated states for years and even lifetimes.

Sexual trauma is particularly corrosive, as its relational components compromise and color so many of our social interactions. Apart from the paralyzing shame and terror preventing us from seeking help, sexual violations—especially those early in life—rob us of a basic notion of safety, and of our sensual innocence and embodied sovereignty. To this day, sexual abuse, assault, and rape carry a severe stigma. No one doubts anyone saying they've been mugged or robbed, but when women or girls share a story of sexual assault, the forces of patriarchy pounce to devalue their testimony: Are you sure this happened? Why were you alone with him? What were you wearing? How could you have been so naïve? Are you sure it wasn't consensual—he says you stopped resisting. You must have wanted it. Why didn't you fight harder?

While most modern societies are clear in their legal definitions of what constitutes sexual harassment, abuse, or rape, there are no laws prohibiting a woman from going out at night, meeting with a man alone, or getting drunk. And yet, many will look first to discredit or blame the assaulted as if she were the one who broke a law. As a consequence of centuries of male entitlement and cultural misogyny, a staggering majority of victims of sexual abuse, assault, or rape never report—*or even acknowledge to themselves*—that they have been violated in the most shattering way.

Our human body and brain's automatic survival responses also play a crucial role in keeping us mute. Nature is compassionate enough to force a shutdown, collapse into immobility, or "feigned death." We enter a state of "oblivion," a zone of "no pain" when our brain recognizes the survival responses of fighting or fleeing as hopeless. This last resort is not a conscious, deliberate choice—we no longer have control when the oldest and innermost region of our brain takes over, causing our heart rate to drop, our muscles to go rigid or limp, and our consciousness to dissociate from the event.

This involuntary immobility haunts victims in the aftermath. Additionally, mainstream culture's widespread ignorance about the ultimate power of our survival biology leads many victims to erroneously conclude that *we* didn't do enough to prevent the assault, to break free, to get away. Together—with the corrosive symptoms of our brain's multiple networks becoming disconnected, its processing capacities becoming impaired, and our nervous-system staying stuck in the loops of fight, flight, freeze, or fawn responses—it's this terrifying doubt that *we* might be at fault or being blamed for what has happened which often stuns, shames, and stupefies victims into a voiceless, death-like vacuum.

In my case, while any memory of the rape remained hidden from my conscious recollection for a long time, my body didn't forget. The assault at the hands of my spiritual mentor would leave my organism and psyche profoundly destabilized and disintegrated for years. Feeling eerily fragmented and alienated from myself, I suffered an unnamable shame and grief, rapidly shifting mood swings, alternating at times between inexplicable rage and depression, panic attacks, and hopelessness. I struggled with brain fog and difficulty staying on task, second-guessing myself even in minor decisions and becoming startled by the most innocent sounds or movements in my surroundings.

At the end of the retreat, I returned to Munich. Once settled into my ordinary surroundings, the delusion of being Brian's special confidante shattered.

I awoke with the pressure of a boulder crushing my chest as an early morning streetcar passed below my bedroom window with its familiar squeaky sounds. The nausea in my stomach alerted me that something appalling had occurred. Catastrophizing thoughts rushed in from all sides: *What happened? Oh my God...I agreed to have sex with Brian! How is that possible? How could I do something like that? It's abominable...feels so incestuous*! *And what about Maggie? I like her...she's always been friendly. I betrayed her. This is a nightmare!* Disgust, despair, and guilt roiled inside of me so powerfully that I could no longer think straight or even cry. I felt shredded into pieces by screaming voices in my head accusing me of being filthy and worthless—shame sticking to me like toxic glue. My body felt heavy like lead: I couldn't get up, so I stayed motionless in bed, paralyzed while clenching my eyes closed or staring at the white ceiling above me as waves of fear and dread pulsed relentlessly through me. Unable to go outside, let alone show up for work, I managed to call the restaurant and cancel my shifts for the next two days.

At midday, the phone rang. To my utter surprise, the woman's voice on the other end announced, "It's me, Maggie." I gasped, followed by a long silence. Maybe Brian's wife was waiting for me to explain or excuse myself, but swamped by immense shame and guilt, my brain shut down and I was left too tongue-tied to utter a sound. I had stopped breathing, my body bracing for impact, waiting for Maggie to explode and yell at me as I deserved, but she stayed quiet for what felt like forever, until she unexpectedly exclaimed in a gentle tone, "Oh my God—you are innocent." She paused. "He pressured you into having sex with him!"

Her words stunned me, even as I felt so despicable that I couldn't fully let them in. "I am so sorry, Maggie. I don't know what to say. It's inexcusable..." I said feebly.

Something of her empathic energy, though, landed inside me and unlocked tears that began rolling down my cheeks. We exchanged no other words and soon hung up.

Several hours passed before it dawned: Maggie calling me innocent even though I hadn't told her how it unfolded could only mean that, indeed, Brian lied about her agreeing to the "experiment for truth." I had no clue how she found out, but not even Maggie's forgiveness or the revelation of Brian's obvious dishonesty could abate my emotional turmoil. My mind and body were paralyzed by terror, helplessness and shame. Besieged by thick, heavy clouds of intense self-loathing, I could no longer find the liberating skylike openness of existence—only an impenetrable, black storm. I'd been crashed from the height of the heavens all the way down to hell with nothing left to suppress or defend against the raging pain inside of me.

After three days of this agony, I reached out for help from the only person my traumatized mind could think of: Brian. I found out where in Europe he was teaching, then called the local organizer to give him the message that Annette in Munich needed to speak to him. Urgently.

It didn't occur to me for a moment that he was the least suitable person to relieve me from my suffering. The same way I had disregarded how much I risked in my life and devoted to gaining a deeper understanding prior to meeting Brian—unduly giving him all the credit for me dropping like an overripe fruit into the realization of my original face—now in my chaotic state I couldn't think of anyone else as a savior. Incapable of even remembering the violent assault, and clueless about my long history of abuse or my tendency to over-idealize Brian as the all-potent healing father figure, I couldn't see that reaching out to him was like asking a fox to take care of a chicken.

YEARS LATER, in my training with Dr. Diane Poole Heller and Patti Elledge on relational trauma healing, I learned that far worse than the traumatizing event is the secondary trauma which stems from not having a safe landing figure available with whom we can process what has occurred. It gets more complicated when our abusers are the same person with whom we previously developed a strong emotional connection—intimate partners, friends, parents, or mentors. The excruciating feelings of existential helplessness paired with the despair of abandonment that often play a role in relational trauma scenarios override our brain's survival instinct to get away from the very source of harm. We are stuck in a trauma-bond which, like Stockholm syndrome, blocks our brain's capacity for rational assessment and compulsively prioritizes feelings of previous emotional connection, safety, or even loyalty, and the urgent need to re-attach to our abusers, expecting help.

Cut off from logic or reason, our short-circuited brain is compelled to return to the traumatizing scenario as if an undefinable force within us is looking for *what*—making the pain undone, or maybe even attempting to master the situation by becoming more conscious? For bystanders, it can be inapprehensible and horrifying to witness how victims of domestic violence "prefer" to cohabitate with their abusive partners, victims of sex trafficking can't muster the resolve to leave their traffickers for good, or followers appear to willingly endure the exploitations at the hands of cult-leaders. "Traumatized minds make traumatized choices."[1]

BRIAN TELEPHONED two days later. "Annette, how are you, sweetie?" His familiar tone gave me immediate comfort. I no longer felt isolated, alone in my pain and helplessness.

"I don't know what to do...since the retreat, I have been having a really hard time. I have all these really crazy feelings. I am just freaked out all the time and I cannot find the peace in the midst of it any longer. There is so much guilt and it feels so...so wrong what happened on the retreat!" I burst forth.

"Well, it's just the mind. Really nothing to worry about. It's just thoughts, remember? But check right now: are these thoughts real?"

His heavy breathing oozed through the phone as he awaited my reply. *Real? Not real? What does that even mean right now?* Brian's intellectual dismissal of my experience made me feel crazier and panicky. I convulsed with dry heaves.

He cleared his throat. "Look...what happened between us, just happened. There is really no problem here. Let it go, you see...Maggie and I are already moving on."

My mind went blank. I was too dumbfounded to counter with anything that seemed a valid argument. The room's light dimmed as if a dark hood was pulled over me. My despair morphed into a cold stupor and complete shutdown. "Okay, then," was all I could utter before hanging up.

It is said that the term "dark night of the soul" means one no longer has any spiritual perspective left. It is easy to be conscious of our true nature in the good weather of our life. It's a

[1] Quote by Deborah Lee, DClinPsy from "Three Critical Insights into Treating Trauma," a NICABM (National Institute for the Clinical Application of Behavioral Medicine) video clip on YouTube.

steeper learning curve to find God in grief, taste love in loss, feel indestructible in the face of fear, or know that our original innocence remains unscathed even in the midst of betrayal. I began to believe that the Heavens I had trusted all my life, the same Grace that had brought me to recognize my heart as the source of the sacred, had forsaken me. Everything which had been revealed, the undamaged openness of reality and unborn ground of existence—held as holy and dear within and without—felt tainted, stained, soiled. I had nowhere to turn.

I'd become homeless in my own heart.

chapter 17

The Feminine and Reclaiming Authority

Meeting our strong feminine energy, we will develop as women, and not as women trying to be like men or asexual beings. We are different, and until that difference is known, owned, and maximized, our true feminine potency and capacity to bring this world into balance will not be realized.

LAMA TSULTRIM ALLIONE, *Wisdom Rising*

In the weeks and months to follow, I fell apart. I could barely drag myself to work. I stopped exercising, chain-smoked cigarettes, and didn't clean the apartment. A sense of being buried alive in an all-enveloping dark tunnel was regularly punctuated by my mind's vile comments and self-condemnation: *How could you have been so stupid to give in to having sex with him? Why didn't you trust your gut and stick to your initial no? What the hell is wrong with you?* I attributed all responsibility and blame onto myself, making it impossible for any speck of self-compassion to arise.

When, four months after the retreat, my emotional agony hadn't lifted, I decided to travel one more time to Tahnee Point in search of resolution. Despite my last contact with Brian, I still nursed the irrational hope that *if I can get through to him*, *making him understand how my torment started with his "experiment for truth" at the retreat, he will see it too, and all will be well again.*

I didn't know that "It is one of the main signs of childhood trauma to, instead of walking away, try to convince the people who are hurting us to treat us better."[1]

Brian was delighted to see me back in Tahnee Point, but the disconnect I now felt between us did not allow me to simply return to the "good old days." Spending time with my friends, like Monica, brought some comfort, yet even with her I stayed stuck in a vortex of voiceless shame, too caught in my spiral of self-blame to mention the hideous consensual sex and incapable of even remembering the rape. The teachings which once had evoked such a profound shift and waves of bliss in me now felt hollow. The silent thread of awareness hadn't disappeared, but I felt helpless and plagued by a heaviness, muddled emotional pain, and chaotic energy shifts during waking hours.

One afternoon, I telephoned Brian at his home. I felt relief as he picked up right away, but he didn't want to hear me out; he continued to gaslight me as he'd done before: "There is no real problem here. It's all in the past. Just let it go."

THREE WEEKS after my arrival in Tahnee Point, together with the rest of humanity I crossed over into the new millennium. There were parties everywhere, yet the exuberated celebrations only exacerbated my sense of alienation.

I was still unsure about any possible next steps in my life, when ten days later, Cecile, a local woman whom I had come to know through satsang, invited me to join her for a public evening talk given by the American author and teacher David Deida.

[1] Adapted from original quote by psychologist, author Ingrid Clayton, PhD, on Instagram @ingridclaytonphd, July 13, 2023: "Did you know that one of the main signs of childhood trauma is instead of walking away, we try to convince the people who are hurting us to treat us better."

Deida had come to Australia to present his work on masculine and feminine approaches to spirituality. At first, I had no energy or interest—listening to something "so dualistic" as feminine and masculine principles did not catch my attention—however, I'd come to appreciate Cecile as a perceptive and mature woman, so after a little nudging I agreed to go along.

The words I heard that night rekindled a long-forgotten spark within me and allowed me to breathe again. Deida's lecture was insightful, thought-provoking, and at times even outrageously funny as he expounded on the differences between feminine and masculine qualities. According to him, these principles were not bound to our physical gender or even sexual orientation, but instead two complementary universal polarities present in all humans. Apart from having both feminine and masculine energies within us, Deida stated that on the spiritual level most people tended to naturally lean toward one or the other.

"Well, how do I know if my spiritual essence is more feminine or masculine?" a woman in the audience asked.

"Good question," Deida replied without missing a beat. "So, you tell me which of these scenarios do you prefer: meditating alone in a quiet room for three days on emptiness, or being ravished and opened to divine love by your sexual partner?"

My head, like all the others in the room, spun toward the young woman who had asked the question. She burst into delightful giggles, her body shivering and shifting on the chair.

"You don't need to answer! We all can see which one you'd choose," Deida quipped, and the entire room erupted in laughter.

I chuckled too, but I wondered: How would I answer his question? I loved emptiness, I loved the infinite openness that no words could ever touch, but imagining a wonderfully present and sensual man loving me entirely also seemed desirable. Was I a strange case in between, or was this model too simplistic, too black-and-white?

As if Deida had read my mind, he explained that he had come

to see that usually ten percent of the population was balanced or rather neutral and could feel their spiritual essence equally at home in transcendent stillness as well as in the moving, immanent field of consciousness. Consciousness, Deida clarified, was the interplay of the Hindu deities Shiva and Shakti. The masculine aspect, Shiva, represented formless transcendence, while Shakti, the divine feminine, was the luminous radiance, love, and ever-changing creative force of life.

"A spiritual seeker with a more masculine essence tends to lean naturally toward practices that foster a single-pointed focus on emptiness. So, from the perspective of the masculine, the ever-changing feminine always seems far too chaotic and complicated," he expounded, emphasizing his point with undulating gestures that provoke raucous laughter from many men in the audience.

"But the realm of form—and with that I mean the whole world—*is* Shakti." As he thundered on, my whole body felt vibrant and luminous hearing those words.

"So, men, you have to make a choice: you either retreat and be celibate living in minimal engagement with the world, which is a totally valid choice or..." here he paused, then deepened his voice, "you choose to engage the world—and with that also all women—fully, as a way of giving your gift!"

The men's laughter subsided in an instant.

"Now, unfortunately for you women or anyone with a more feminine essence," I perked up in my seat, "most spiritual traditions have been shaped and passed on by men, and this male preference toward emptiness has never given equal weight to the feminine. Her radiance and power are eroded by spiritual practices focusing only on transcendence." And then with slight disdain, he added, "To me these spiritual teachers can sit in consciousness 'til the cows walk on the moon,' but they are deeply hurting women!"

Deida's last sentence shook me to the core. I thought of Brian's teaching style and his erosion of the feminine aspect of spirit. My thoughts harkened back to moments in satsang when he belittled his female audience members' questions about intuition or fear, or when he ridiculed and mocked my longing for being in a relationship. For the first time in months, I felt a slight, but nevertheless encouraging energetic uplift in my being.

A FEW days later, Deida's message reached even deeper for me when Cecile invited me to her house to join her and three other women for tea. The relentless Australian sun was not as blisteringly hot as usual, and it felt luxurious to sit in Cecile's shaded backyard garden and chat the afternoon away. All the women were native Australians, fifteen to twenty years older than I was—and except for Cecile, who was a multimedia artist, worked as therapists or holistic healers. We had all attended Deida's talk and a lively conversation about his lecture ensued, flowing between light banter and more serious topics.

When the conversation shifted to how Deida's teachings applied to the practical aspects of intimate relationships, something unexpected occurred. In an unusually bubbly way, I voiced my hope of finding a romantic partner again one day soon. All the women fell quiet.

Cecile broke a short but awkward silence, "I don't know how to say this, Annette, and I really don't mean to hurt you, but the thing is that...I really can't feel much of a romantic bone or even feminine flow in you."

Stunned, I felt my face freeze as my body stiffened. I stared at Cecile, trying to digest what I heard and how the other three women seemed to agree with her striking statement. It took me a moment to realize there was no need to become defensive, as Cecile's overall demeanor and words conveyed no ill will.

I swallowed with a dry throat, then replied, "Wow...that's weird. I am shocked you see me this way." The thought of people perceiving me as so radically different from what I believed myself to be was unsettling.

"What is your experience of yourself?" Cecile urged.

Her eyes exuded empathy and I was thankful for her warm presence. I glanced again around the circle at the women who all looked at me soft-eyed. I felt safe, which allowed me to see that there was nothing wrong with me, only that *something* must have gone wrong in some way. My experience this very afternoon contrasted with Cecile's remark. I'd felt nourished and even downright happy again in this exclusively feminine company. The re-awakening of my feminine flow had been evoked by listening to Deida's talk, and this afternoon it had become even more palpable. It was as if my cells began to remember an inner effervescence which had been pushed to the periphery of my daily life for too long, and now, by spending connected time with these seasoned and heart-felt women, I was softly returning to an almost forgotten territory of my being.

"Mm...honestly, if I look back, I have always thought of myself as having a bit of a girly-romantic streak, but maybe I haven't been able to be myself lately?"

Over the next few days, I reflected on this conversation and what transpired for me since Deida's lecture. I looked at my emotional turmoil and depressive states from a new angle: Was there a connection between my overall sense of dis-ease and having drunk Brian's Kool-Aid for too long? He always loved to say that he was sharing the truth of "non-duality"—meaning reality was one undivided whole, free of distinctions—but now it seemed that maybe it couldn't be quite so non-dual if for thousands of years the male way of defining Spirit or wholeness had become the default perspective! Was it this overemphasis on transcendence, of spirit over matter, and the disregard for the immanent, living field of consciousness as form, which had led me to disconnect from my more natural flow and feminine expression?

Rather than embracing the totality of who I was—emptiness as form, pregnant no-thingness giving rise to my precious human life—these days I mostly felt de-spirited, dull, deadened, and restrained by some invisible shackles.

The final push to sever my unhealthy relationship with Brian and his disembodied teachings came during the last week in Tahnee Point before my return to Europe.

I sat in satsang in the furthest row in the back of the audience, my eyes mostly closed in meditation, when out of the blue the strident voice of an older woman up front erupted with, "What I really want to know from you is who is that bitch that slept with you while you were in Europe?"

A gasp rippled through the sangha of around fifty people and then, eerie silence. I, too, was perplexed, but for a different reason: *How does she know? Maggie must have confided in someone who then revealed the news.* My heart raced and searing heat rose in my body. My back row position provided some protection from curious eyes—everyone had their gaze fixed on Brian in the front, eagerly awaiting his response. I too waited, naively expecting him to publicly clarify and defend, without giving away my name, that "this woman" was not a "bitch," but had been of immense help to him. I was terrified to be found out and, in my cowardice, preferred Brian repeat his deceptive storyline. But he kept quiet, nevertheless fidgeting a bit and adjusting his posture.

"Is this true? It cannot be!" several quieter voices blurted out at once.

I could hear their tone of disbelief: their beloved, perfect teacher possibly chose to have sex with anyone other than his wife. Someone in the room started to sob loudly.

"Who is that bitch? Do I know her?" the first woman shouted now louder, her voice simmering with repressed rage.

I realized she didn't have the slightest intention of challenging

Brian. Like many women raised within and conditioned by the patriarchal paradigm, she was used to over-accommodating and adapting to men's needs, preferences, and desires. And finding her self-identity and self-validation through the eyes of men, she believed "one of these lowly kind of women" must have seduced him.

I broke into a sweat. It was like being transported into one of the terrifying witch-hunt scenarios I had seen in movies about the Middle Ages. Waves of fear rattled my trembling body, as my mind produced archetypal images of being ripped into pieces by an angry mob. It was clear, no one in this sangha had any interest in hearing my—the woman's—side of the story. *What is my side of the story, anyway?* I still felt unclear and too muddled to define, let alone, stand in my truth. Minutes passed while I waited for Brian to put an end to the cacophony of voices and crescendo of emotional chaos.

Only when a feisty woman in her sixties attacked him personally accusing, "How could you cheat on your wife like that?" did his grandiose veneer of "supreme equanimity" crack.

He lashed out angrily at her, "You don't know that! I was in my truth!"

His outburst sent shockwaves through the room and the energy in the hall roiled, chaotic. I didn't know whether his reaction or words were able to convince his devoted audience—for sure, they didn't cut it for me. The emperor no longer had clothes! Like brittle glass fragmenting into a thousand pieces, Brian losing his self-aggrandizing "spiritual composure" and acting like a little boy in a fit of anxious defiance, shattered my projections of him as the unconditionally wise and ego-less being. I saw how self-serving and self-centered he was, and how little he cared about how his actions impacted anyone else. *I've been delusional to continue to sit in his satsang—a so-called gathering of truth!*

And, as if the universe were throwing me a lifeline, Brian—incapable now of quieting the chaos around him—prematurely closed the session for the day. Using the general commotion as cover and drenched in sweat, I swiftly stood and walked as if on stilts toward the back exit before anyone could engage me.

The words "utter lack of integrity" formed in my mind. It was a stumbling, humbling, but first step in finally re-claiming my authority. Over the next few hours, a long-overdue healthy indignation and moral outrage erupted in me, morphing during the following weeks into waves of hot-coiled rage. After this, I descended into a pit of grief and throbbing hurt. I didn't know which was worse—the pain of disillusionment of having given my devotion and power to someone who didn't deserve trust, or my having acted against my better instinct and my own heart's integrity.

IN THE last three decades, I have met several dedicated spiritual practitioners who either were subject to or witnessed grave mistreatments or unethical behaviors at the hand of their spiritual mentors. Whether the abuses were emotional, physical, sexual, or financial—the wounds of betrayal cut deep. In most cases, students don't just feel let down by their fallible mentor, they are haunted by an overall loss of faith in the validity of teachings they received or even their overall purpose. In the gravest cases, our most precious values feel so violated and our soul's compass so contaminated that we no longer trust ourselves at our core and suffer an existential loss of all meaning. This[2] is not unlike war veterans who initially set out for a noble cause to serve something larger than themselves—defending their country or standing up for justice or democracy—only to find themselves forced to commit actions or witness situations that betray their conscience

[2] Based on my conversations with Jack Saul, PhD, psychologist, specialized in offering individual and collective services to heal moral injuries and collective traumas. Also, inspired by the work of Jonathan Shay, clinical psychiatrist, and Bill Nash, PhD, who work with veterans suffering "moral injury."

and ethical code. Not only do they struggle with PTSD, they suffer even more from the intense shame and guilt escalating into self-hatred and driving them into social isolation.

Paradoxically, what is easily identified as unethical or blatant abuse of power in the worldly arena is often completely normalized in spiritual circles. There is a poignant Zen koan that addresses this error: "There is no right and there is no wrong, but what's right is right and what's wrong is wrong." Still, some teachers, upon being confronted with the facts, claim the "truth of emptiness" to deny the existence of relative suffering or use conceptual landing places like "There is no real doer" or "It's all perfect and divine anyhow" to conveniently dismiss personal accountability. Others go as far as to say that their abusive acts are only proof of a superior compassion, aiming to serve a deeper healing process in their followers.

The justifications often go both ways. I remember a client of mine, a licensed psychotherapist in her sixties who laughingly defended her guru's self-serving, constant recruitment of sexual partners from his pool of young female devotees with the words, "He can't help himself. He just likes women! What's the big deal?"

"Look, I don't believe that spiritual teachers have to be celibate saints, but don't you think it would be more reasonable," I asked, "to hold them to the same or even higher ethical standards than lay professionals?"

Just like me two decades earlier with Brian, I could see how her sincere devotion was muddled with juvenile infatuation—leading her to overlook everything she learned in her own profession about inherent power-differentials or the necessity for clean boundaries. When I gently prodded her to reflect on whether she would respond so nonchalantly if one of her therapist colleagues had sexual relationships with a client, her eyes went big, but she remained quiet.

Whenever I work with clients today, I am aware of a thin line between spiritual seeking and the unresolved traces of complex trauma. The deeper our psychological injuries run, the more we are inclined to idealize and submit to spiritual "authorities." Equally, our sincere motivation to "dissolve into God" can be an indicator of distorted life-energies and unconscious attempts to escape excruciating childhood pain. Spiritual guides or meditation teachers don't need to be licensed therapists, but if they are not acknowledging or addressing the importance of working through their own or their mentees' unresolved psychological baggage, they are ill-equipped to deal with unhealthy power dynamics and parental projections.

It is only human to enjoy having our offerings and contributions appreciated, but teachers with moderate or severe narcissistic personality traits—egocentric, grandiose, manipulative, and capable only of shallow, performative empathy—cannot survive without gobbling up their followers' adulation. Beyond this, they establish parasitic relationships with those who are naturally empathic, devotional, or "love to serve." Taking their role personally, demanding sexual favors, reveling in expensive gifts, or requiring substantial donations as proof of their undying devotion—these are all bright-red flags. So are the setting of double standards like asking followers to renounce sensual pleasures or intimate relationships while secretly initiating sexual relationships with some of them. The Indian mystic Padmasambhava, who introduced Buddhism to Tibet, warned practitioners in the eighth century against these transgressions: "View as vast as the sky, conduct as fine as barley flower!"

In the East, traditional gurus are often seen and revered as "an earthly incarnation" of divine wisdom or primordial presence and tend to fulfill their specific role and societal function by not mixing it with any other kind of worldly relationships—such as picking personal friendships, sexual, or business partners from their flock of devotees. This boundary has often been blurred in our times: either by western-born "gurus" with little clarity, training, or interest in how to relate to the culturally foreign guru principle in a wise—namely, impersonal—way, or by native teachers from India or Tibet with little understanding of the unique psychological make up, deep emotional wounding, or developmental trauma of their western students. And since the #MeToo movement has gained considerable traction, it has become obvious how this cultural mismatch paired with outdated patriarchal structures has brought more guru-like figures to publicly fall off their pedestals.

Shocked and stunned by the shadow sides of spiritual teachers or communities, the nuances often break down and many conclude that one shouldn't rely on outer teachers. Yet, the idea that we don't need any teachers at all—"You are your own guru"—is as simplistic and erroneous as the opposite statement that "It is impossible to awaken without a teacher." There is no need to toss out the baby with the bathwater and rob ourselves of the treasures of ancient or contemporary wisdom practices and the skillful assistance of those who know the map or have travelled further ahead. I believe that we often do better with less hierarchical structures and more contemporary views of our spiritual teachers who, no matter how profound their wisdom, are still human and therefore as fallible as the rest of us.

PART THREE
Return

All that I yearn for is to die
To soften my lips in an ultimate sigh
To melt completely with the motionless motion
That silent beat of my innermost heart
All that I long for is to die
To give up this world of notion
To be drowned beyond the waves of time

And yet
Is not already life itself
When fully lived and wholly embraced
The break of the spell which seems us to enchain?
What if I just laugh and dance 'til I faint
And kiss with devotion
My sorrows and pain

When I recall
Even the darkest ghosts onto the stage
Meet them with compassion, a clear look into their face
Then, life and death start to be intertwined
And the universe unfolds in a mystic's dance

Where everything is possible
Yet nothing takes place

So, let me be gifted with that trust
To lay aside my foolish mask of fear of life and petty demands
Let me pour out joyfully every cup placed here in front of me
And savor the flavors of this exquisite wine
Let me be life's insane lover
Allowing Innocence to love
While I die

chapter 18

Fresh Start and Solace in Amsterdam

There is no such thing as failure. There is only a rearrangement of plans and the surrender of ego. There is only the twist on the road we never expect. As long as we remain true to our vision and ourselves, we simply cannot fail. That is all that we have to remember.

SUZANNE FALTER-BARNS, *How Much Joy Can You Stand*

AFTER EXTRICATING myself from Brian's influence and sphere, I felt compelled to make a fresh start. I chose Amsterdam in the Netherlands as my new home base, drawn there by the multicultural atmosphere and the fact that, being European, I was allowed to work legally.

Two Dutch women who I knew from my travels generously let me crash on their couches for a month until I found a tiny but lovely studio in the attic of one of the canal houses in the city center. After scouting job listings in various newspapers went nowhere, I walked through the commercial streets looking for work. I was drawn to a job where, for the time being, I didn't need to churn my thinking mind too much and, anyway, I didn't speak Dutch yet.

On the second day of my search, I almost dashed past the

small "help wanted" sign in the window of a Japanese inn. As I stepped inside, *"Irasshaimase!"*—the traditional shout to welcome customers in Japan—erupted from the kitchen in the back. I waited for a staff member to appear in the front space made up of only a few wooden tables and benches. On the walls hung Japanese ink drawings and next to the cash register sat the typical porcelain cat figure with its waving paw.

A Japanese man emerged from the kitchen and smiled as he walked toward me, cleaning his hands on an apron. His black hair was beginning to gray at the temples. He introduced himself as Yoichi, which I repeated, adding the honorific "san" while also bowing respectfully. We exchanged little pleasantries before I handed him my resume. Yoichi-san was in dire need of a sous-chef, as his current one would return to Japan in three weeks due to a family emergency.

When he didn't see any professional experience in a restaurant kitchen on my resume, he looked surprised. He respectfully let me know I wasn't suited for the position. "However, I am a really good cook, I love Japanese food, and enjoy feeding others!" I blurted, smiling. I felt an inexplicable certainty that his kitchen was the place I was meant to work.

"I see," Yoichi-san nodded, trying not to look bewildered lest he offend me before politely thanking me for coming in. But then two days later he rang me up, saying he was willing to try it, and I shouldn't set my hopes too high.

The next three weeks were an intense crash-course in Japanese cooking and food preparation. Overall, we were both surprised how fast I learned the necessary skills and methods and how much we enjoyed working together. It turned out Yoichi-san was also a seeker. He had defied his conventional Japanese upbringing and travelled the world for years until he fell in love with a Dutch woman with whom he settled in Amsterdam. Even with my occasional accidents of burning chicken on the stove (maybe because I didn't eat meat?), Yoichi-san remained patient and kind. Through many hours in his caring presence, whether teaching me the traditional way to wash sushi rice or how to hold and cut a tomato while breathing in unison with the movements of my knife, my faith in humanity began to return.

Something about breaking away from Brian's disembodied teachings and being in a more grounded and stable environment allowed for more post-traumatic symptoms to surface. While I'd had some success in pushing myself to be more functional again, I also became aware of how fragile and fragmented I felt underneath it all. Even worse, on any given day, I might be overtaken by intense crying fits and feelings of angst and despair which seemed unrelated to anything occurring around me. Obsessive thoughts about the so-called experiment for truth and Brian besieged me at random moments and I was attacked by harsh voices in my head: *How stupid of you to agree to having sex with him! That was where everything started to go wrong.* On other days, the fury turned toward Brian. *What a selfish, sleazy asshole! I trusted him with all my heart, then he lied and manipulated me.*

No matter from which direction these rageful thoughts and emotions struck, there was no relief from the barrage. On top of it, the voice in my head screamed at me for failing so miserably in living up to my deeper understanding. *How can I feel so lost and in agony after "waking up"?*

I eventually pushed through my shame and fear enough to disclose to a friend how much I was struggling. When no amount of talking brought respite, she recommended I seek professional help from someone who understood this kind of matter. Still, it took me several weeks to muster the courage to make an appointment with the person she referred me to: a well-known workshop-leader in Rotterdam who was available for private spiritual counseling.

But then when I told her about the spiritual mentor who hadn't respected my boundaries on a retreat, she retorted, "Boundaries? Sweetheart, there are no boundaries!" There it was again. The frightening black hood rendering me mute and paralyzed with a dismissal of my pain and experience. I don't recall our sparse conversation after her glib words; and when I was on my bike again, I wept all the way home.

I realized I needed help from a professional who might not know anything about spirituality or transcendence but would at least not make me feel crazier. I applied at my Dutch healthcare plan for paid therapy sessions with a clinical psychologist, and a month later sat in the office of Mevrouw van der Meer. A short-haired, slender, and extremely upright-sitting woman in her late forties, Dr. van der Meer seemed somewhat stiff at first sight, but her firm handshake, the strong boundaries she established around our sessions, the predictable timetable of our weekly appointments, and her genuine care and witnessing provided a much-needed anchoring. She encouraged me to acknowledge all feelings and not judge or blame myself for having trusted my old mentor. She welcomed my indignation about Brian's breach of trust and pointed out the inhumanely high standards which I'd put on myself to "get it all over with" faster. All this kindled a spark of self-compassion, but despite Mevrouw van der Meer's skill in her talk-therapy approach, my panic attacks and intrusive thoughts about Brian—what I still believed to be fully a result of my naïve consent to the "experiment of truth"—endured.

After spending an entire afternoon seized by another emotional meltdown and panic attack, I was at my wits' end. That night I fell and lay in bed in the dark, and had an urgent desire to pray.

I needed to give words to my despair and helplessness, and with tears streaming down my face I whispered into the night, "If there is anything out there that can hear me in this Universe—Tara, or any angels—please, please—I need help! I need some clarity, guidance or—whatever. I don't know what to do any more..." Allowing myself to pray again and ask for comfort softened and calmed me. More at peace, I fell asleep.

The next morning, I opened my eyes to a luminous, piercing-blue sky through the attic's window above my bed. Yet what staggered me most was the lingering vividness of the experience I had before I awakened. It felt so real that for a split-second I was not sure which happened—the experience of waking up in my bed or the experience of standing on a high mountain's plateau. Which of these belonged to the waking or dreaming state?

I closed my eyes again to revisit and savor what had transpired: I stood on top of a mountain surrounded by nothing but vast sky. A Tibetan monk appeared, and we faced each other without saying a word. We bowed, and the monk handed me two books. I bowed again to thank him, and he turned and disappeared. That was it. I sat up in my bed, still dazzled, and then I remembered...

Was my dream the answer to my prayer?

chapter 19

Dream Come True

I don't actually know what spiritual authority is, but it has to do with someone who studied hard and practiced for many years, who has run into all these ghosts and dreadful places and can say, "Watch out there! Go this way, read this, consider this."

ENKYO O'HARA, *Most Intimate*

TWO DAYS later, I was sitting in one of my favorite spots in the garden of our canal house, resting my back against an immense copper beech tree which had become a healing ally. Just looking at her, with her crown touching thirty feet into the sky and powerful roots reaching into the earth, reconnected me with an embodied quality of grounded strength I desperately needed. When I rested close to her smooth strong body, like today, her majestic canopy of deep purple leaves held me almost lovingly.

"Hey, Annette. How are you?"

I opened my eyes. There, stood Sandra, my fifty-year-old landlord holding a basket of washed laundry; the bloomy fragrance of the detergent wafted from her arms. Sandra was warm-hearted, gentle, and always incredibly poised. She had been interested in meditation and transformative inner practices for a long time and being born into a wealthy Dutch family allowed her to follow her path without needing to worry too much financially. These days she lived comfortably from the rent that the various apartments of her family's canal house brought in.

"I'm good, thank you. Soaking up some peace and calm here before heading to work."

"Ah, yes." Sandra looked up the trunk of the copper beech and smiled. "She's a beauty!" and then continued on the little path toward the clotheslines at the end of the garden where she placed the laundry basket on the ground. "Oh, I forgot to tell you something!" her voice then shifted into a slightly higher pitch. "The weirdest thing happened yesterday morning. I got a phone call from a Tibetan Buddhist center here in town."

Upon hearing the word "Tibetan" I perked up.

"I don't even know who gave them our number," she shook her head slightly as she fastened another white bed sheet to the line with a clothespin, "but they asked me, if by any chance we had a space available to rent for a couple weeks. Apparently, they have an important teacher, a 'Rinpoche,' as they called him, coming from out of town. The accommodation they had originally planned fell through, so they're looking for alternative lodging."

My arms prickled with goosebumps. The images from my dream became vivid again. I gasped, but Sandra didn't notice my reaction. "And?"

"As you know," she continued, "the apartment below your attic is vacant for another month, as I still need to do some renovations on the windows and..."

"I mean, what did you tell them?" I interrupted her.

"Well, I told them 'Yes.' That he can stay here with us. He should arrive in four days."

I HEARD movement and voices coming from the apartment below me: *It must be the Tibetan teacher*.

I was curious who he was, but felt uncertain if he had any real connection to my dream. Maybe it was a coincidence? I didn't want to fool myself, so I let it go. *We'll meet eventually; no need to bother him.*

The afternoon after his arrival, walking down the stairs in our hallway on my way to the supermarket, I passed his apartment door. I wondered if there was anyone looking after him. *He arrived late yesterday, and he must have come from far away, maybe even India? What if he needs something...like groceries?* I paused for a moment, torn between letting it be or asking him directly.

He opened the door almost immediately after my first tentative knock. The man in front of me reminded me of some of the Tibetans I had met during my time in Dharamsala. He wore his pitch-black hair short, had high cheekbones, olive-brown skin, and shiny dark brown eyes. He was not wearing robes like the monk in my dream—instead, he was dressed in brown slacks and a mustard-yellow silk shirt.

"Yes?" he asked with a neutral expression.

"Ahem...sorry to disturb you...I live above you." I gestured toward the ceiling, not knowing how much English he spoke. "I was wondering...you see, I am on my way to the supermarket, and I was wondering if you have everything you need? I mean, I could bring you some groceries, some food if you'd like?"

My question hung in the air.

"Thank you," he replied, while continuing to look me up and down with open curiosity.

"Wait!" he declared and disappeared back into the apartment, leaving the door slightly open.

Good! He is probably making a shopping list.

"Okay," he reappeared with a sunny smile, now wearing street shoes. "Let's go." He slipped out of the apartment and locked the door.

"Oh...no, you must be tired, you don't need to come!" I

exclaimed. "I can bring you what you need, you see, I am going anyway. All I need is your shopping list."

"No, I'm going with you to the supermarket," he replied in fluid English without missing a syllable.

We descended the creaky wooden staircase, then stepped onto the Keizergracht, a scenic copper-stone-paved street along one of the bigger canals in the town center. It was an unusually warm spring afternoon and some of the tree branches were starting to reveal their first tender green buds. The supermarket was a ten-minute walk to Amsterdam's Waterloo Square. As we treaded along the canals, he introduced himself as Tenzin Wangyal and then peppered me with questions about who I was, my occupation, and if I had been born in Amsterdam. His curiosity went beyond courtesy; his genuine presence and openness showed in how attentively he listened to my answers. We hadn't even arrived at the supermarket when the conversation shifted to what was most important to him and me: the dharma.

From that moment on, it seemed we never stopped talking, and in the following three days over numerous meals, he shared anecdotes of his life—his extremely close relationship with his spiritual teacher growing up as a child in Northern India, his extensive global travel to teach the ancient practices of healing and awakening from his lineage, the Tibetan Bon tradition. His homebase was in the U.S.; he pulled up his cell phone to show me photos of his U.S. retreat center, his Tibetan girlfriend, and his two dogs.

On the third day, I finally shared that I'd prayed for guidance as I was struggling with some extremely upsetting energies inside of me and that it was hard to stay present at all when I felt overcome by them. I revealed my dream of meeting a Tibetan monk just days before his own arrival. He listened with great interest, then kept quiet for a while. When he spoke again, he declared, "There could be many causes for your afflictions. There isn't a one-size-fits-all answer to this." I clearly wanted his advice, but by not offering a ready-made formula, he made himself even more trustworthy.

"Why don't you come to my teachings? My week-long program starts tomorrow. Please come as my guest! Maybe you'll find some answers there."

I nodded, thanked him, and said I would consider it. And that night, sitting on my bed, I began thinking about the possibility of opening myself up too much to another "spiritual authority." This made alarm bells in my brain ring berserk and my body break out in sweat.

The next morning, I felt thin-skinned, frazzled, indecisive—but resolved it wouldn't do any harm to get on my bike and at least cycle toward the teaching venue, an old church in the city center. I watched from a safe distance as people entered the building. I took a deep breath, unsure if I should follow them. Then I spotted Tenzin. When he noticed me, he smiled, waved, and cheered, "Ah, good to see you. I'll see you inside!"

I sheepishly got off my bike and locked it up. Inside, I was surprised to see a large crowd of about ninety participants. Tenzin walked straight to the podium in front, where a bald, tall man and a grayish-blonde-haired woman in their late fifties welcomed him with beaming faces. I heard someone nearby say they were his Dutch organizers. I found an empty seat in one of the back rows.

Tenzin stepped onto the podium where he sat cross-legged on a meditation cushion. In front of him was a low table covered with an embroidered Tibetan silk cloth and at his back a richly decorated altar with more silk covers, various bowls, candles, and images of Tibetan teachers. Colorful Thangkas depicting Buddhas and Tibetan deities hung on the side walls of the church. Even though none of them depicted white Tara with whom I had connected so strongly back on New Zealand's South Island, for me, they evoked her presence.

After welcoming his audience and offering a short chant in

Tibetan to request his lineage's blessings, Tenzin began, "The teachings of this week center around the five elements—earth, water, fire, air, and space—which, in the ancient Bon tradition, are the underlying energies from which all our experiences of the physical world, our bodies, our emotions, and our minds arise. I will present levels of teachings, also called vehicles. In the Bon tradition, the three levels of teachings and their correspondent practices are divided into the vehicles of Dzogchen, Tantra, and what in the West is often called Shamanism, however in the Bon tradition we don't exactly use this word. These distinct levels can help us to heal as well as realize and abide in our true nature."

I had heard the term "shaman" before mostly as related to the Indigenous culture in Siberia. Later I would learn it was more precise to designate the word shaman for someone entering into altered states of consciousness through rattling, drumming, or imbibing medicinal plants, but that many nature-based Indigenous healing practices such as the ones presented by Tenzin Wangyal Rinpoche were not about "altering" one's consciousness but engaging the sacred energies of nature in a direct way.

During my time in Dharamsala I had discovered that the word "Tantra" meant something quite different for Buddhist practitioners than what most westerners knew as techniques to enhance one's capacity for sexual pleasure. Tantric teachings were about transforming egoic habits through breathing exercises, yogic movements, mantras, or visualizations. The last of the vehicles that Tenzin mentioned as "Dzogchen" was translated as "the Great Perfection." This was the Bon tradition's non-dual path, aiming at realizing and continuing to abide in the natural state or silent wakeful openness.

Tenzin further explained, "In Tibetan Bon, the word 'shamanic' refers to practices meant to harmonize the relationship between the individual and the environment through working with the raw powers or sacred energies underlying all nature. These practices are not primarily concerned with enlightenment but with the removal of obstacles in life and the lessening of suffering we experience through interaction with external forces. However, shamanic practices can also help Dzogchen practitioners overcome obstructions to spiritual practice, which makes it easier for the practitioner to abide in the natural state once it is recognized."

I sat up straight, my interest piqued. According to these teachings, even once we've recognized silent aware openness, there is still ample room for various kinds of skillful means. Brian had laughed off any questions about the need "to do anything at all." Also, listening to Tenzin speaking about nature as a healing force, I thought of my relationship with the copper beech in the backyard garden of our canal house. Sitting close to her allowed me to access a deeper sense of stability within my being. It was soothing and grounding to attune to the tree's presence, but at times I wondered: *What exactly am I doing?*

I listened with increased attentiveness to how the five natural elements didn't exist solely on the level of form, but also more subtly as vital energies within us. While in practical reality we could derive physical nourishment from drinking water, we could also experience the energetic presence of water in its cleansing or comforting qualities and restore a visceral sense of ease within. The element of fire was not just an open flame, the radiant light of the sun, or the digestive fire in our guts, but on an energetic level it could be experienced as the qualities of inspired creativity or warmhearted joy. Too much or too little of any element, he explained, produced an imbalance. Too much fire energy could make us prone to irritability or having a hot temper. Too little fire, on the other hand, could result in feeling uninspired, dull, or lacking joyful resolve with our projects in life. And on an even subtler level, Tenzin expounded, the five elements were also intrinsic aspects of our true nature. Most subtly, water was the mirror-like capacity of awareness akin to the calm surface of a lake that reflected all appearances without distortions. The element of space was the wisdom of emptiness, fire represented the lucid, discriminative quality of awareness, air was all-accomplishing wisdom, and earth was non-reactive equanimity.

According to his teachings, we were typically born with individual energetic constitutions with one element more predominant than others, but any of the five elemental energies could also be nourished or depleted by life circumstances. Catastrophes, crises, or shocking events like war, loss of a child, divorce, rape, or even witnessing these brutal acts could create a degree of imbalance in our energetic body causing us to shut down, feeling lost or de-spirited. In the Bon tradition, this was called "soul loss" and often required—apart from working with the natural elements—the more elaborate intervention of a soul-retrieval ritual at the hands of a trained practitioner.

Hearing the term "soul loss" from Rinpoche's mouth made my ears buzz! In an instant, what was happening to me—my crying fits, my sense of fragility and fragmentation—made perfect sense. *My struggle isn't "just thoughts" as Brian suggested. I am likely suffering from what Rinpoche calls "soul-loss," or trauma. And here are teachings that offer remedies for my predicament!*

I attended each of Tenzin's teachings for the rest of the week. And even at dinner after we ended for the day, he patiently answered all my questions. I believed I was in dire need of what he referred to as a soul retrieval, but I didn't dare mention it. He had already been so generous, and I didn't want to ask for any more of his attention or time.

After completing his weeklong program, Tenzin prepared to travel to teach his students in Poland. On his last day, as the taxi waited in front of our house, we hugged each other goodbye. I felt full and enriched by his teachings and presence, and a little bereft at the prospect of being on my own again. He was about to get into his taxi when he turned around, reached into his bag, pulled out two books, and wordlessly handed them to me. Perplexed, I thanked him with a bow, as the taxi whisked him off.

Once I climbed the stairs to my attic, I looked closely at the books. I discovered that Tenzin himself was their author, and I was moved by his handwritten dedications on the inside covers. Only then did it dawn on me that even though I'd never mentioned this detail to him, *these are the books from my dream!*

chapter 20

Subtle Body Insights

The body is the shore on the ocean of Being.

SUFI PROVERB

EVEN NOW, it is difficult to put into words how auspicious the appearance of Tenzin Wangyal Rinpoche in my dream as well as my waking state turned out to be. The depth and clarity of his teaching, streaming so effortlessly from his well of study, experiential knowledge, and embodied wisdom were an unmeasurable gift. I was most transformed by learning about the subtle body—a term I hadn't heard before, even though I had already experienced subtle energies many times. When I listened to classical music, or prayed to God as a child, the ensuing experiences of ecstatic expansiveness had been my subtle body's energies. Similarly, what I'd previously thought of as me being depressed had been my subtle body's energies being blocked or shut down.

On an average day, our subtle body can be experienced as our basic sense of aliveness. It is our individual vibratory field which is intimately interconnected with the basic lifeforce animating all entities—humans, animals, plants, rivers, or mountains—similar to what electricity is to a light bulb. In China, this essential energy is known as *chi* or *qi*, the yogic traditions of India call it *prana*, while in Tibet it is called *lung*. Depending on various conditions, our subtle body energies can feel vibrant or depleted, flowing or clogged, centered or frazzled, speedy or calm, hyper-agitated or depressed. A delicate interdependence exists between the state of our subtle body and our intentions, thoughts, feelings, and behavior; how we breathe, speak, or move both affects and depends upon our subtle body's states.

Listening to Tenzin, I remembered again how I had already worked with my subtle body in a deliberate way in Madrid in my early twenties. Then, I had often sensed a soothing centeredness while practicing Tai Chi and Hatha yoga, and these provided some respite from my bouts of depression. My first yoga and Tai Chi teacher in Madrid hadn't taught much of the theory behind the physical movements and postures, but now I grasped how these body-mind practices were a direct way of loosening energetic knots in the subtle body, thus enabling us to experience greater harmony with the forces beyond our individual idea of self. I remembered how natural it already felt back then to attune to these invisible but potent currents.

It is easy to believe that meditation is something we exclusively do "in our minds" because mainstream western culture adheres to the centuries-old belief of the mind being separate from our energetic or gross body. Upon closer examination, though, we all can detect how our mental-emotional content is reflected in our immediate embodied experience. Even neuroscientists support what we know intuitively, that while thinking "happy thoughts" our energies and body can feel light and expansive, and our step gains more bounce, while worrying about worst-case scenarios causes the space around our hearts to constrict, our breathing to turn short and shallow, and different areas of our bodies automatically tense up. It happens the other way around, as well: bodily states of hunger, physical pain, or extreme tiredness tend to churn our minds more easily into worrisome or self-critical thinking, as our brain registers our physical state as being more vulnerable and less capable of fending off potential threats.

Over the years, my understanding of many concepts I first encountered through Tenzin Rinpoche—the reciprocal interdependence between silent aware openness, the subtle body, and thinking mind—has become more refined. Today, when I teach, I use an analogy of the different dimensions in the ocean to illustrate the "territory of consciousness." I compare silent aware openness with the absolute stillness at the ocean's depth, remaining unaffected by any movement of the surface-waves. The passing waves represent the world of name and form as well as the dimension of our finite thinking mind. Below the constant up and down on the surface we find the broader flow of oceanic currents which are our subtle body energies and essential life force. In reality, there is no actual separation between these dimensions—it is essentially all made of the same water—but having a map can be helpful in navigating the landscape of our experience.

While there is much we can learn about the deeper anatomic minutia of the subtle body, it is enough to recognize that the energetic currents flow through its myriad paths or channels. When channels are relatively open and un-constricted, and subtle energies can move in a balanced way, we more fully experience the wisdom qualities of our being, such as: love, contentment, compassion, calm, trust, strength, curiosity, or even our innate worth. One reason we often feel disconnected from these essential qualities is because our subtle body's channels are congested by unprocessed events or imprints or from the past. Imprints work like the files or folders on our computers: when we click on the icons, they open, and their content overtakes our computer's screen.[1] When our imprints are triggered, in an instant we might feel enraged, shut down, ashamed, or panicky.

Even though it's not at all necessary to resolve or repair our

[1] I heard this analogy first in a public talk by Alberto Villoldo, PhD.

imprints or trauma to recognize silent aware openness, our ability to source our everyday life from the completeness and clarity of our innermost essence often depends on how much or little we keep getting entangled by the kinks and knots in our subtle body. Silent aware openness remains unconditionally okay and shines forth amid all experiences—pleasant, unpleasant, or neutral—yet the subtle body is where we experience the blossoming of wisdom qualities in our life.

As I learned more from Rinpoche about the five elements in connection with the subtle body, it became clear that my primary focus should be to reconnect with the earth element. Earth was not only the ground underneath my physical body, but also that energetic sense of stability that I had felt so acutely lacking since Brian's abuse of power and authority. To remedy that, I followed one of Tenzin's practices wherein I connected with earth through an image. The copper beech in our garden had already become a trusted ally, so in my mind's eye I followed her roots deep into the dark, fertile soil beneath. I could sense my body inadvertently settling and releasing some of that unnerving jumpiness within. As I let the image dissipate and gave myself over to the visceral experience, the felt sense of earth's stability pervaded more of my body—and then, eventually, spread to everything around me. The ultimate step was to recognize and affirm, on the subtlest level, earth element as the inherent non-reactivity of silent aware openness and allow myself to rest in that unconditioned equanimity.

Sure enough, after several weeks of diligently connecting with earth in this way, my out-of-the-blue panic attacks and crying fits subsided. Just as in my childhood the sound of wind rustling through the canopies of the trees, the warm breath from a horse's nostrils, or a clearing summer thunderstorm had imbued me with connection and all-surrounding sacredness, nature again provided an invaluable resource, helping me to trace myself back to my true identity.

In the following year, my practices with the natural elements helped to further stabilize my energies, and the agonizing notion of having fallen from grace evaporated. However, my overall experience in everyday life or in formal sitting practice was still encumbered by an obscure emotional agony. Before the insidious "experiment for truth," the felt presence of silent aware openness had been prominent, which allowed for any rambling thoughts passing through to be noticed in the mere periphery or ignored with greater ease. In contrast now, the presence of my true being felt often reduced to a tiny, bare thread of awareness amid the cacophony and clusters of obsessive, anxious thought patterns.

Even after being treated so kindly by Tenzin, I couldn't shake off a persistent sense of hypervigilance, and as I stayed in touch with some of his students, I observed almost wistfully how they could openly express their love and gratitude—*I also longed to return to that unencumbered innocence*—but my heart was clogged with grief and I was terrified to lose myself again. Inwardly, I grappled with the conundrum: *What are the signs of a wholesome connection with a teacher versus the indiscriminate naivete and unbridled adoration that misled me so cruelly? Could one err on having too much devotion? Or where is the line between blind faith and genuine trust? If a teacher betrays their follower's trust to further their own agenda—where is the responsibility of the student in all of that?*

These questions sobered me up enough to recognize I needed more help on a psychological level, as well as further insights from outside the Eastern wisdom traditions.

chapter 21

Touching the Untouchable

To be whole, we need to include, accept, and connect all parts of ourselves. We need acceptance of our conflicting qualities and the seeming incongruity of our inner and outer worlds. Wholeness does not mean perfection. It means no part left out.

FRANK OSTASESKI, *The Five Invitations*

I BEGAN to regularly peruse the shelves in the psychology and self-help sections of the American Bookstore in Amsterdam. I read volumes on how to dialogue with one's subpersonalities, befriend one's inner critic, and bring more consciousness to one's shadow parts—and was stunned to discover how my "inner parts" were still so stuck in the past and yet made themselves so vividly felt in my present. Opening Pandora's box was overwhelming at first, but I was desperate to try whatever could help me get a better understanding of my psyche's landscape. I chose to practice some of the integrative methods I read about, and they fostered a healthier sense of self-agency. Still, despite a growing capacity to skillfully identify and analyze my conditioned patterns, not much was changing in my experience of them.

One visit to the psychology section of the bookstore, though, brought an unexpected discovery.

After the already grizzly-grayish afternoon burst into sudden, heavy rainfall, I stayed longer than planned. Wandering the aisles, a thin book on display above my head piqued my interest. Its title—*Focusing*—didn't sound particularly enticing, but I remembered that my landlord Susan mentioned it once as a useful therapeutic modality. Curious, I plucked it from the shelf and opened to the first pages.

The author was Eugene Gendlin, an American philosopher who, with a lot of research and under the guidance of famed psychologist Carl Rogers, developed a psychotherapeutic approach proven to effect lasting change. His position was that if clients not only analyzed and worked with their thoughts, emotions, or behaviors but also accessed a nonverbal "bodily felt sense" around their issues, old limiting patterns could open quickly. Just reading the phrase "bodily felt sense" elicited a surge of gentle warmth in my energetic field.

According to Gendlin, our felt sense was not an emotion but an innate ability of our human consciousness to be in touch with something on a more subtle dimension. The bodily felt sense around an event or issue first seemed vaguer than our thoughts and feelings about it, and yet it held and included much more than what we thought or felt about our challenges. Strangely, there was an unequivocal impression of "rightness," even though on a cognitive level we couldn't pinpoint the why. *Maybe this Focusing method can augment my subtle body practices as another way to work through my confusion and muddled pain?* I bought the book and in the following days and weeks diligently studied and practiced the various steps of the Focusing method.

What struck me most was the first phase, called "clearing a space," which invited one to consciously engage the internal landscape by asking within: "What is the main thing for me right now?" And then, instead of letting my thinking mind serve up a fast reply, I waited for my body's slower response to emerge. Once the issue had made itself known, it was suggested one stand back by acknowledging "Yes, that's there. I can feel that." This naming process created a tangible space between me and the issue, which I experienced like a soft disentanglement. I would inquire again (and again) about what else wanted to be known until all my concerns had been honored and palpably lifted off my chest—instead of huddling like an undefinable weighty lump in the underbelly of my experience.

Once the space had been "cleared," I checked within to determine which of all these topics needed my focus most urgently. This was not an invitation to deal with it as usual—feeling full throttle any emotions or mentally analyzing the issue—but again, to stand back and drop below any related thoughts or emotions and attune to the wider bodily-felt field around them.

Subtle but welcome shifts occurred in my experience. I also noticed a growing capacity to remain more settled and softer inside while bringing awareness to unwanted experiences. Instead of being overwhelmed or bogged down by familiar mental-emotional barrage, I felt equipped to consciously engage any painful content, like loneliness or hopelessness, and listen into the uncharted territory of my wider being with a fresh, kind, and curious attitude. It was marvelous! It was like learning a new language and yet, at the same time, my experience was rather effortless; it seemed so natural to be in this intimate communion with my embodied sensitivity!

Surprisingly, in the process of engaging with the bodily felt-sense of any issues, my thinking mind and its speedy urge to deal with it all quieted on its own. Even though there were none of the huge breakthroughs or emotional catharses like the ones the therapists in the Pune ashram had pushed for, it was so soothing to be able to slow down and become aware of many little cues and bits of information that I'd previously overridden or missed. With each little "aha," I experienced a further opening of my bodily field and the subtle release of pent-up restrictions and tensions.

Eventually, this discovery led me to Hendrika, a psychotherapist in Amsterdam who not only offered individual therapy sessions but facilitated group trainings in Focusing for personal or professional application.

Hendrika's session room exuded, as usual, a warm and welcoming atmosphere as I sat in a circle with seven other trainees. In addition to the therapist's safe presence, soft lighting, high ornate ceilings, and a floor covered with plush, cream-colored woolen carpets offered a comforting environment. Through large windows, the evening sky darkened, waters of the Amstel River flowed by, and cyclists spun past, bundled up in thick jackets, scarves, and mittens. Hendrika finished filling our mugs with steaming herbal tea and sank into her armchair.

"Good. Let's start." Her softly wrinkled face, framed by white-blondish short curls, lit up with her smile. This was our fifth Focusing training session and by now I could tell how much she loved to share this body-centered approach. We all put our mugs down, sat back, and closed our eyes.

"Let's arrive here first by sensing our body. Take a moment to feel your feet on the ground...become curious about the sensations of pressure at the contact points..." Hendrika always took ample time to guide us as we connected with our embodied experience and extended a warm, silent "hello" within to whatever sensations and energies we momentarily encountered. After ten minutes, she checked in with each of us to hear how we'd integrated what we learned during the previous week. Tim, a teacher at a school for "emotionally challenging" children, buzzed with excitement to share first.

"I had a kind of explosive situation happening in my classroom two days ago," he burst forth. "Jurek, a ten-year-old boy got very triggered by something another kid said to him and before I could utter a word, he had grabbed a chair and jumped onto a desk. He held the chair high over his head and screamed at full lungs at all the other kids, '*I am so angry, I will kill you all!*'" With his arms, Tim replicated the boy's menacing stance.

"Before, I would have tried to calm him down and make sure that no one got hurt. You know, I would have tried to defuse the situation by convincing him that killing everyone wasn't a good idea and maybe not what he really wanted to do. But this time, something clicked. It was so different..." Tim shook his head, still astounded.

"What happened?" someone exclaimed.

"Well...I just acknowledged his experience. Without making him or his behavior wrong in any way, I simply repeated his words: *I can see that you are very angry and that you want to kill us all.* I saw instantly in his face how he softened when he heard his own words echoed back. So, I just said it again: *I understand you are very angry and that you want to kill us all.* I mean, he still stood there with the chair over his head, but his aggressive stance had cracked." Tim glanced around our circle for a moment. "When I repeated these words a third time, his arms went limp! He lowered the chair and stood there, as if snapped out of a spell. I believe that also the other kids could feel the change. He looked so innocent and vulnerable." Tim teared up. "It was remarkable!"

Hendrika and the rest of us nodded in agreement.

"After that, I knew I could go over to him. I simply took the chair out of his hands and helped him get down onto the ground." Tim shook his head again, still amazed, but also smiled about the efficacy of his intervention.

Hendrika beamed, pleased. "That's wonderful, Tim. I am so happy for you and also for that boy in your class. This is exactly how focusing can work. As we learn to turn toward and connect with our bodily felt sense, we can also meet others in more helpful and fulfilling ways! Would anyone else like to comment on..."

Hendrika's voice faded into the background as my attention turned to my inner epiphany: the boy's stance reflected my experience. In his hurt and helplessness, Jurek's last resort of defense had been to lash out in rage. As Tim spoke, empathy with the boy swelled up in me, followed by a warm wave of relief when Tim had not fought against his anger but welcomed it for what it was. As I drew a comparison between Jurek's feelings and my wrestling with bitterness about Brian, the loving compassion toward the kid shifted within *me*. The presence of compassion felt so intimate, yet vast. Its gentle warmth enveloped and swirled around my dense knots of animosity and resentment without pushing against them—touching them like soft, sensitive hands with no other agenda besides allowing and accepting them like an unloved child. My eyes moistened, my chest opened, and layers of constriction and rigidity in my torso loosened.

In an instant I was reminded of the absolute love I experienced in San Francisco after falling to the ground in my room, and again while encountering first the female Buddha Tara depicted on the thangka in New Zealand. I recalled finding the bird's rotting corpse on Tahnee Point's beach shortly after my first satsang and realized the profound, impersonal love pervading all of creation—now, right here, it was coming alive and online again within and *as* me. Nothing was ever separate from this all-encompassing compassionate love—only my linear brain's interpretation could make it appear to be so! I remembered a quote attributed to the late Indian sage Sri Poonja. When a student asked him how he could hold on to the experience of bliss, he retorted: "Ocean is ocean. If you want to have a different experience than the one you are having, you end up on the shore!"

This further validated my understanding that abiding as silent aware openness was not about cocooning in sublime transcendence, but rather allowing its innate compassion to touch all the bits and pieces within me starving for kindness and presence. Just as the undisturbed stillness at the bottomless depth of the ocean didn't need to fight or turn against its own currents or waves, this absolute compassion was accommodating and permeating everything like an infinitely benevolent Mother—nothing was too unbearable or unacceptable to be included.

This was different from the times when I had experienced *relative* compassion arising in the context of witnessing someone else's suffering. And often my empathic concerns had pulled me outside myself in an urge to fix someone else's pain. I could now see that my motivation hadn't always been altruistic but stemmed from an incapacity to face my hurt or helplessness triggered in that instant. *It is so much more comfortable, even falsely empowering, to be the caretaker of somebody else rather than face the flames of my chaos and vulnerability.*

This slightly embarrassing insight evoked a surge of heat in my body accompanied by prickly sensations akin to a small army of ants crawling over my torso to the top of my skull. Unbidden, the judgment arose: *I should have known better*—and with it a clamping and dampening down of my body's energy and a drooping of my shoulders. I didn't move an inch. I could see the naiveté of my mind's statement because the reality was: I hadn't known better—until now! Without dwelling further on self-judgment or adding self-referential commentary, I let the tactile experience be what it was, without trying to remediate or resolve it. Yes, the sensations were unpleasant but gradually they changed and then dissipated, like a cloud in the sky revealing and morphing into its insubstantial openness. *Wow—I didn't even need to try to fix my bodily feelings! The less "I did" to change them, the better. And, without adding any label or interpreting what the embodied experience supposedly meant about "me," I was free...* What remained was silent aware openness sensing and expressing itself as tiny droplets of sweat on the body and a patch of itchy skin on the scalp.

⁂

"ANNETTE…IT'S your turn." Hendrika's voice reached me from afar, calling me back. "Annette, are you okay?"

I opened my eyes and nodded.

"Would you like to share how your week has been?"

A bit at loss for words after what had transpired, I excused myself from sharing. For the rest of the evening's session, I leaned back and listened while steeping in that effortlessly compassionate heart of existence and my true being.

I didn't know it yet, but in the weeks, months, and years to come this radical compassion would continue to gradually meet and mend so many of the bits and pieces within me that had felt so separate from love and acceptance for my entire life.

chapter 22

Heart-Mind Awakening

That unshakable deliverance of the Heart: that, verily, is the object of the sacred life, that is the essence, that is the goal.
SHAKYAMUNI BUDDHA

UNTIL THE pivotal realization during Hendrika's training, I had defined silent aware openness as "being in satsang." For me, this hadn't just meant the in-person gathering, but also knowingly connecting with the vast silent presence within and all around us. Unwittingly, the old label morphed into what I called from then on "the free Heart" or Heart-Mind. Even today, over twenty-five years later, I still find the term Heart-Mind apt, as it encompasses the silent knowing openness of our being as well as its absolute compassion. In fact, in some Buddhist traditions, it is often warned that any insights into emptiness are incomplete without the realization of compassion. As the Tibetan Buddhist sage Marpa pointed out: "Nonconceptual compassion and the primordial nature of emptiness are inseparable in the nature of simplicity." In other words, if our spiritual view lacks heart, is it even spiritual? And—don't we all benefit from the medicine of compassion in times of pain, struggle, or adversity?

Despite my genuine realization of absolute compassion, implementing the insight into living reality was, as it is so often, easier said than done. Like many moderns growing up with predominantly left-brain education systems, over the course of my life I became proficient at not feeling what I was *really* feeling. I learned to numb my body to override or cognitively bypass inconvenient, uncomfortable, or "unacceptable" experiences. Overthinking was my well-trodden escape route allowing me to mask fear, bury sadness, and bottle up anger. To be fair, this was not entirely due to my disembodied upbringing, or the emotional illiteracy at my childhood home—in general, infants and children often have no choice and even good reasons to disown, dissociate, or distract themselves from too much distress and overwhelm, because developing brains and bodies don't yet have the capacity to tolerate intense experiences. This is further exacerbated when there is no positive or "safe enough" holding environment available (in the form of attuned and well-regulated adults) who can help process upsetting feelings. Besides, it is counterintuitive to turn toward our disturbing experiences and more natural for sentient organisms to recoil from pain and distress as a survival response.

I became more conscious of my mind's seemingly innocent commentaries such as *Oh, this feeling again? I thought we dealt with that already* or *Sigh...will this ever come to an end?* and *I can't take this anymore*. It was clear: giving any validity to these complaints was unhelpful. Yes, my mind didn't like what came onto the plate, but by ignoring its opinions and objections and instead asking Heart-Mind if it could *please help to hold "all of this,"* there was an instantaneous softening and more room for the fear, sadness, or anger to be included. My calling on the deeper dimension of my being didn't make away with the excruciating experiences, but it took the sting out and allowed them to be met and felt cleanly. This didn't detract from the fact that when meeting with an undisturbed attitude my unwanted experiences could feel at times like sitting on hot coils or riding a razor's edge. It reminded me of the work of firefighters who willingly put themselves at risk to protect others' lives—only it was my original sanity that I was trying to reclaim and save.

I explored other cues, like *Would it be okay to just feel this?* or wrestling with particularly gnarly knots like *Would it be okay if this feeling would never end?* The open-ended nature of these questions usually evoked a spontaneous *Yes,* but also at times a rebellious *No!* However, even in moments of my mind's ingrained resistance, there was no need to argue, because Heart-Mind had equally infinite space for the *No* to be allowed—prompting a further opening and un-knotting of tougher spots in my emotional-energetic landscape.

Learning to attune with this radical but gentle honesty of my nitty-gritty emotions and bodily constrictions turned out to be as humbling as it was healing. As the inner split between unpleasant experiences and my mind's defenses against them diminished, a lot of inner conflicts abated. Also, prior to my recognition of absolute compassion there had still been a hankering for getting back to the honeymoon of lofty blissfulness I had first experienced in Tahnee Point, but now a deeper inner knowing conveyed in no unmistakable terms that the medicine was to be found *in* the wound—not by trying to fix or ignore it.

As crucial as it was to recognize and familiarize myself with the centerless openness and essential okay-ness of my being, it felt of equal importance to let all my experiences unfold and flow forth without interference or attempting to improve them.

As I increased my capacity to no longer react by running from the dark and difficult, I learned also that by letting go of my mind's labels and self-referential interpretations around challenging emotions or sensations—i.e. irritation meant I was an angry and therefore a "bad person," or a sinking feeling in my gut was interpreted as not being good enough—it was even easier to surrender them. Removing the label and ignoring that habitual self-talk circumvented my mind's automatic tendency to attach a permanent sense of self to the arising mental images, thoughts, or feelings. Instead, I *became* the raw texture and pure suchness of the experience—stripped of that subtle sense of "me" or managing observer identity with an agenda or idea of relief or resolution. Uncomfortable experiences disentangled and changed on their own accord: sometimes first intensifying or slowly dissipating, and at other times giving way to another emotion—like anger revealing underlying hurt or fear, or sadness turning into tenderness. But increasingly, unpleasant experiences would burst open like a bubble on contact—revealing their fundamental insubstantiality and inseparability from silent aware openness or absolute love.

The thirteenth-century Zen master Dögen knew this well, teaching: "If you cannot find the truth right where you are, where else do you expect to find it?"

LOOKING BACK at that pivotal time in Amsterdam, I see how much trauma was still slumbering in my body—no recollection yet of the rape or any understanding about the impact of earlier sexual violations or being raised by a borderline-narcissistic mother. Today, after getting trained in various somatic approaches and relational trauma resolution, I understand better why my most significant injuries were not as easily unpacked on my own. When our brain and body are highjacked by chronic dysregulation and too much dissociation, having someone experienced in how to safely unwind the trauma from our neurobiology while providing an anchor of embodied presence is priceless. And it doesn't always need to be individualized attention, as being part of a conscious community where pain or confusion can be unpacked, shared, and held in non-shaming and non-pathologizing ways can be profoundly therapeutic. We cannot heal everything on our own.

However, for me in those early days the visceral knowing of absolute love as an intrinsic fabric of my being restored an enormous amount of trust and invested me with bravery to begin thawing the unconscious "permafrost" in my body and psyche. The most reliable resource and refuge was already within me. I thanked the heavens for Tenzin Wangyal Rinpoche's presence and teachings—but the erroneous sense of being separate from love, was foremost about "me" needing to close this inner loop and learning to examine my struggles and welcome all of my apparent obstacles without judgment.

I continued with my inner healing work—silent sittings, subtle body practices from the Bon tradition, and focusing training—but also returned to a daily practice of yoga asana at home. As I no longer felt so helpless in the face of all the overwhelm and turmoil within, my body re-emerged as if out of a long, dark tunnel. It had been waiting to be re-engaged, *asking* to be felt and sensed without aggression, to be moved without any ideas of perfection—and all of this felt so right and enlivening that I included weekly group classes of other conscious movement practices. These allowed me to let momentary embodied experiences be, unfold, or morph into swirls of aliveness and a seamless cognizant field beyond any ideas of good or bad.

For the first time since the fateful retreat in Germany, there was more room to wonder about my future: *How might I contribute more to the life of others?* I enjoyed my work with Yoichi-san, but he'd mentioned his intention to soon expand into a bigger restaurant. This would mean longer evening shifts and getting home later at night. I couldn't see myself having a long-term career in gastronomy, so as I attended public yoga classes in town I seriously contemplated becoming a yoga teacher myself. Until then, I'd only made a frugal income by working part-time, and a yoga teacher training would require saving up some money. I decided to fall back on some of my old skills that had worked quite well in the past.

THE RAIN splashed my face and my clothes were getting soaked, so I cycled faster than usual that late morning. I was already accustomed to the Dutch habit of not letting rain, cold, or even snow prevent me from getting around by bike. It was one of things I appreciated about living there: being out and about no matter the weather. Direct contact with the living elements rarely failed to rekindle in me the simple but visceral joy of being alive.

I was on my way to the Herengracht in the center of Amsterdam, the seventeenth-century canal ring area known for its large, majestic houses built by bankers, merchants, and regents during the height of Dutch colonialism. But I was not interested in history on that day. As I pedaled along the Herengracht, I slowed down to check out the house numbers. I was looking for 470, where the German Cultural Institute—also known as Goethe Institute—had one of its many international outposts.

The downpour had morphed into a light drizzle as I arrived. I locked my bike on a chain close to the sandstone façade of the institute's ground floor and rang the buzzer. As the door attendant inquired into the reason for my visit, I asked politely in my native language if it was possible to leave a flyer offering German tutoring to private students. It was a bit of a gamble, but he let me in. He noted that someone would have to approve my post, then pointed me toward the Institute's blackboard in the cafeteria on the same floor. My flyer mentioned my credentials as professional interpreter and translator as well as my international teaching experiences.

In the cafeteria sat a few people, sipping coffee or reading German magazines. Through the windows I saw a large backyard terrace and garden populated with bushes, a cherry tree, and tall, magnificent elms. *What a gorgeous place for anyone to study or work!*

It was a week later when I received a phone call. To my surprise, on the line was not a potential private student but the director of the language department himself with an invitation to an interview. I was overjoyed to be hired as a part-time German teacher. My new job allowed me to keep up with my schedule at Yoichi's restaurant and to put some money aside for future yoga teacher training. I marveled and was grateful for how life continued to support me, and I sensed myself getting evermore unstuck from old, encumbered patterns.

I was still saving up for my six months long yoga training a few months later when, during a quick run to the health food store, something grabbed my attention. As I picked up a shopping basket, I noticed a black-and-white photo of a woman pinned on the community announcements board. "Pamela Wilson," the flyer read. She would be teaching in town soon. Her smile and eyes drew me in, but as I spotted the word satsang below her photo my enthusiasm deflated. It wasn't only the unfavorable association with Brian that turned me away; I had developed more of an affinity for Buddhist teachings. The heartfelt energy coming through the image of this female teacher was not enough to convince me to attend another satsang ever again.

Life had other plans.

The following weekend, my landlord Sandra and her sister invited me to come over for breakfast and meet Philippe, a young meditation teacher visiting from out of town. Over a spread of croissants, jam, fruit, yogurt, and a big pot of brewed tea, we four talked about consciousness, dharma, and meditation. Then, a long-haired blonde woman floated into the kitchen.

She nodded a deep smile in our direction, but Philippe stopped mid-sentence and declared, "Oh, Annette, let me introduce you to my friend Pamela. I always attend her teachings when she is in France, and this time I followed her all the way to Amsterdam."

Pamela beamed in my direction, then Philippe exclaimed

enthusiastically, "She holds incredible profound satsang gatherings. Maybe you can join us for her last one here tonight?"

It dawned on me then: this was the Pamela from the flyer I had seen at the health food store! That seemed more than a simple coincidence—and so, my evening plan was set.

My cheeks stung from the ice-cold evening wind as I fastened my bike in front of the entrance of De Ruimte, the little seminar house and cultural center at the Amstel River. Earlier that afternoon, Pamela had asked me to take her for a stroll to one of my favorite cafes. In the few hours we spent together, there had been an immediate ease and palpable depth of connection—I had sensed the beginnings for sweet dharma sisterhood. I learned that, for many years, she had been an instructor of a psycho-spiritual approach called the "Sedona Method." She had studied with Robert Adams, a direct disciple of the late Sri Ramana Maharshi and another teacher, a Polish American woman named Neelam. After Pamela underwent her own awakening shift, the simplicity of wakefulness had become the core and heart of all her teachings.

As I entered the upper floor seminar hall, I found about sixty people gathered; some were chatting, others sat quietly with eyes closed in chairs and on meditation pillows on the floor. A cozy light bathed the room and a chair and small side table for the presenter were positioned at the back. I took a seat in the last row and closed my eyes to drop in. Slight astonishment rang through my body—*of all places, I've found myself at a satsang gathering...again.* All chatting subsided as Pamela entered the room and sat down.

"Welcome to satsang. Let's sit first in silence together," she said, then closed her eyes.

The silent openness that was always present amid phenomena—thought, feelings, sensations, and perceptions—came vividly to the foreground, enveloping the room. From the outside it appeared as if nothing happened for thirty minutes, but this kind of "nothing-in-particular" was one of the hallmarks of resting in and as our true nature—the sense of being complete. This moment was as good as the next; sitting without wanting as nothing was lacking or needed to be enhanced.

My eyes remained closed as Pamela announced, "For anyone who is new today: satsang is a gathering of people to honor Truth, to rest from the conflict and confusion of the world and take refuge in the Heart. When we take refuge in the Heart, we are not asking for thoughts or feelings to stop. The Heart is infinitely welcoming to all that passes through...and when we allow the Heart to function in its natural kindness, even fear and confusion and perturbing emotions can rest in its embrace."

What a balm her words were! She exuded a unique, profound, embodied kindness which I'd never before encountered. Not only did she speak the language of my heart—the compassion that had re-awoken here in Amsterdam within my being—her teachings were imbued with an unequivocally feminine energy. For the rest of the evening Pamela guided us, often humorously, from the "needing-to-analyze-everything mind" into the other kind of knowing—bare wakefulness to one's moment-to-moment experience, as well as letting attention rest and relax into its wider source. I continued to sit and steep in clear presence until at some point something prompted me to open my eyes again, and when I did Pamela was looking across the distance straight to me; we held each other's gaze silently and intently, drinking in the unborn silence.

After Pamela left to teach in the UK, we stayed in close touch over email and phone; when we met again in person, she asked me directly, "Annette, will you come to the U.S. one day and teach? I will arrange everything—your accommodations and sending invitations—all that is required is you saying yes." She looked at me with twinkling eyes.

Even as I observed my mind silently formulating *No. No way!* my heart opened, and my lips uttered, "Yes." The great Sufi poet Jamaluddin wrote once: "Who says words with my mouth?" In my case, it was the bigger heart speaking in that instant, and Pamela beamed at my answer.

chapter 23

Devotion and Doubts in New York

The world is illusory, only Brahman is real, Brahman is the world.
SRI RAMANA MAHARSHI

I FLEW to the United States to facilitate my first teaching under the name "the free Heart," deliberately choosing not to label it as satsang. What was I thinking? The truth was, I wasn't. I didn't grasp yet what it really took or meant to be a "spiritual" guide. There is a clear difference between knowing or speaking one's native language, and then teaching it to others. I was showing up in the role of the mystic who was aware of the paradox of being a character in a dream and supposedly helping the other characters to wake up. Today, it is easier to see how much I was still grappling with the unresolved pieces of my own psycho-spiritual integration, yet there I was, on my way to share the underlying essence of reality in public for the first time.

My flight from Amsterdam touched down at New York's JFK airport on a warm summer evening. In the Arrivals terminal, three women from Pamela's New York Sangha were waiting to pick me up. A petite, slender woman in her late fifties with short salt-and-pepper hair, recognizing me from the flyers, waved enthusiastically as I came out of customs.

"It's so nice to meet you, Annette!" she exclaimed joyfully as I got closer. She introduced herself as Marge and hurried to take the big duffle bag out of my hands, but I didn't let her—she was not only my elder, but also two heads smaller than me. She kept insisting; Marge had spent decades around an Indian guru, so the traditional attitude of deference to the teacher was engrained in her.

"This is Belle and Laura," she said, introducing the other women, both with chin-long light blonde hair, and we all shook hands. On our drive into Manhattan, I discovered that Belle and Laura were psychotherapists and had been a couple for over twenty years. Their grounded authenticity, sense of humor, and sharp intellect typical of New Yorkers immediately drew me to them.

My first teaching event in Manhattan took place in a spiritual bookstore close to Canal Street. Apart from being surprised about the size of the audience of around sixty people, I was astonished to not feel the slightest bit rattled. I had certainly suffered from severe performance anxiety at countless points in my life, but now the unconditional calm and larger presence of being came to the foreground of my experience. I noticed a few warmly smiling faces in the audience. *It does help to feel welcomed.*

I used Pamela's method to guide my audience—accustomed to her style of teaching—into a silent sitting of fifteen to twenty minutes. However, afterward I felt the need to continue with a more intellectual talk to set a foundation and provide more clarity. I wanted to express the importance of living in recognition of something deeper than our familiar surface reality.

"Commonly, we feel ourselves to be a somebody—a person of a certain gender and ethnicity who has been born into a particular family and society. And depending on these relative circumstances, we learn or are told how to become happy or that our happiness has a lot to do with getting what we want and accomplishing our goals. Now, just to be clear: there is nothing wrong with having desires or goals, but I believe it's helpful to gain or refresh some basic discernment around them, as we often look for what we really want in all the wrong places.

"I'd like to borrow a teaching from the Upanishads—the ancient sacred Hindu treatises—that has helped me to be clearer around my own motivations." I took a deep breath. "The Upanishads explain that there are four natural pursuits in a human life. The most basic one is our desire for material means or securities, such as food, shelter, health, working skills, or education. And, unless we are a cave yogi or a full-time contemplative who is supported by society or a religious organization, we all need money."

Someone in the audience chuckled.

"The second human pursuit is to experience leisure, play games and sports, or take pleasure in the beauty of nature, art, music, or bodily sensuality. Leisure and pleasure are not only enjoyable experiences in and of themselves, research shows they are also beneficial for our physical and mental-emotional health, right? For example, I learn faster when I love the topic of my studies. However, just chasing pleasure blindly without measurement or care can lead to harmful results or destructive behavior."

A few heads nodded in agreement.

"The third pursuit according to these ancient teachings is about our values, or what we personally give deep meaning to, but it also includes our contribution to others and ethical ways of living. And ideally, I am sure we all agree, the best way of obtaining our material needs and enjoying pleasure is by not inflicting harm onto others.

"Now, these first three pursuits all have to do with having a body-based identity living in a world and striving to fulfill or improve these three legitimate goals or desires. The problem is, we commonly confuse these pursuits with acquiring a permanent sense of fulfillment, or even freedom and love. For example, we often superimpose the experience of lasting freedom or security on the purchase of a home. Owning our own four walls can give us more privacy, independence, or even material stability, but we also discover that the extra work, money, or time needed to afford the general upkeep, insurance, taxes, and so forth add more stress and struggle to our life. Marketing makes effective use of our mind's fallacy to superimpose objects with attractive qualities, right? The way money tends to represent freedom, romance equals happiness, youth implies beauty, or designer clothes and expensive cars symbolize status, style, or even superiority."

I paused to let it all sink in.

"Similarly, we also attach an improved sense of self, a 'better me' to these relative, external conditions—which can change in a heartbeat! The flashy new car gets dented, relationships fall apart, our savings can be depleted by illness or unemployment. But most important, we erroneously believe our external circumstances have something to say about who we *essentially* are. Our innocent misunderstanding is that something in the realm of changing conditions has the power to make us permanently complete or adequate *someday*."

Noticing my mouth becoming a bit dry, I reached for my water bottle and took a sip.

"Once we recognize that the first three pursuits for material means, leisure, our values and ethical ways of living are totally legitimate but can only grant temporary fulfillment at best, it gets a bit easier to stay clear of unhelpful societal influences and reduce unnecessary suffering."

Everyone seemed to be listening with interest.

"So, in that regard, the teachings say, the fourth pursuit of a human life is very distinct from the first three. The fourth is about being freed from our mistaken identity and the ignorance of our true essence, because our human dilemma is believing ourselves to be somebody who we are not: a self that is fundamentally incomplete and separate from love; a self that must add or subtract something in order to *become* okay, lovable and complete.

"Now, I don't know about you, but if you are just a bit like me, then you too have suffered often or a lot, because you believed yourself to be essentially unworthy or flawed in some way. Right? But here is the catch: if we genuinely believe ourselves to be deficient, unlovable, or unworthy, how could anything change our *essential* condition? We either are fundamentally inadequate and unlovable—or we are not!

"It's like, we can choose to dress up a broomstick in beautiful clothes but underneath it is still and always will be a broomstick. Therefore, all our striving to *become* adequate or complete *someday*, once we have fulfilled condition x, y, or z, or our attempts to *become* lovable and free by any external means is fruitless. However, the good news is, according to the teachings, we are already inherently okay and complete. So, the invitation tonight is to recognize and uncover this inherent truth of our being—not as something new to be created, acquired, or accomplished, but simply that which has been missed, forgotten, or overlooked. This means we want to see through the layers of our mistaken identity and learn to relax into the openness and love of our innately free being and Heart."

That was more than enough. I paused, taking another sip of water.

"So, let's explore this all a bit more. I know from Pamela that many of you have been sitting in Satsang for some time, but feel free to add your own comments to what I just laid out or ask any questions."

Silence.

I noticed my heart beating a bit louder in my chest, stemming from a mix of my passion about the teachings, the unusual expenditure of energy of public speaking, but also some nervousness about my new role. I glanced into the audience: most people were looking at me attentively and a few were sitting in meditation with their eyes closed. Then I noticed a young woman maybe in her late twenties in one of the back rows tentatively raise her hand.

"I do have a question."

"Yes, please. Would you mind telling me your name?"

"Sure, I am Bridget. My question is...not sure how to phrase this..." She paused. "Okay, so sometimes there is a lot of talk in satsangs about the world being an illusion..." Her voice cracked, but she picked up right where she had left off, "I wonder, if you could you say more about that?"

I intuited that this meta truth had triggered pain in her. It was important to address that in a more experiential way, instead of conceptually explaining that it wasn't the world which was an illusion, but our interpretation of it as inanimate matter, populated by solid objects and separate beings, all devoid of sacredness.

"Thank you, Bridget. This is a really good question. And, if you don't mind, let's maybe not go so much right now into what other teachers or people have said, because it didn't seem for whatever reasons that helpful to you. Is that right?"

Bridget shook her head. "It only confuses me." I could see her eyes had begun to fill with tears.

"I get it. If someone else's experience doesn't resonate with us, we often hold that against ourselves. I remember when I was spending time in an ashram in India where many people there seemed to benefit from a particular meditation style. It involved a lot of movement and emoting, and even though this didn't work for me at all, I forced myself for quite some time to do it anyhow. I thought it would be useful to at least give it a try, but then I mostly succumbed to peer pressure as my mind kept comparing me with the others and berated me: '*What's wrong with you? Everybody else is so into this!*'" Somebody snickered and chuckled in the audience.

"Fact is, the mind loves to compare. And then this kind of

looking for 'Where am I in all of this' and 'Who is better or inferior' slips also into our spiritual path. But if anything, spirituality is about coming home to ourselves as we already are." I looked at Bridget. Her eyes had widened a bit and her body had perked up.

"So, is there any kind of spiritual teachings that spontaneously touched you on a more intuitive level?"

"Mm...I love Rumi, you know, the poet." Her eyes showed more gleam. "Especially that poem called 'The Guest House.' Maybe you know it?"

"Oh, sure, Rumi! Yes, I agree, that's a profound poem. Could you maybe track what helps you when you read 'The Guest House'?"

Bridget took a deep breath, and she gazed upward as if trying to remember.

"Well, there is a lot in there. I mean, Rumi's words about welcoming all feelings, even the hard ones, like shame or...he mentions 'sorrows.' But, I guess, I love the ending where he says something like 'Every experience has been sent from the beyond'?"

Her voice had gone up a pitch at the end. She wasn't questioning the accuracy of her memory, but rather the real meaning of that last line. I didn't remember the last line too well myself, but that was beyond the point right now.

"So, how does the line 'every experience has been sent from the beyond' help you? Not so much what you believe Rumi wanted to say, but how or why it moves *you*."

"Mm...it's like, it points to that there are really no wrong or right experiences, as they all come..." she hesitated for a bit "... from the same source." This time she ended her sentence on a lower pitch, signaling she wasn't doubting herself.

"And if *everything* comes from the beyond what does—?" I couldn't finish my question.

"I too come from the beyond!" Her lips cracked into a little smile, the tone of her voice now gentle but firm, "And that I too am okay, just the way I am."

I could hear that she wasn't talking conceptually; she had touched into the deeper truth of her own being. "Beautifully said, Bridget. Thank you."

After a few more weeks teaching in New York, I flew to New Mexico where Pamela lived. On one hand, I felt positive about my first teaching experiences, but there were also doubts arising within about whether I really fit the job description of "spiritual teacher." I felt much aligned with Pamela's heartful style of teaching and she had officially invited me to share the free Heart, but she was also seen as a guru in the traditional sense by her followers, and I was clear about not wanting to take on that role. I wasn't sure if this came from a realistic assessment of me not having enough experience to responsibly guide others, or if it was due to my discomfort around the traditional guru setting and the unhealthy power dynamics which could ensue. An incident with Marge, who had met me at the airport in New York, illustrated how tricky the terrain was.

Marge had attended every one of my teachings for nearly two weeks and approached me at the end of one evening asking for a few minutes of private conversation. When we sat down, she looked at me with teary eyes, speaking almost inaudibly, "Annette, you don't know how much you have helped me in the last few weeks." Immediately, I felt uneasy; my gut told me that whether she had really been helped by the teachings or not, she was caught in her long-standing identity of a submissive and dependent devotee.

"And...I want to surrender more! As an expression of my devotion, I want to offer something. I am currently selling my apartment here in the city...I don't yet have a clear idea where I want to move, but tonight during satsang I just knew..." She paused for a moment, holding her breath, then released it, "...that I should donate all the monies from the sale to you!"

I was aghast. Her expression signaled she was dead serious and expected me to express delight or humble gratitude. She did not strike me as particularly wealthy, and I imagined she would likely need the money for her retirement, which seemed imminent.

"No, no. Look, you don't need to give me anything." I shook my head. "In fact, thank you for the generous offer, but I dare say that this is not a very sensible thing for you to do."

She looked at me perplexed, with eyes wide open, retorting, "But I want to surrender to you..."

"No," I replied more vigorously. "You shouldn't surrender to me! And quite honestly, from where I see it, no one should ever surrender to another human." My voice carried clear tinges of my own experience. "It's not about the outer teacher. I'm more like a waitress in a restaurant bringing you food. The food is the teaching—not me! Does that make sense?"

She squinted and tilted her head to the side.

"The teachings are about what is already within *you*, Marge—that silent knowing and loving space of your own heart—that's the real deal, the teacher that is always here and cannot leave or betray you."

She nodded, but I could tell she didn't like my answer. She thanked me but left the hall looking forlorn. And as I rode the subway home to my host's apartment on the Upper West Side, I felt unsettled.

For the following three months, as I continued to teach in the U.S., I grappled with many questions: *What can I do differently, to prevent any extra fuss around my persona or a pattern of codependency and disempowerment being played out? Should I address that topic in my teachings? How? I don't feel I've explored these issues thoroughly enough within myself to guide others through the maze, nor do I know experientially of ways to grapple with this issue. Maybe change the traditional classroom set up and have us all—space permitting—sit in a circle?*

I spoke with Pamela about my concerns; she listened empathically, but had no qualms about it and was fine with playing her part. She was aware of the need for emotional integration but had no objection to the traditional ways of teaching. She summed it up by saying, "Consciousness gives satsang; it's not me."

I concluded that the form of sharing Heart-Mind needed to feel true or more authentic to me, despite not yet knowing how that would ultimately look or come about. For the next two years, I travelled to the U.S. a couple of times more to teach, despite not feeling entirely comfortable or sure about it all. I ultimately resolved I was better off pursuing my original plan of becoming a yoga teacher, as this allowed me to infuse the wisdom of dharma into my classes but within a far less hierarchical setting.

There was another reason for my resolve. Instead of continuing to travel back and forth, I was ready to plant roots more firmly, establish a permanent home, and even open my own yoga studio. And I hoped one day to meet a man who could turn out to be a life partner. However, expectations never yielded tangible results—other than briefly dating a few men during my travels, and being overcome at times by hefty surges of longing for a significant other. It was a challenging conundrum to grapple with, as my yearning wasn't a mere and neutral "being open to a relationship," but bore tinges of my childhood's thwarted desires for affection and unmet needs for safe connection. It helped to no longer let my mind indiscriminately entertain hopes and fantasies of a desirable future, but instead to drop below this narrative and let the love of Heart-Mind hold hands with the intense sensations and urgent feelings of lack underneath.

Over time, the experiences became more manageable until one day it dawned on me that it would be more coherent to come to terms with the possibility that a partner I could seriously fall in love with might not exist in this life. I had never given much credibility to belief systems promising "You can have it all," nor did I feel drawn to the whole philosophy of "manifesting." It felt truer to squarely assess my current reality: there was no man. Instead of arguing with that or letting my life energies collapse into waiting, I rested in the moment-to-moment truth of a reality which brought not only more peace and joy to my every day, but also restored a sense of healthy self-stewardship: I didn't need to let myself be bogged down by languishing hopes; I could focus on creating the life I wanted for myself—with or without a significant other at my side—as well as the emotional nourishment I found in close friendships with other women.

And yet, as I was completing my six-month yoga teacher training in Amsterdam, I accepted another invitation to teach in the U.S. *One last time,* I told myself. In recent years, I had developed an interest in exploring the more feminine aspects—which meant including and highlighting more of the embodied aspects of the spiritual path—and this would provide an opportunity to do so. Besides, the date fit nicely with my summer break from the Goethe Institute and the invitation had come with two co-facilitators—my friend Pamela and her teacher, Neelam.

What I didn't know when leaving Amsterdam was that much grander scales were tipping toward a lifelong "yes." I would soon meet the man with whom I'd share my life. He, in fact, was already aware of my impending arrival.

chapter 24

Unforeseen Destiny

All journeys have secret destinations of which the traveler is unaware.
MARTIN BUBER, *The Legend of the Baal-Shem*

THE TEACHING event with Pamela and Neelam was scheduled to take place over a weekend at the Omega Institute, a large holistic learning center in upstate New York. I had visited Omega a few years earlier as Tenzin Wangyal Rinpoche's assistant during one of his weeklong retreats. I fondly remembered the bucolic campus that stretched over 200 acres nestled around a large lake with water lilies, sprawling meadows, and a forest. During the breaks in Rinpoche's retreat, I'd taken every opportunity to go for hikes and soak in the surrounding beauty, and at one point even exclaimed to the trees, "I wish I could live here one day!"

It was a Friday afternoon in June when Pamela, Neelam, and I climbed out of the car that had transported us the two hours from Manhattan to Omega. I looked around while stretching my legs, shoulders, and arms in the parking lot that was filled with comings and goings—hundreds of people leaving after their weeklong retreats, and new ones arriving for weekend programs.

I was chatting with Pamela in the check-in line when I caught a glimpse of a tall, slender man approaching us at a determined pace.

"I am looking for Annette Knopp...does anyone know who Annette Knopp is?" I heard him ask, still twenty feet away. Then he fixed his eyes on me. "Are *you* Annette?"

"Yes, that's me," I answered, while wondering what this was all about. *Has there been a change in the program?*

"Oh, so happy to meet you," he reached for my hand, shaking it heartedly with both of his while slightly bowing his head. "My name is Stephan and I just wanted to welcome you," he beamed. "I will see you around soon!" Then he turned to greet Pamela and Neelam, and off he walked.

"Nice eyes!" Pamela commented. We shrugged, unsure what else to make of this encounter.

Our teaching venue was a large classroom at a quiet end of the campus, with white walls and a view through its large windows of the trees' dense green foliage. The quiet presence of the forest created a harmonious setting for our group of forty to fifty people.

We all checked into our rooms, ate dinner, and were then sitting at the front of the cabin on chairs facing the participants in our first teaching session. I caught sight of the man from the parking lot all the way in the back. After the teaching ended, I felt content and pleased—my co-facilitators and I had enjoyed an easy flow among ourselves, and the participants had asked great questions. I sensed that we were off to a good start with each other and ready to go deeper during the following days.

Walking outside to retrieve my shoes from the rack on the wooden veranda, I sensed someone looking at me: it was Stephan, his back leaning against the wooden balustrade. I nodded and smiled a little in his direction. "I enjoyed your teaching," he said, approaching me as I strapped sandals onto my feet. "Would you be free to have some tea with me at the café?"

"Now?" It was already dark, and I planned to return to my cabin and leisurely get ready for bed.

"Yes, if you'd like." He smiled.

I paused, sensing into my body. The evening air was still warm, and after taking another look at his face, my body felt quiet and open, so there was nothing standing in the way of a quick cup of tea.

Even at 9 p.m., the Omega café bustled with workshop participants enjoying conversation over late evening desserts, cappuccinos, and juices. We sat down in a quiet corner on the outside porch. As soon as we were by ourselves with our cups of tea, I was startled to notice that the space between us had no barriers. I didn't feel a romantic chemistry—it was more as if a vast energetic corridor had opened between us, a palpably naked presence which put me instantly at ease and made any kind of social posturing or monitoring of words or feelings superfluous. I sensed Stephan's relaxed, embodied composure and our conversation flowed in an easy back and forth for thirty minutes as we spoke about spiritual teachings and shared personal details.

"So, what kind of a path have you been on?" I inquired.

"I started in my early twenties sitting Zen practice during the last years of college and medical school. I also studied Sufi teachings for many years. And then I was lucky to be accepted for a fellowship in a hospital in Mussoorie, a remote town in the Himalayas in Northern India, where many of the Tibetan lamas and refugees had crossed over to escape the Chinese invasion of Tibet."

"Wow! When was that?"

"I arrived at the beginning of '73 and stayed for four months."

"Did you get involved with Tibetan Buddhism?"

"Not at first. I was moved by the presence of these lamas and felt real kinship, but I had been directed by my Sufi teacher to meet one of his own teachers, who lived on the floor of a temple near the hospital where I worked. He was already in his late eighties by the time I met him, having become a renunciant after working as a professor at an Indian university. He had also spent time in prison—incarcerated with Mahatma Gandhi for involvement in his Satyagraha movement."

"Oh, that must have been a remarkable man."

"Yes," his voice cracked, "as soon as I finished my daily rounds in the hospital, I would rush off to spend the rest of my day with Bhagwan. That was what the villagers called him. I was fortunate to have such exclusive access, because he wasn't interested in having followers or taking formal students."

"What impacted you most during this time with him?"

Stephan didn't hesitate: "The wisdom and simplicity of his being. It just shone forth. He emanated something I had never felt or experienced in any other person. He was...present. He embodied the adage of 'Nowhere to go, nothing to do.' And I was able to bask in his luminous presence."

We both fell quiet, and aptly, rested for a moment in silent beingness. I noticed my body beginning to feel tired and I was ready to make it an early night. I thanked Stephan for the tea and conversation and we said goodnight with a friendly hug.

The next morning, I bumped into him again at the breakfast buffet. When he also appeared next to me in the dining hall at lunchtime, I was curious. "How is it that our paths cross so often? There must be at least four hundred people on the campus right now."

"Oh, it's not a coincidence," he said with a twinkle. "I've been looking for you. My friend Michael who attended some of your teachings in New York City thought that we should meet."

My heart made a little jump. I was pleasantly surprised, but "Oh, I see" was all I could reply as I heaped more salad greens into my bowl.

"Do you want to have lunch with me, Annette?"

"Sure, why not?"

We sat down on the warm lawn outside the dining hall, close

to the trunk of a splendid catalpa tree that shaded us from the midday sun. I examined Stephan more closely. He had a slender, athletic body and seemed at ease in his natural masculine presence; but from the way he expressed himself—his words and gestures—I sensed he was also in touch with his emotional-intuitive side. During our conversation I learned he was seventeen years older than me, and that despite having veered off mainstream society's conventional, well-trodden path by spending time in India, had kept both feet firmly planted on the earth. He had opened a medical practice in the mid-'70s in upstate New York, combining modern medicine with holistic approaches such as acupuncture, nutrition, and mindfulness to help his patients become and stay well—a radical endeavor at the time. It also grew clear he wasn't just another retreat participant or visitor, as I had assumed, but—that together with his Sufi teacher Pir Vilayat Inayat Khan—was one of the founders of the Omega Institute.

"So, how did you come up with the idea of creating all of this?" I let my eyes sweep around the campus lawn in front of me and its several buildings to each side.

"It was just a natural consequence of what was happening in my life back then. A few years before we founded Omega, my Sufi teacher asked me to become the organizational head for our spiritual community and search for a good location where we could live and practice together. We eventually came across an old, abandoned Shaker Village about an hour north from here and about a hundred of us moved in from all over the country. As the leader, I had to figure out how we all could actually survive there. Everyone needed to work and bring money into the community. Being a physician, I worked weekends in a hospital emergency room, but not everyone had a profession or clear way to have an income, so we created new businesses that would sustain us and our kids living in the middle of nowhere." Stephan's face flickered with amusement. "We opened an organic bakery, a fruit stand, began to sell woodstoves, and my ex-wife ran a school for kids from outside and within our community. Oh—" now he chuckled, "And we also had a Volkswagen repair garage!"

"Why a repair garage only for Volkswagens?"

"Well, you know, we were all hippies and that was the kind of car many of us drove back then, but also one of us was an actual Volkswagen mechanic."

"Ah, I see. Mm, I still don't understand how you got from that community up north to Omega here?"

"Okay, so, Pir Vilayat had always held a vision of recreating the ancient library of Alexandria, a place where wisdom teachings from all the world's religions and traditions could be taught. As we further developed the idea, I went for a hike one day with my philosopher friend Eduard Gauthier. We both loved the teachings of Pierre Teilhard de Chardin, and as we sat on a hilltop looking for a suitable name—we didn't think Alexandria would be right—we talked about Chardin's concept of the Omega point which symbolizes the interconnectedness of consciousness."

"Wow...interesting!"

"So, at the beginning Omega was just us offering a few weekend workshops in the community for people from the city and later, as we gained more traction, we also rented a boarding school for a summer and then even Bennington College in Vermont. Finally, it became clear to me that we needed a bigger, more permanent, location somewhere independent of the community so that we could invite more upcoming teachers—many of whom are now actually household names."

"Who were they?"

"Well, like Ram Dass, Elizabeth Kübler Ross, Deepak Chopra, or the mindfulness teacher Jon Kabat-Zinn."

"And then we found this land here," he gestured at his surroundings. "Back then it was an old Jewish cultural camp in disrepair that had gone bankrupt. So we took out a loan and I signed it."

Listening to Stephan life's story I realized I'd rarely met a man quite as clear and successful in his mission in combining worldly and spiritual life. However, he was also humble and truthful about his shortcomings, because when I exclaimed at one point, "Wow, you are accomplished in so many things!" he countered, "Well, not in everything. No one gets a free ride in life. I do have something to learn about intimate relationship. I experienced some dark times as I went through two difficult divorces. I asked Ram Dass once for advice regarding relationships and he told me 'Hold on tightly, let go lightly.' I think I mostly got it the other way around." His lips parted into a little smile.

I was a bit surprised—not one, but two divorces. I was feeling into his words, and these revealed new layers to his life. I wasn't quite sure what to make of it. I had never met a double divorcee, but on the other hand most of my friends had never even been married. In Europe, the committed couples I knew lived mostly without official papers, and sometimes these relationships didn't last despite everyone's sincere efforts. "Do you also have kids?" I asked.

"Yes, three sons," he beamed. It was obvious: he reveled in fatherhood. "The two eldest are already living on their own with their partners, and my youngest is twelve and a half; he lives part-time with his mom and me. What about you?"

I shook my head. "No. Never married. No kids."

Over the next two days, as we kept meeting during my meal breaks, Stephan often made me laugh out loud as he drew me into stimulating conversations about consciousness and life—and our mutual kinship as intrepid fellow explorers continued to deepen.

After our weekend retreat ended on Sunday, I had three more days in New York before I planned to fly back to Amsterdam. Stephan surprised me: "I would love to have more time with you, to get to know you better. I have a trip to Brazil planned in a couple of days, but if you could extend your stay for another week, I'll cancel my flight to Sao Paulo right away!"

My heart swelled in a wave of warmth as proverbial butterflies danced in my belly. Nevertheless, this was the moment when I needed to voice a concern. "You know, I had such a great time with you over the last few days, but there is something I have a bit of trouble with. Sorry to be so blunt, but you strike me as someone who seems quite confident with women."

"Yes, that's true, since my divorce I've done my share of dating," he replied without hesitation. His straightforward way of acknowledging the obvious—with no attempt to defend or convince me of the opposite—was disarming. Then I felt more open, and my misgivings subsided. I noticed a surge of vibrant aliveness welling up in my body: *There is nothing and no one waiting for me in Amsterdam. What is there to lose in getting to know him better?* The Goethe-Institute's language department was closed for vacation and the new summer intensive courses would not start for another month and a half.

I felt my face light up as I finally responded, "Okay, I'll postpone my departure for another week."

Over the following seven days, Stephan drove from his home in upstate New York to see me in Manhattan four times, even though the commute was two hours each way. A part of me couldn't yet comprehend what seemed to be developing between us and how the heavens had all of a sudden let this man to cross my path. Yet I noticed ripples of joy, a sense of adventure, and expansiveness in my heart—and whenever the thought of him arose, I couldn't stop smiling. When we kissed for the first time in a little Cuban restaurant in downtown Manhattan, I experienced something startling. It was beyond anything I had before—his lips on mine felt so utterly familiar, as if we'd known each other long before we met. It felt like a whole different kind of coming home.

chapter 25

Relational Dance and Love's Growing Pains

The great paradox of intimacy is that our capacity to remain close rests on our ability to tolerate solitude inside the relationship.

TERRENCE REAL, *How Can I Get Through to You?*

AFTER THE extra added days, Stephan and I extended our time together even further. Six weeks later, it became clear I would simply fly back to Europe to put things in order for my eventual return to the U.S. to move in with him. Neither of us had much interest in a cross-Atlantic, long-distance relationship. I was overjoyed by the idea of being close to the man for whom I already had developed such depth of feeling.

The enormity of this life-change occasionally gave me pause. Three months later, after Stephan picked me up from the airport in New York and we arrived at his home in Woodstock, he pointed to the guest room which would become my office, then carried my two large duffle bags up to the master bedroom. I followed him into the walk-in closet where he had emptied half of the space. "Here—you can hang all your clothes." And after pulling out several, empty drawers, he declared, "And here is more space for you!"

I was touched by this gesture and appreciated the obvious practicality of the arrangement, and yet replied that I would unpack later. In this moment, the full extent and weight of my intrepid step had dawned: I was not just moving into Stephan's home, but into another human being's very full life. *Am I acting too hastily? What if it all falls apart?* A frown creased my forehead. My elatedness of being with him was dimmed by underlying caution. This man didn't just run a large operation like the Omega Institute, he was also involved in many projects and non-profit organizations centered around spiritual transformation. His two ex-wives happened to both live in the same town, he had two sons in college and graduate school, and a third twelve-year-old one, who lived half of the time with his mom and the other half with "us." I, on the other hand, had followed my own compass for the last nine years without needing to ask anyone if it was okay if I turned left or right. I'd downsized and simplified my life drastically so I could go wherever I felt drawn and stay in the places that suited my intentions and needs at any given moment. I'd followed my own bliss. *Am I ready for this full immersion?*

Two weeks after my arrival, I still hadn't unpacked. One morning, as I finished my yoga practice, Stephan asked if I would like a cup of tea. As I rolled up my mat, he handed me a steaming mug: "Do you have a moment to talk?"

We sat on the living room couch. Outside under the crisp blue autumn sky, the foliage of the ash and birch trees in the garden around us had begun to turn yellow; soon this would become a feast of luminous amber-golden, warm-orange, and bright-red colors known as Indian summer here in Upstate New York. "Are you okay? You still haven't unpacked your bags," he asked gently.

A knot twisted my stomach, and my body slumped a bit. I pulled my legs up to my chest. "Well, it all feels a bit daunting. I guess I am rattled by this radical shift in my life."

"I get it. Yeah...it's obviously easier for me. This has been my home, my life for a long while." He took a deep breath and stayed quiet for a moment. Then he chuckled. "I have an idea—what if we just pretend that you are here on holiday with me? I mean, in that case, would you still just live out of your bags?"

"No," I cracked up in loud laughter. I realized in this moment that I felt so safe, seen, and met by him—and that it was less scary than my mind made it out to be.

A few hours later, I unpacked my belongings.

In the previous nine years, I hadn't had much opportunity to work through my deeper attachment wounds in the context of a committed intimate relationship. We can keep the subtle but profound implications of early attachment trauma hidden from ourselves, as they are formed during the pre-verbal phases of our development. We live with these implicit imprints for so long that they are like a wallpaper we no longer notice—familiar as an intrinsic part of ourselves, or the impression this is how life is supposed to feel.

In the first year after moving in, I was confronted with needing to change my old script about family life. I had never actively sought this arrangement because I hadn't trusted it. "Family" had never been a haven and still registered as fraught with chronic disconnection and disappointments. It was obvious that raising a precocious teenager wasn't exactly a piece of cake, but seeing how Stephan kept showing up with a clear head, deep care, and affection toward his youngest son was inspiring as well as confronting me emotionally with all that had been amiss in my upbringing. I got to directly witness how a parent could interact with a child in healthier ways: Stephan rarely missed an opportunity to praise him; shepherded him in making his own decisions; set clear boundaries when necessary; encouraged him to openly speak about his emotions, doubts, or challenges; and also sat for hours on end helping his youngest solve particularly difficult math homework. It was earthshattering. When, after a couple of months, I realized that my visceral bracing for the other shoe to drop wasn't necessary, the grief set in. The grief I hadn't been able to face and feel as a child about everything so starkly awry or missing at home.

Also, as expected, over time the swoon of our new love was punctuated by the reactivation of old relational imprints. I remember beginning to experience Stephan no longer being as emotionally available as I desired. There was a kernel of truth in my perception: he was prone to being standoffish in an attempt to find more space for himself, while in comparison I had a fuzzy warm persona and the desire to establish more closeness. During our first attempts in consciously addressing and navigating the mismatch of our preferences and needs, I didn't lose my cool, but after a couple months I was blindsided by the growing emotional pain his attitude evoked in me. I was overcome by an increasing childlike despair which—despite my better knowing—compelled me to lean ever further toward connection. This left only one direction and route for Stephan: to move further away from me.

This scenario played out during a couple of romantic dinners in one of our favorite restaurants in Woodstock. After ordering our meals, I unwittingly looked to Stephan to meet me in my desire for romantic closeness after a busy day, but my unspoken expectation triggered him to seek more space. His eyes avoided mine for a moment, prompting me in a nano second to unconsciously lean further in and toward him. No words, yet the invisible world of energies, subtle facial cues, and bodily gestures broadened the apparent distance between us into a harrowing emotional abyss. The onset of hurt felt so overwhelmingly existential that I couldn't help but burst into tears. I was slightly ashamed for being so overreactive, but Stephan didn't judge. We amicably talked about our emotional gridlock, but no matter how much we tried, we couldn't create any opening shifts. We were at a loss about how to better work through our disconnect and triggers.

Today, with my deeper understanding about early attachment imprints and abusive family environments, I see how much I was still in the grip of an unhealed trauma response described as "attach and cry for help." This is often seen and mislabeled by many as "needy." It's not a mere desire for affection, but a child's earliest relational survival response. Even for mental health professionals it can feel intrusive or challenging when this strong neuro-biological charge is projected toward them by a client. It requires a lot from the therapist to stay regulated, hold their ground, and meet clients with warm empathy, yet without trying to rescue them from their pain. The client needs to be guided out of this highly dysregulated state and then lovingly empowered to develop their inner resources.

When old pockets open, our brain can become so flooded by the unleashed energies or so numb and shutdown that we are unable to remain mindfully engaged with the intensity or pain. So, we need to practice intelligently. Instead of fighting or staying entangled with the overwhelming experience, we can resolve to re-direct our attention to something or somebody that evokes a felt sense of safety, comfort, or at least neutrality. We might orient towards one area in our body—like the palm of our hands or our thighs—that remains unaffected by the distress and feels already relatively calm. Or we can recall the image of a trusted friend, mentor, or a beloved pet—and as we hold our "safe ally"[1] in awareness, our brain begins to receive this regulating piece of information that allows it to gradually reconnect with a more settled state. Other helpful interventions include taking several rounds of extended exhales or a self-hug while speaking to ourselves in soothing ways.

While the traces of trauma are often more easily discharged in the presence of a somatically trained therapist or counselor, who can hold a safety rope while we go down into our inner well,

[1] "Safe ally" is a term created by Dr. Diane Poole Heller, expert on attachment trauma resolution.

it doesn't take away the fact that it's ultimately up to us to learn how we can meet our younger feeling parts carrying the old emotional injuries and distorted beliefs.

Eventually, we need to wise up and become the ideal loving parent who was not available back then. We cannot undo what has been, but when the past shows up in our present, we best not ignore it but find inner or outer resources to provide the healing response to the parts of ourselves that have remained frozen in time. After all, the quality of our adult relationships rests primarily on the quality of the relationship we have with ourselves.

BACK THEN, a conversation with Pamela pointed me in the right direction and helped me see my relational dilemma in a new light. "Look, a pattern is created and maintained by two," she said as she stretched out her arm with her palm facing toward me and invited me to do the same. Our palms eventually touched. "Now press firmly against my hand," she invited.

"You see, the more you press, the stronger our palms are glued together! The good news is—" and without any warning she pulled her hand away and for an instant mine hung in midair and then collapsed "—it just takes one to break a pattern!" She twinkled.

Shortly afterward, I had an opportunity to put that insight into practice. It was evening and Stephan had come home from a basketball game in town. Feeling the urge for closeness stirring within, I mustered the determination to not follow the compulsive inclination and familiar yearning to reach out—and stayed put in my seat. He didn't know I was home, so instead of getting up and greeting him as usual, I remained quiet, while I sensed my heart beating faster, as a surge of heat and waves of dread and anxiety engulfed my body. I closed my eyes and willed myself to take several rounds of slow belly breaths while gradually letting the exhales become longer than my inhales. This was a way to signal my brain that there was no imminent threat to my life.

Only when I felt myself more centered did I sense, with kind curiosity, neck downward into the larger field of my body: the familiar feelings of agony—a harrowing pain of isolation and abandonment, a bottomless sense of hopelessness and grief locked in my heart. Too big to meet head on! I opened my eyes again to get my bearings as I believed that I had no capacity to get closer without getting too overwhelmed by the pain. I drew in a deep breath. "You can do this," I encouraged myself in a whispering voice. "This is from the past...all this wants and needs is just presence...and love, remember?"

I looked around the room, consciously noting familiar, non-threatening objects like the art on the wall, books on the shelf, the colors and subtle alive energy of the plants. I methodically named to myself what I saw, then also named the sounds I could hear—the faint sound of the washing machine spinning, the wind rustling in the trees outside. This allowed me to anchor my body and brain even more in the present and create the necessary space between me and the overwhelming emotions. Then I noticed where my body felt supported: the soft cushion on the sofa, a plush pillow in my back. A sigh of relief escaped my lips and I let myself linger in the pleasant sensations of my body becoming ever more settled.

Then I placed one hand on my heart and closed my eyes, and inadvertently the image of three-year-old me in the family kitchen arose: my mom on her hands and knees cleaning the floor with all her force and me feverishly crying to be held. *This makes so much sense!* My heart space filled with compassion for that little one I once was, and my eyes moistened.

"Oh, sweetheart..." I whispered to her. The truth and warmth of my words were a balm. Tears rolled down my cheeks and I let myself savor this softening for a good while—until the image dissolved and the sharpness of the pain began to dissipate of their own accord. I intuited this was more than enough for the time being.

In the following weeks, slowly but steadily, I harnessed more capacity to sit still and open my heart toward the unbearable feelings and sensations of abandonment and isolation whenever they arose. It was intense, but by bringing my heart to all the places and parts in me that felt so existentially separate from love, I sensed how my inner holes began to fill with the warm presence they had yearned for all along.

It must have been about two or three months later when Stephan commented with a tinge of surprise in his voice, "I feel that something has shifted between us. I'm really glad...now I can be closer to you again." He was right: the trance had been broken and I felt deeply loved by him as well as reconnected to a much bigger love.

PART FOUR
Whole

How can I say
How precious this is?
How deeply Life loves
When you allow
To crack open?

How will you know
How wide are your wings
And gentle the wind
To the one
Who seems broken?

While death is on its way
To bereave you of form
Love wants to love
No word
Needs to be spoken

When will you see
The innermost "me"

Alive as the world thru the light of your eyes?
Sun and moon are only your shadow—
Don't hold the flood, leave all fear behind

chapter 26

Black Cat Medicine

What we do not realize is that this patriarchal denial affects not only every woman, but also life itself. When we deny the divine mystery of the feminine we also deny something fundamental to life. We separate life from its sacred core, from the matrix that nourishes all of creation. We cut our world off from the source that alone can heal, nourish and transform it. The same sacred source that gave birth to each of us is needed to give meaning to our life, to nourish it with what is real, and to reveal to us the mystery, the divine purpose to being alive.

LLEWELLYN VAUGHAN-LEE, *The Return of the Feminine and the World Soul*

THREE YEARS after moving to the States to live with Stephan, I was feeling well-settled in my new life. With the help of Pamela's non-profit church—The Fellowship of the Heart—and its director Kurt Johnson, I'd been sponsored to be in the U.S. on a five-year religious worker visa, and when Pamela and I weren't collaborating on facilitating women's retreats in the U.S. or Britain, I offered classes on meditative inquiry, yoga, and other transformative processes at Omega or smaller venues. Stephan's youngest had upgraded me from "Dad's girlfriend" to "stepmom" and I also felt warmly welcomed by Stephan's parents.

There was one funny moment in the first three months of our being together at his parents' home on the Upper East Side of Manhattan when the larger family—Stephan's siblings, sisters and brother-in-law, an aunt, uncle, and a few cousins—gathered for a luscious dinner. As it often was, the conversation was lively as well as intellectually stimulating when it circled around Jewish history and the Holocaust. One of Stephan's sisters-in-law turned toward me and asked in all innocence: "Annette, you are from Europe, right? Where are you from, again?"

Everybody in the room fell quiet and looked at me.

I no longer felt personal guilt about my country's horrid acts. The atrocious suffering of millions of innocent people could never be undone, but I had come to see how as a collective, my people had finally grappled with their shameful past and continued to make amends. I also understood that evil acts can only spring from a basic ignorance of our true nature as essentially interconnected—no matter the nationality, religion, gender, or ethnicity. All of this allowed me in that instant to reply quite neutrally, "Germany."

You could have heard a pin drop; the silence lasted a few seconds, but then everyone carried on as if I had remarked "Denmark" or "France." It probably also helped that Stephan's sister once disclosed to me that their mother had remarked, "I like Annette very much—and this means a lot, considering she is German!"

I PARKED my car in front of our two-story home in Woodstock, grabbed the grocery bags from the backseat, and walked along the meandering stone path through the garden to our front door. As I slipped off my shoes, I was captivated by a haunting melody coming from the living room. I'd never heard this kind of music before—it emanated such otherworldly beauty that I hurried to the kitchen island, set down the groceries, then sat to close my eyes, allowing it to envelop me. A male voice sang in Portuguese, which I didn't fully understand, but my knowledge of Spanish allowed me to pick up the meaning of some lyrics here and there. The singer offered praise to Mother Nature, to the wind and the waters, and the purity of devotion in the song brought tears to my eyes.

"Hey, darling, I didn't know that you were already back."

I opened my eyes. I hadn't even heard Stephan coming downstairs from his office. "What is this music? Who is singing?"

"Oh, that's Carioca, you know, the Brazilian shaman I've told you about..."

"You mean *this* is the shaman that you have been doing those *ayahuasca* ceremonies with all these years?" I asked.

When we first got to know each other, Stephan told me about the plant medicine journeys he participated in over the previous decade, mostly in South America. Indigenous tribes in the Amazon used ayahuasca—a foul-smelling concoction prepared by mixing two different plants with sacred and psychotropic capacities—to access heightened states of consciousness for insight, transformation, and healing. Stephan asked if I'd ever wanted to explore this, but I had never felt any inclination to use substances to access different states. My most valuable realizations in life had come through other doorways. My disinterest also stemmed from my time as a teenager when friends who got high by smoking joints, taking cocaine and acid, never struck me as particularly illuminated while under the influence. Nor did they seem better able to navigate life's challenges afterward.

The way Stephan described taking this plant medicine, though, had nothing to do with a pleasant or recreational experience. "Doctor Ayahuasca," or "the grandmother" as it was also called, was considered a medicine for the soul. From all accounts, it sounded rather scary to put oneself under the brew's influence. Most people went through phases of deep physical purging and retching; the ritual space featured plenty of buckets placed strategically so participants could safely empty their stomachs' contents. After this, ayahuasca began to open long locked doors in one's consciousness, rendering ineffective defenses that tended to hold back unprocessed painful or overwhelming experiences. Many people felt deeply shaken by the effects of the medicine and often compared it to the experience of dying. Yet most emerged at the end of a ceremony feeling renewed, broken open, or viscerally interconnected with all sentient life. In fact, some held the opinion that one night of ayahuasca could be as healing and clarifying as years of therapy. Stephan trusted the plant medicine and his shamans so much that, many years earlier, he even brought his own teenage sons deep into the Amazon to take the medicine as their rite of passage into adulthood.

"You told me once that this shaman comes to New York?"

"Yes, Carioca usually passes through in August or September."

The mystical songs of the Brazilian shaman filling our house removed any objections I might have felt about trying the medicine. My heart and body gave me a clear signal. "Good. Could you help me sign up?"

Stephan's eyes widened. "Are you serious?"

"Totally."

A FEW mornings after I had set my intention to take part in an ayahuasca journey, an unusual energetic presence surrounded me. It reminded me of Carioca's music: an ancient, earthy, motherlike gestalt that was both powerful and full of love. *This can only be the spirit of ayahuasca!* I felt such awe and natural respect that I intuitively started to bow to her within me and continue to do so until the very day of the ceremony itself, one month later.

Stephan invited Carioca to lead the journey at our home and

twenty of our friends joined us. I was glad that my "maiden journey" wasn't happening in a random place or stranger's home.

On the afternoon before, we prepared by clearing all the furniture from the living room, leaving only the plants, artwork, and large candles to be lit, as the ceremony would take place during the night. We lined up two long rows of meditation cushions and back-rests along each side of the opposing walls, so that the women and men faced each other during the journey. Carioca and his musicians would sit with their backs toward our fireplace, giving them a full view of everybody in the space.

We started at 9 p.m. Carioca motioned to drink my first cup of the thick, unpleasant-tasting liquid, and I felt like a young girl on my way to first communion. The initial signs that the medicine was taking effect appeared when I saw the colors of my surroundings drastically change. It was already dark outside and the light from the candles was sparse and dimmed, yet the whole room glowed bright gold as if the midday sun forgot it was nighttime and had come out to cast her radiant luminosity on us.

Unexperienced as I was with hallucinogenic substances, for a moment I was so disoriented by this change of perception that I leaned over to a friend and whispered, "Do you also see the golden light everywhere?" She didn't answer, but with eyes firmly closed continued to sit still and steady in a cross-legged meditation posture. I remembered then that we were asked explicitly not to interact with other participants during the ceremony. Carioca's two assistants were ready to move quietly throughout the room to help whoever asked for help. Their commitment to serving everybody was heartfelt and palpable.

Soon after, an incredibly strong nausea overtook me. Stephan had reminded me to let all experiences unfold as freely as possible, including any urge to throw up. It sounded like a good meditation instruction! That helped me perceive the movements in my belly as reminiscent of a river's gurgling waters steadily rising. When it was time, I reached for the nearby bucket to empty myself. As I did, I felt lighter—not just physically, but energetically—as another perceptional shift occurred. I felt myself projected into the middle of an Amazonian jungle as our living room filled with the presence of gigantic ancient trees, woody vines and spiraling lianas, vibrant orchids and heliconia and other curiously shaped flowers. Fleeting visions of colorful birds and undulating snakes flashed to life around me with an almost overwhelming cacophony of sounds that I couldn't name.

A black jaguar appeared. She looked straight into my eyes, then jumped without pause directly into my body. Her breath became my own, her presence so supple yet immense, she seemed to fill every inch and cell of my being. Strangely, there was no fear; instead, I was awestruck at being permeated by such a fierce and graceful spirit. I hadn't given too much attention to what was going on for anyone else in the room, but now with the jaguar within me my perceptional capacities increased dramatically! The powerful feline was looking out through my eyes, smelling through my nose, and listening through the pores of my skin and my entire body. All sense perceptions were lucid, brilliant, and awake, allowing me to take in everything at once through multiple channels as it all happened within as well as around me.

In an instant, my attention was drawn to a man sitting on the opposite side of the room, a neighborhood acquaintance I didn't know well. His eyes glued onto me with a fixed stare. *Can he see that I have become a jaguar?* As I met his gaze, his eyes made me uncomfortable—I realized they were filled with a voracious lust that had no regard for boundaries.

It re-activated the experiences of other lecherous men from my past—decrepit guys in Pune on the hunt for fuck-dates, the neighbor who tried to rape me, even Dr. Mahl. Repelled I averted my gaze in an attempt to disconnect from that predatory sexuality, but it didn't help. Unexpectedly, I sensed myself shrinking, becoming younger and younger, regressing into different ages of my life, reverting to my sixteen-year-old self, then twelve or thirteen, and finally much younger, maybe seven. *The ages when men from our neighborhood molested or assaulted me.* I felt violated *again*, and squirmed to free myself from the invasive, foul forces, but the more I tried the more powerless I became.

I was about to call one of Carioca's assistants for help when the jaguar inside me growled and in a guttural voice directed, "Use my medicine." *The jaguar can speak!* Then, "Use my medicine!" she insisted in a stronger tone. *What on earth does this mean?*

The spirit cat repeated her command until I grasped that she was asking me to feel her presence as my own—to let go and lean into her vast power. As I obeyed, a sense of unbridled strength surged within. *Oh my god...it feels so good!* As I opened to the healing presence of that quality, I felt emptied of the horrid forces, akin to vampires fleeing at the first light of sunrise. My physical body shook and trembled as frozen feelings of helplessness and terror unwound, released, and drained out. I was cleansed of the gropes and sexual attacks that had cloaked my sensual innocence from so early on. It was incredibly freeing.

Once the cleansing process seemed complete, small tendrils of roots appeared, growing within my womb. They swiftly became bigger and stronger, then wound downward into the ground below my body—only I sensed that this was not just the material, physical earth, but a bigger, alive, potent field...like a cosmic Earth Mother herself! There was nothing I needed to do or make happen. Mesmerized and feeling utterly safe at the same time, I surrendered into the experience, marveling at this unaccustomed sense of rooting endlessly downward. My belly and gut filled with currents of power from below until I was satiated by a blissful, luminous darkness—any notion of separation between the Earth Mother and Annette had dissolved.

Later during the night, I checked what had happened to the man opposite me. Unsurprisingly, he no longer represented any threat. He now sat haplessly with eyes closed and his body slumped, on his own healing journey with the medicine. For the rest of the ceremony, I remained immersed in the magnetic power of the earthly Feminine.

UNTIL THE ayahuasca ceremony, my spiritual insights had been about the essential insubstantiality of reality, the silent aware openness and pure compassion of Heart-Mind, and the ever-deepening journey of unwinding old fixations from my subtle body. I had no map or vocabulary, though, for this new and unbidden opening from my gut downward into that earthy Mother presence, which I would later glean was known as *pachamama* in the Amerindian languages of the Aymara and Quechua.

Back in Amsterdam, opening to the Tibetan Bon teachings, I had first attuned to the five natural elements in form, energy, and awareness. Now, through the plant medicine journey, this invitation had transformed in another, unexpected way. Beyond connecting with the wisdom energies of my subtle body, I encountered the fierce and sentient sacredness of a much larger body beckoning me: Mother Earth. It was also a powerful balm; no one looked out for me when I was sexually molested or assaulted, but now the powerful black jaguar had come to protect and defend me. Apart from helping me release layers of intrusive sexual energies, a more vital connection within had become palpable and I felt safer in my own skin.

I wondered if there was something else I needed to do with all of this. Immediately after the ceremony, Carioca left town, so I hadn't been able to ask him directly for feedback. It only then occurred to me to download images of silky-furred black jaguars onto my computer's desktop. Looking at the graceful felines during the following weeks and months allowed me to call up the creature's energetic presence and in this way connect with its qualities present in my being. I had no further knowledge of any other practices around spirit animals, but also didn't feel any inclination to attend other ayahuasca journeys for the time being. I resolved to honor the ceremony and the jaguar's appearance as a powerful, but one-time occurrence—yet the black feline had other ideas.

I didn't discuss my experience with anyone other than Stephan and a close friend, but I was reminded of the jaguar's presence in unexpected moments. While Pamela and I were teaching a retreat together, she pulled a small saffron-yellow object with little black dots out of her bag. "Here," she said with a cheeky smile, "a client of mine gave this to me a while ago. She got it on her journey to Ecuador, and when I packed my bags for the retreat, I felt it was for you to have!" My heart jumped—it was a beautifully carved wooden head of a spotted jaguar, with dark black eyes, open fangs, a blood red tongue, and even real whiskers sticking out from under its nostrils.

On another occasion, while in Chicago attending a Yin yoga training, I shared my hotel room with a woman I had never met. I opened my eyes one morning as she blurted, "I know this sounds very weird, but during the night I woke up and there was a huge black jaguar with you, right here in our room!"

I searched some more on the internet and learned that in the cosmology of ancient pre-Columbian Mesoamerican and South American cultures such as Mayan, Aztec, or Inka, the spirit of jaguar had always held a significant role. It represented the fearlessness and power needed to confront enemies or face our own fears as well as seeing in the dark, both literally and symbolically, giving priests and shamans the ability to make predictions on a worldly level and also to track and heal what lay in the underworld—similar to our Western understanding of the unconscious or shadow material. Even an entire city, Cuzco, in Peru's famed Sacred Valley which had been the Inkan empire's physical, political, and spiritual center, had been constructed in the shape of a gigantic Jaguar.

That all sounded wonderful...but it didn't give me an answer as to why this animal spirit didn't seem to want to leave my side.

chapter 27

Snake's Message and Soul Retrievals

To see all of Nature as sacred and as a part of ourselves engenders...respect and responsibility.

ELIZABETH B. JENKINS, *The Fourth Level, Nature Wisdom Teachings of the Inka*

TWO YEARS later, the dots began to connect. I was sitting in the faculty dining room at the Omega Institute, having lunch with my friend Beth. Together we had cocreated and facilitated weeklong women's wellness programs. A holistic MD with a background in acupuncture and the spiritual practice of yoga science, Beth taught nutrition, energy medicine, and yogic breathing—while my part was guiding women through the practices of meditation, yoga asana, and cultivating self-compassion.

Beth and I were preparing our morning session when the door to the faculty room opened. My attention was drawn to an unusual presence. Turning around, I saw a tall woman with blond hair, wearing a knee-length black silky dress and colorful cowboy boots. Three men and a woman followed her, all around five feet tall, with dark skin and pitch-black hair. They wore wool ponchos, each a different mixture of patterns and combinations of luminous colors of bright fuchsia, pink, red, yellow, or purple that contrasted with shapes or stripes of brown, gray or black. Two of the men had colorful woolen pompom hats, while the heads of the third man and the woman were covered by caramel-brown brimmed hats held in place with colorful ribbons. Their unusual attire piqued my curiosity, but it was their magnetizing presence that reached my core. Not wanting to stare, I turned to face Beth as the group sat down two tables away. I heard the woman speak quietly in Spanish as I tried to decipher why their presence of peaceful power felt strangely familiar. Then it hit me—*they feel like that rooted Earth Mother from my ayahuasca journey!*

An Omega staff member told me these Indigenous people were direct descendants from the Inka tradition, also known as Q'ero *paqos*[1] (the men) or *ñust'a paqos* (the women), who lived in the high plateaus of the Peruvian Andes and were part of a program taking place on the campus.

A FEW days later, Stephan asked me to join him for dinner with a couple from South America who were passing through New York. I learned they were practicing shamans who shared the teachings of an Andean Indigenous tradition in a three-year curriculum that took place in various parts of the U.S. as well as Peru. I was stunned when they mentioned that some of the elders with whom they trained were from the Q'ero nation.

The woman must have noticed my energy field lighting up when the Q'ero were mentioned, because she turned to me and prompted, "Maybe you should train with us?"

"Oh, thank you," I stammered, flustered. "That sounds interesting, but I am not so sure that's really for me." While I couldn't deny the presence of these Indigenous men and women had left

[1] Paqo is an initiated practitioner and student of this Andean Mystical Tradition.

a mark on me, the idea of a modern Westerner born in Germany becoming a "shamanic healer" felt odd.

Her invitation returned to mind a few weeks later through some synchronistic encounters. Stephan and I flew to Costa Rica, where we were in the process of building Blue Spirit, a retreat center on the northern Pacific coast, and rented a small apartment on the top floor of a three-story building in the little beach town three miles from our construction site. One morning, as I opened the door to leave the apartment, I spotted a slender, two-foot-long snake. Both the animal and I stayed still, observing and sensing each other. I was too curious to feel fear, and after a few moments, the reptile turned and slithered away.

A couple days later, I came face to face with another, smaller snake crawling up the last steps on the stairway to our apartment. In my four or five years of coming to Costa Rica, I had never before encountered any snakes, and while they were an intrinsic part of the thriving fauna, I couldn't help but wonder what on earth convinced these creatures to leave the safety of the jungle and climb up three flights of stairs in a building full of humans.

Then, after returning home to Woodstock, a coiled copperhead struck out at me as I raised my foot to step over a fallen tree in the woods. Chills overcame me—partly out of relief for not having been bitten, but also because I was perplexed by so many snakes showing up in my proximity of late. *What is this all about?* There in the woods, I recalled a detail from my dinner conversation with the South American couple—they commented that the serpent was one of the archetypal animal spirits in Andean energy medicine practices.

I finally paid attention to the signs, and a few months later began my shamanic studies in the Southern direction of the medicine[2] wheel, known for its "Snake medicine." Even though I felt

[2] A medicine wheel is a sacred circular symbol used by many ancient Indigenous cultures for healing and a deeper understanding of reality, pointing to the interconnectedness of all things and the cyclical nature of life. The four quadrants or spokes are often aligned to the cardinal directions and can represent

reluctant at first, once I committed to these practices and studies, I was surprised by how it felt like slipping back into comfortable shoes. Over the next two and half years I immersed wholeheartedly in receiving a wide array of teachings in the U.S. and Peru. I learned how to track imbalances in someone's subtle body, extract dense energies, guide soul retrievals, perform death rites, and pacify upset spirits connected to the land.

During that time, I was unaware the teachings I was receiving were not purely from the ancestral Q'ero lineage, but more a compendium of diverse energetic healing practices that the South American couple had put together. However, their courses provided an important steppingstone as I became exposed to crucial elements of the Q'ero cosmology. It was during the curriculum, for example, that I first heard the term *ayni*—Quechua for "sacred reciprocity"—and so much of what I had intuitively felt out of line in many modern satsang teachings suddenly fell into place. For a paqo, one of the most essential laws and ethical guidelines is to be in right relationship with the living cosmos, in other words: *If you give, you will receive and if you receive, you must give back*. This extends to all areas of our lives.

Elizabeth B. Jenkins, spiritual teacher of the Inka Nature Wisdom Tradition and cofounder of the Global Paqo School[3] with her Indigenous Q'ero brothers and sisters often points out that trees, plants, or even marine algae can widen our perception of innate inter-existence. With each inhale, we receive the oxygen they produce, and by breathing out we return sustenance to them in the form of carbon dioxide. Even taking a few minutes each day to breathe mindfully and open ourselves to the alive nectar from plant beings, acknowledging their presence and sentience

different stages of life or aspects of one's being as in physical, emotional, mental, and spiritual.

[3] Global Paqo School was founded by Elizabeth B. Jenkins, MA, MFT, in conjunction with the Global Paqo faculty hailing from Hatun Q'ero, known as the last Inka Village in Peru, https://www.elizabethbjenkins.com/programs-1/global-paqo-school.

by sending loving affection back, lets the world around us sparkle and come alive. Showing our awe and appreciation for nature is not only fair, but counterbalances our brain's negative bias toward what's wrong with the world, you, or me. Cultivating high states of joy and gratitude rewire our neurophysiology toward greater resilience and well-being, and help us embrace the paradox of reality with more flexibility. Side by side with the obvious challenges, hardship, and pains of life co-exists so much goodness and unfathomable beauty.

I VIVIDLY remember receiving an early transmission rite known in Quechua as *karpay,* in which my subtle body was "irrigated" with energies that initiated my conscious, reciprocal relationship with the natural world. Then I was asked to keep nurturing this inter-existence by making sacred offerings to the pachamama and other nature beings with which I would develop a more personal connection.

Now, bear in mind, I always considered myself an open-minded skeptic: somebody not tantalized by extraordinary phenomena or particularly interested in anything deemed to be supernatural. Opening to the immediacy of life and knowingly living from Heart-Mind offered more than enough potency. Furthermore, I had never been keen on spiritual transmissions or empowerment ceremonies, as they are called in Tibetan Buddhism.

However, something happened during my first traditional Q'ero initiation rite that blew my mind wide open to the transference of living information. I was seated with my eyes closed in a line of other students, but could sense in an instant the palpable presence of the Q'ero woman with her *misha*[4] stepping behind me. What happened next is difficult to describe, but as

[4] *Misha*: traditionally woven ceremonial cloth in which paqos keep their *khuyas*, or healing stones.

she uttered words in Quechua which I didn't understand and tapped my skull again and again with the healing stones wrapped in her ceremonial cloth, I felt as if my head had turned into a vast funnel through which luminous, non-verbal cosmic wisdom currents were being poured. The hair on the back of my neck stood up as I sensed liquid black light streaming into my spine and a smokey yet intoxicatingly pleasant taste in my mouth, together with another rather indescribable experience. I am not sure if ancient wisdom can even have a fragrance, but if it does, then to me in that moment and the subsequent hours and days, it beheld the sweetest scent I had ever come to know in my heart! I was left humbled by the little that I ultimately knew or understood—and prayed I would make good use of this medicine for the benefit of others.

chapter 28

Truth's Relief and Grievance's Release

Be patient toward all that is unsolved in your heart and try to love the questions themselves, like locked rooms and like books that are written in a very foreign tongue.

Do not now seek the answers, which cannot be given you because you would not be able to live them.... [T]he point is, to live everything. Live the questions now. Perhaps you will then gradually, without noticing it, live along some distant day into the answer.

RAINER MARIA RILKE, *Letters to a Young Poet*

IT WAS pitch dark when I stumbled out of my cabin with a flashlight, my rattle, *misha*, medicine bag, and the several twigs that we had been asked to bring to the ceremony. I was grateful for my warm down jacket, as the temperatures in the California desert dropped significantly at the end of the day. All around me the night was pierced by the flashlight beams of other apprentices making their way toward the large firepit behind the Joshua Tree retreat center's adobe buildings.

That morning, our group leaders instructed us to make a list of all the teachers in our lives. "Think of those who deeply inspired you...and remember the ones whose impact was challenging or painful. Whether they were spiritual mentors, family members, spouses, lovers, or strangers, go out into the desert and find a twig for each of them. Then bring all your teachers to tonight's fire ceremony. It will be quite different from all the ones before." I applied myself with enthusiasm to this mysterious assignment and wandered throughout the desert landscape gathering twigs for hours, the sun searing above me. The water in my stainless-steel bottle had already come to an end when at last my eyes fell upon a particular gnarly stick in the sand ahead of me. "Yes, this should do," I mumbled to myself.

Instead of bending down right away to pick it up, I paused and sighed. This was the last and heftiest twig among all of them. For a moment I let my eyes sweep the arid wilderness, sparingly inhabited by desert scrub oaks, cheatgrass, and the peculiar-shaped yucca palms—also called Joshua Trees—that give this part of the earth her name. By taking in the bigger picture, I connected viscerally with the wider space and openness of being that accommodated even that gnarly twig in front of me with ease. To me, it stood for Brian and that piece of my past that even now, over a decade later and after all the deep insights and inner work, could still weigh me down. I didn't understand why; I genuinely felt that over the years I had sufficiently dealt with the pain, shame, and confusion. The most difficult had been when I temporarily lost faith and trust in what I cherished most: Spirit! I also believed I had found forgiveness and taken responsibility for my part—and yet that muddled heartache clung to me like a shadow. *What am I missing?*

I looked up and let my view mingle with the cloudless firmament above. As my gaze widened to match the expanse of blue sky, the sensations of pressure in my chest gradually dissipated. At last, I lowered my eyes toward the portentous twig. I squatted to lift it from the earth and buried it deep inside my medicine bag.

⁂

I EXPECTED our ceremony to be held as usual around the large communal firepit, but as I got closer was surprised to catch sight of Don Francisco, Lee, Dan, and the assistants awaiting us by the blazing flames of seven single fires. When all of us shamanic trainees arrived, we split into smaller groups of five to six and positioned ourselves around one of the fire pits. I burst into loud laughter upon viewing a student lugging two heavy plastic bags spilling over with hundreds of little branches—obviously representing all of her life's teachers. She winked and grinned back at me.

Lee, a tall, blonde woman from the Southwest, shook her rattle to get everyone's attention. "Today, as we gathered all our sticks, we had time to contemplate the lessons and teachings that we have received, and how they've impacted our lives. There will always be teachers, elders, and wisdom keepers from all times, but eventually everything we've learned can become an obstacle to sitting with Spirit, to sourcing ourselves from stillness and our direct connection with timeless wisdom within. Yes, we honor all the teachings, but to become self-referencing shamans we need to release our teachers—the good ones as well as the ones that taught us what not to repeat."

My body shivered at her last words.

"Only when we can release all our projections and reclaim our true authority and inner wisdom will we no longer cast a shadow. We are like the sun. And, tonight, as we all burn our teachers, we ask you to make your own vows with Spirit, to take your seat at the fire and step into the circle of wisdom keepers of this Earth."

I knew this wasn't empty talk. During the last two and half years of study, I had appreciated how wisdom and truthfulness could be shared in a spirit of sister and brotherhood. Instead of worshipping or giving power over to a guru or special someone, each of us was encouraged to become self-referential, to trust our innate spark of clarity and walk a path of the ethics of interconnectedness with everyone and everything. It was about the Sacred expressing itself in its multiplicity, it was about "the many—not the one."[1]

Following Lee's lead, we opened sacred space for ceremony. First, we turned our bodies to face the South, calling on the medicine of serpent. In the West we honored the teachings of the jaguar spirit, in the North we asked for the blessings of our ancestors and the hummingbird-spirit, then from the East we called on the spirit of the condor. Then we knelt and asked pachamama—our cosmic Earth Mother—to hold us sweetly in her embrace for our ceremony. Finally, we lifted our rattles, turned our faces toward the sky, and called on the moon, sun, stars, and the unnamable all-pervading Spirit. After sacred space had been opened, one by one, each of us stepped up with our medicine bags to our fires. When my turn came, I knelt in front of the flames like the others before me. I retrieved my seven twigs and lay them on the ground in no particular order.

During the day, while gathering sticks representing my teachers, I'd journaled about the lessons from each of them, and then tracked in my body any feelings and sensations that arose. I contacted and became present with the residual energies and then sent a gentle breath to surround and permeate any obvious densities with fresh energy. Finally, I blew and transferred all of that "energetic information" through my breath into the corresponding twig.

Now, it was time to honor the lessons as I gave them over to the fire. I was compelled to first pick up the twig representing my father. I felt deep gratitude toward him for having nourished my devotion to the Sacred from early on, and honored our generational differences and difficulties as opportunities to grow. After blowing these memories through my breath into the twig, I offered it to the flames to symbolically set us both free from any remaining entanglements or projections.

In a similar manner I proceeded with the next two twigs—one

[1] Here, I'm pointing to an insight from *Feminine Courage: Remembering Your Voice and Vision Through a Retelling of Our Myths and Inner Stories*, by Meghan Don (Muirgen Books, 2021)

representing my mother and the other Sergio. Then there were three twigs for my spiritual guides: Tenzin Wangyal Rinpoche, the next representing a female shaman elder, and one for the late Indian sage Sri Ramana Maharshi, whom I had never met in person but whose teachings impacted my journey. Each exemplified a particular wisdom quality for me and I felt immense appreciation. Acknowledging that they were also profound mirrors of my innate clarity and wisdom, I blew their energies into their correspondent twigs and called my positive projections back as I flung them one by one into the flames.

When only the last and heftiest of my twigs remained, my eyes filled with tears as I was overcome by a mix of feelings. *My last twig stands for the spiritual mentor who taught me what not to emulate.* The familiar ache rose in my chest more intensely than usual and, as best I could, I opened to the layer of grief that, despite all the years and healing work I'd done, seemed still reluctant to let go of me. With as much reverence as I could muster, I blew the heaviness into the gnarly twig, asking Spirit to help me unlock what I still failed to see. Looking up into the vast night sky engendered in me the trust that whatever it was around Brian that was still slumbering in the underbelly of my conscious experience, would be revealed when I was ready.

Once our ceremony concluded, the participants closed sacred space together by facing the four directions of the medicine wheel and expressing our gratitude to pachamama and the source of the Sacred. The overall mood was festive and exuberant. As it was tradition to guard the fire until its glowing embers had extinguished, a few of us remained by the flames until our teachers and projections had turned to ash.

THERE IS often no rhyme or reason to when buried memories or unprocessed pieces of trauma re-surface. We might lean with all our truthful conviction and heartfelt intention to not walk completely asleep through life, and yet, ultimately, we have little control over when the unconscious becomes conscious. Human beings can live for years, even a lifetime, in total oblivion of what lies hidden in their depths. The symptoms and traces of unresolved experiences can be mild or nerve-racking companions in everyday life, or only become re-activated in moments of great adversity and extreme stress. I have come to appreciate the more mythical analogy from the Q'ero, who say that shocking events force pieces of vital energy to disconnect from us, and these "splintered-off-energies" remain safe with pachamama until the day they are retrieved.

Trauma is part of human life because duality is in itself traumatizing. I dare say that everybody will undergo an incident at some point that exceeds their organism's capacity to digest and process the experience. And many hold a greater amount of undischarged trauma and invisible wounding due to having been exposed to violent combat, systemic racism, religious persecution, sexual violence, everyday homophobia, misogyny, or childhood abuse. Trauma, though, doesn't need to torture or confine us for the rest of our lives.[2] The recognition that something in us has remained undamaged all along is vital, and together with energetic and somatic-centered approaches or community healing rituals, we can reclaim one moment at a time the lost territory of our instinctual intelligence, mend old fragmentations, and restore our trust in life and human connection. More than this—once our vital energies are resurrected, they often become the most powerful breathing parts of us and can carry immense maturity or healing medicine for others.

For me, a pivotal resurfacing of what had been hidden from conscious recollection for nearly sixteen years unraveled in a strangely unassuming way a couple of years after the "burning of my teachers" fire ceremony at Joshua Tree.

[2] Inspired by Peter A. Levine, PhD, the developer of Somatic Experiencing.

I was in Costa Rica sitting on the beach, as I did on many evenings, watching the sun set. With my arms slung around our Rhodesian Ridgeback Kaya, and without any announcement or fanfare, like a curtain being silently withdrawn to reveal a movie screen, the images and sounds of the long-repressed morning in Brian's room played out, unbidden, in my inner eye. I was as much stunned by the clarity of the events unfolding as by the realization that these missing pieces of information didn't feel new. No.... they had traveled with me all this time. I was so stupefied by this unexpected unraveling that I could barely move, so I continued to sit in the sand long after the sun disappeared on the horizon. Only when the beach was empty of the local sunset devotees did Kaya and I get up to go.

As I returned to our house, Stephan looked up from his laptop. "Good time at the beach?"

I was too shaken to immediately reveal the secret I had carried for so long. I feared that verbalizing the ugly truth and receiving a reaction from Stephan in the form of outrage or shock was too much to handle in that moment. Whether it was irrational or not, I believed that if I said it out loud, all the fuses in my brain would short circuit. Stephan was too tuned into me, though, to not notice something was up.

"What's going on?" his facial expression shifted in instant. He was already up from his chair and coming toward me. "What happened?"

I stammered: "It's okay. I mean, I am not okay...but I will be. Oh geez, that is probably not helpful. Okay, here it is: Please don't worry! I need a moment or maybe until tomorrow to collect myself. I will tell you then, for sure. Thank you, love."

He frowned and nodded. "Whenever you are ready, I am here."

For the rest of the evening, I found myself going through the motions of my routine. Retired early and as I lay dazed in the dark, I felt nothing other than being gripped in a freeze response.

Hearing Kaya snoring softly at the foot end of our bed invited me to shift my focus, and as I took in her calming presence my body softened and I eventually fell asleep.

When I awoke the next morning, I realized it would be best to begin by unburdening myself with someone neutral and professionally trained in somatic trauma work. I called my close friend Suma, a wonderful bodyworker and SE practitioner, and she was free and happy to meet with me. As we sat together, nausea surged and my guts cramped—a sign that my nervous system and body were beginning to thaw out of a state of shutdown. I had the sudden insight that writing the words first, instead of needing to face and tell Suma directly, would be a helpful in-between step. Without further ado I put my pen on a tiny piece of paper and scribbled one simple sentence: *Brian raped me.*

I dropped the pen, rushed to fold the paper up and handed it to Suma. She opened it, read the words, and looked at me with wide eyes. She knew of my past struggles around Brian and understood in an instant—and at last, it felt safe enough to let loose and wail. She knew me well enough to get up and hold me at once, while my body writhed and shook with sobs. I wept until snot was running down my nose and I was emptied of tears—both of us ending up lying on the floor, Suma holding me tightly and silently in her arms.

While a part of me was still aghast, there was also a tremendous sense of relief. Now, it all made utter sense—the panic attacks and hypervigilance in Amsterdam, the emotional meltdowns and unnamable despair, the struggle with obtrusive thoughts around Brian, my inability to trust a wonderful teacher like Tenzin Wangyal, the spirals of self-doubt and shame, even the subsequent years of adrenal burnout and insomnia. I had made it through all of this. I had survived. The rest would be easy.

⁂

In the following weeks and months, with Stephan's steady presence and further sessions with my supervisor Patti from my somatic attachment trauma training, I processed and released layers of shock, shame, and dysregulated states from my body and brain. As strange as it might sound, I was grateful for having uncovered the truth, no matter how ugly it was. I felt coherent and liberated by the missing piece at last slipping into place.

Once I had it all fairly well digested, I let myself contemplate whether to do something with this revelation. It became clear that it wasn't my path to now spend my life's energy going after my former mentor legally. However, it was important for me to hold him accountable by putting him at least on notice. Through an intermediary, I sent Brian my written recollection of the assault, and for two-plus months I heard nothing back. Then, the short reply, delivered through the intermediary, that "the incident was remembered differently."

While this was unsurprising, it nevertheless felt like a slap in the face—first pain, then indignation, anger, and resentment arose as a response. I allowed these experiences to be what they were—neither feeding them nor suppressing their energies and sensations in my body. I couldn't help thinking of the countless other women throughout all times and cultures who were exposed to that kind of power abuse and spiritual betrayal. When I noticed bitterness wanting to settle in and take up residence in my heart, I knew I had more work to do. I didn't want to stay burdened with heaviness or harshness. I wanted to be free.

Ever since gaining deeper insight into the inseparability of existence, the concept of forgiveness no longer held much weight for me. With the risk of sounding as though this was spiritual bypassing, the question naturally became: *Who is there to forgive whom?* Our thinking minds tend to get stuck in solidifying victim and perpetrator identity, or even the roles of teacher and student—but ultimately, everything is an experience of our own conditions and mind. Just as I discovered in Japan that there was no inherently solid separate self—now, whenever I looked into the deeper underpinnings of reality, I couldn't find anything or anyone independently existing "out there."

With that, the idea of having to "practice forgiveness" toward my mother or father for their less-than-perfect parenting, or the men who had sexually violated me, fell away. Even on a more relative level of reality, it was clear that we all are made of the same absolute love—but either utterly ignorant of that truth and blinded by delusions of separateness or trying our best to work through them and our unhealed trauma. I knew well, though, that holding the compassionate view didn't mean one should condone harmful actions or refuse to right wrongs when possible and necessary.

As I explored my resentment toward my former mentor more closely, I noticed that at first it felt empowering, but it was a false sense of power: it would never set things right or change what occurred. Neither could resentment protect me or anyone else from being on the receiving end of unethical or abusive behavior in the future. If anything, it only prevented me from accessing the softer tissue of sorrow beneath it all.

Whenever a client or retreat participant asks me about forgiveness today, I always point out that the concept is often convoluted and obscured by unhelpful assumptions. For one, we should never be prematurely forced to forgive, because true forgiveness is a process of maturation. It happens as an organic consequence of grieving the losses and hurt we've suffered—and coming to terms with the fact that pain, adversity, or injustices are part of our human collective dream. The questions become: What do we do with what can seem or feel so unbearable? What do we do with the dreadful and difficult—the poison? Do we continue to feed it, or do we make medicine from it? How can we dream a better world into being?

Once we realize that forgiveness is never about another person, we are on the right track. Forgiveness is, in its essence, an inside job. This realization frees us because it means letting go of resentment doesn't need to hinge on involving the perpetrating party. We don't need to change them, "heal together," or even directly reconcile. The person might not care at all, have a different version, find no fault with what happened, or no longer be alive or available to offer apologies or make amends.

In my own process of forgiving Brian, I took the often quoted saying, "Resentment is like drinking poison and hoping it will kill your enemy" deep to heart. I reflected on the many Tibetans tortured by the Chinese military; the deep practitioners who didn't allow for hate to root in their hearts amid the most barbaric and excruciating circumstances. The countless victims of racial injustice or people sitting falsely accused on death rows in prison—and despite it all, having found peace and restored their dignity by not feeding hatred in their hearts. At last, I thought of the great Nelson Mandela, who found forgiveness for his apartheid jailers of twenty-seven years, and I resolved that I could let go too. Whenever thoughts of Brian or the rape arose unbidden, I plunged below the mental content and straight into the intense raw energies of my heart...until one day, what had happened was no longer a source of pain or grievance. It was something that had changed the course of my life but could no longer hurt or define me.

chapter 29

Sacred Sovereignty

And did you get what you wanted from this life, even so?
I did.
And what did you want?
To call myself beloved, to feel myself beloved on the earth.
RAYMOND CARVER, *A New Path to the Waterfall*

I LET myself drift. Floating on my back, offering belly, chest, and face to the cloudless sky, my body feels inseparable from the luminous transparency of the green-blue waters. The sun will reach its zenith in a few hours, but already the droplets on my face evaporate fast under its steady heat, leaving my lips with a fine tinge of salt. I am mesmerized by finding myself so unperturbed suspended in the ocean, while the lush verdant jungle framing the sandy shore is teeming with coatis, iguanas, and armadillos rambling through the bushes, or common garter snakes and boas slithering onward with their bellies touching the earth. High up in the ceiba or laurel trees, howler monkeys dangle from branch to branch with their broods in tow, pausing to munch on leaves or holler sudden roars so loud, one can mistake them for a jaguar attacking its prey.

I feel the ocean, the earth, the wind, the trees as much as they feel me. Each having their unique personality, energetic temperament, and healing wisdom. I am not even their guardian; I am nature too; we are intra-woven as and through the cosmic intelligence that animates us all. I have found belonging here, which only has deepened ever since I first came here twenty years ago.

I swim toward the shore and wade out of the water at the quiet south end of the three-mile-long Guiones Beach. In the distance I glimpse the silhouettes of kids from the fishing village playing soccer on the sand. I pat my skin dry with a towel, step into the shade of the almond trees, and slip into my flip-flops. Then I make my way past the coconut palms through the gardens further up with the old majestic mango tree, hibiscus bushes, and ginger flowers sheltered by the tall canopy of tree crowns, toward the main building of Blue Spirit.

Two decades ago, Stephan's vision of creating a retreat center in Costa Rica had begun to take shape when he finally found the piece of land that he was searching for. We had just met a few months earlier in New York and he brought me to the small Central American country to see how I felt about this place. Standing high up on the then still parched grassy hill, the view over the long coastline below was nothing less than spectacular, but there was something else I sensed that made me wring for words: "I'd want to say that this land feels so...healing, but that's not it. It's different. Interesting...it's beyond the concept of broken. The right word is *whole*, this land feels so whole!"

Here I don't take for granted the extreme fortune of my circumstances: I have landed in a part of this world that allows me to live free of the usual disconnects, distractions, and speediness of modern urban living. I am also aware that for so many of us, by choice or not, the brunt of life passes in closed-in spaces: we commute in cars or trains to school or work; spend our days in an office, store, factory or clinic; exercise in a gym or yoga studio; seek solace in meditation halls, temples, or churches—while at night we close our eyes under our roofed homes. It is no wonder we no longer feel the natural living world as interwoven with ourselves. To this day, many earth-based and Indigenous cultures—as well as our own direct ancestors—experience this sacred inter-existence in their hearts and bones, but mechanistic and patriarchal worldviews have succeeded in objectifying Earth as a commodity to be exploited, degrading our pulsating cosmos into inanimate concepts and categories, mere measurements and molecules bereft of any sentience or soul, beauty or breath, magic and mystery.

None of us needs a shamanic training or journey into altered states of consciousness to at least acknowledge that it is nature who is keeping us alive with her air, water, sun, or the food we grow on her soil! However, *everything* we as modern humans have—our laptops, smart phones, books, the clothes we wear on our skin, the buildings and art on our walls, the cars or trains transporting us to work and planes flying us around the world—are *all* made of her. She is not just (literally) matter, she is *Mater*—Latin for mother—our genuine and only Earth Mother.

How much we are intra-connected with nature and how she even heals us has never become clearer than on one of my trips to Peru. On this occasion, I joined a small group of twelve western paqos to make sacred offerings and do ceremonies together with six paqos and six ñust'a paqos from Q'eros at different places throughout the Sacred Valley for ten days. It was on our fifth or sixth day when our little bus stopped in the middle of nowhere in the Chinchero valley at 12,000 feet, surrounded by high mountain peaks in the distance, far away from the sprawling city of Cuzco or other human settlements.

Fredy Conde, our Quechua translator and one of our Peruvian paqo brothers, scouted in silence the parched meadows and ochre terrain until pointing our group toward a three-foot-high mound of earth covered with dry grass. The spot appeared inconspicuous—nothing like the other traditional Inka sites—the ancient nature altars hidden in the mountains, the famous temples, or deep lagoons—where during the previous days we had paid our respects to nature by making offerings as had been done so for centuries.

"Okay, here is what we are going to do," exclaimed our western group leader, Elizabeth, in her raspy voice. "One after the other, you all will lie down on your back over this mound, holding your misha of healing stones against your belly's eye and connect with all the nature beings present. Pull in the potent sami of the surrounding mountains and collect it in your gut. The rest of us will form a circle around the paqo brother or sister stretched out over this mound and we will harass them energetically, disturbing and distracting them from harnessing the powerful energies. Once the person lying down feels they have retrieved enough energetic strength, they will channel that into their voice through a loud shout from their belly to push the intrusive energies from us out of their way as they jump up. Any questions?"

I didn't want to rush to any conclusions, but my hunch was that this little exercise wouldn't be as easy as Elizabeth made it sound.

Connecting with that grounding power in my belly had been one of my steepest learning curves. The many times when my sense of sovereignty was violated—the physical, verbal, and emotional abuses at home, the sexual groping, assaults, and rape—had conditioned my brain into choosing safety over standing out and shining too much or resorting to appeasing and over-accommodating others instead of acting from a place of inner authority and authenticity. From my somatic studies I learned to identify that neuro-biological reflex as a "fawning" mechanism and part of the five F's: fight, flee, flop, freeze, fawn. This kind of "rolling over" and submitting wasn't solely my personal trauma response, but so pervasive in women and marginalized communities all around the globe trying to survive in the hostile environments of power over culture.

When it was my turn, I lay down as instructed, and feeling the connection with the surrounding mountains, channeled the powerful energy into my belly. Despite my strong intention, only a half-hearted scream emerged from my lips. I got up and tried not to give it too much meaning. But as a couple other women struggled with the same challenge, Fredy suggested a ritual to bring the practice to fruition.

We formed a circle and moved around by stomping our feet and shouting in unison with each of our steps the names of two mountains in the Sacred Valley: "Asun-gate, Sal-kan-tay, Asun-gate, Sal-kan-tay, Asun-gate..." Our group fell into a joint pace and sing-song rhythm. In an instant, I sensed the energies of the mountains becoming stronger in my belly, but instead of feeling supported or filled by their power, it was as if my energy field was being "cooked" by them. I noticed my voice and steps getting weaker and unable to keep up.

Without warning, my legs gave way under me, and I collapsed onto my knees at the side of our moving circle. I became unglued by uncontrollable sobbing and abysmal recognitions. *No amount of "power" or using my own voice has ever been enough to protect me. I have been run over by my much stronger assaulters! Why should I have even cared to have a voice? What difference does it make at all?*

Then I sensed being held by two arms, and the gentle voice of the friend who had joined me on this trip, uttering: "I am here, I am here. For whatever you need...." Her soft presence affirmed and encouraged without words the younger part of me that needed to weep without holding back. My body kept shaking, the crying ever louder...until suddenly, a deep roar unleashed itself from my belly. The power of the voiceless vacuum that up to that moment had sequestered itself as condensed dead matter, a black hole in my gut, was so monumental that it thrusted me straight up into the air off the ground where I had been cowering and whimpering. Akin to hot lava smoldering for years under the surface and then ejecting itself from the center of the earth, the unbridled force kept lifting and flinging me around for several minutes.

My body became a wild roaring animal.

Elizabeth also came to my aid, offering containment within her arms, but nothing or no one at this point had enough strength to wrestle with me. I had become a mouthpiece for this earth, and nobody could take control over her—the untamed forces of nature *were me* and letting everybody know in no unmistakable terms that *I* was a force to be reckoned with!

Gradually, I could hear my voice losing its volume, then turning hoarse as my body succumbed to being held and rocked in Elizabeth's and my friend Gisela's bodies and arms. When it all felt complete, Elizabeth whispered in my ear, "I know there is still another scream in there. It doesn't need to happen today. You'll know when it feels right..."

She spoke the truth, but I was not going to give up: "I want to do it now!"

I picked up my misha, held her against my body, and lay one more time on the small grassy hill. My paqo sisters and brothers encircled me again sending disruptive energies toward my body. In an instant the mountains and pachamama's power became my own, and this time, I didn't need to decide to shout—it was all right there, deep in my gut ready to emerge, to express, to give itself. The pure, unbroken lifeforce roared and jolted me up without the slightest effort—only to be caught in midair by the arms of one of my sweet paqo kin. We held each other in embrace, humbled by the truth and medicine of our truest nature and being. Everyone stayed quiet for a moment—until a younger paqo sister exclaimed: "I want what she has!" and our circle erupted into raucous laughter.

I sensed into the vast space and rooted power: *the Earth's and my sacred sovereignty are free of all shackles.* And then I chuckled too.

epilogue

Flaws and All

It's so easy to get hooked on the practices, on the spiritual highs, on a sense of breaking through patterns and making some sort of progress, on the pride of doing things correctly. But eventually we have to let all that go. We need to stop doing and simply be. We need to simply trust the spark within us.

TSOKNYI RINPOCHE, *Open Heart, Open Mind*

THE MORNING sun illuminates our classroom as I hear the faint sounds of waves of the Pacific rolling against the shore of Guiones Beach below. It is the last day of one of my regular weeklong retreats where, like in all of my teachings, we explored what keeps us seemingly at a vast distance from ourselves and each other; what prevents us from feeling at home in this very existence which offers herself so abundantly, afresh in each moment, to be honored and experienced in all her shades and nuances through our feeling bodies. None of my classes are ever the same—as the willingness to bring honesty, vulnerability, and generosity of spirit and the unique heart intelligence of everyone in the group co-creates the compassionate field which allows us to dissolve our inner and outer sense of dividedness and find true connection. As we learn to gently unpack our mistaken pain-identities that perpetuate suffering and also honor what is already profoundly okay within, we forge a safe healing tribe and sacred community.

Two assistants and I prepare the space for our last group session. We light the candles in the center of a circle and rearrange the surrounding blankets and meditation cushions for everyone. I am often told that my teaching style bears an unequivocally feminine fragrance. I believe this is because I emphasize not repeating the old power-dynamics that are still so painfully present in our world. And as the feminine doesn't hold on to power but rather returns it swiftly to whom it belongs, I always conclude longer teaching programs with a particular ritual.

As soon as everyone settles into their seat in the circle, I guide us into our last meditation. We have a final check-in as the group and then I begin the talk I have given for many years:

"I have been in the role of the guide during our week together. I believe that we all need at times someone in the form of a mentor, peer, or friend who can hold up a mirror that supports our remembering of our inherent goodness and natural openness. To have a heart-felt bond with our dharmic friends, as I like to call them, also helps us staying committed and trust their compassionate feedback when the terrain gets rough, when we are caught in distorted thinking, too overwhelmed to unpack painful material by ourselves, or in need of straightforward advice. And yet, from my own experience, I know how the comparative mind can be quick to over-idealize and project a picture of perfection onto someone in some type of authority position. No matter how much respect or gratitude we might feel for our mentors, it is so tempting to put them up on a pedestal and permanently transfer our inner gold—our innate wisdom, love, and power—onto the outer 'expert.' And while love and goodness is our very essence, it should go without saying that no matter how much wisdom I appear to have gained or spouted out this week, believe me, I am just like you: a human with all the frailties and fallibilities of our species. So, in that regard, I find it essential to have a clearer understanding of what is happening in the precious relationship between ourselves and a mentor."

I hold up a little book titled *Inner Gold*.[1]

"The Jungian analyst Robert Johnson understood the power of projection and therapeutic transference well. He acknowledges how we all at times need others to carry our 'inner gold.' When we are still unaware of our inner gold, or it still feels too mighty for us to carry it by ourselves, a spiritual guide can reflect and hold it for us until we are ready to re-claim it. There is nothing inherently wrong with projecting our inner gold onto others as long as both parties are conscious of this alchemical contract."

I pull out the bookmark and read Johnson's words aloud: "Carrying someone's gold is a fine art and a high responsibility. If you are the recipient of someone's gold, hold it carefully and be prepared to give it back within a microsecond's notice. Unfortunately, there are people who collect gold and refuse to give it back. It's a kind of murder. They collect an entourage or followers and exploit them."

I close the book and put it aside.

"So, in case you have been projecting your inner gold onto me during this week, I am not interested in keeping it. It never has been mine to begin with, so I would like you to take it back tonight during a fire ritual that we will have on the beach. In fact, for the rest of the day, I invite you to contemplate or journal about the question: *who have been my teachers, the mentors in my life?* Not just spiritual ones, but also the friends, therapists, lovers, colleagues, or bosses who taught you valuable lessons. Good lessons as well as the ones that taught you what not to repeat. To whom have you given over your innate authority and light? Are any of these people still carrying your gold? And then I would like you to go out and gather little sticks and twigs from the ground. Find

1 Robert A. Johnson, *Inner Gold* (Koa Books, 2017).

a stick for each of your teachers—and tonight, you will burn them in the fire. We all will release our projections and own our inner gold."

There is often one participant who asks, "Just to make sure: should I also burn you in the fire tonight?"

"Yes, do us both a favor!"

We share a hearty laugh.

Sources

- Allione, Lama Tsultrim. *Wisdom Rising: Journey Into the Mandala of the Empowered Feminine.* Atria/Enliven Books, 2018.
- Buber, Martin. *The Legend of the Baal-Shem.* Princeton University Press, 1995.
- Carver, Raymond. *A New Path to the Waterfall: Poems.* Atlantic Monthly Press, 1989.
- Chödrön, Pema. *When Things Fall Apart: Heart Advice for Difficult Times*. Shambhala, 2005.
- Dass, Ram. *Words of Wisdom: Quotations from One of the World's Foremost Spiritual Teachers*. Mandala Publishing, 2023.
- Erdrich, Louise. *The Painted Drum.* HarperCollins, 2009.
- Falter-Barnes, Suzanne. *How Much Joy Can You Stand? How to Push Past Your Fears and Create Your Dreams.* Beyond Words Pub Co; English Language edition, 1999.
- Jenkins, Elizabeth B. *The Fourth Level: Nature Wisdom Teachings of the Inka.* Pu'umaka'a Press, 2013.
- Levine, Stephen. *A Gradual Awakening*. Knopf Doubleday Publishing Group, 2010.
- Lorde, Audre. *The Cancer Journals.* Aunt Lute Books, 1980.
- Minium, Alice. *I Said No.* https://medium.com/@aliceminium/i-said-no-b7247c618292, 2018.

- Occelli, Cynthia. *Resurrecting Venus: Embracing Your Feminine Power*. Agape Media International, 2014.
- O'Donohue, John. *Conamara Blues: Poems*. HarperCollins, 2009.
- O'Hara, Pat Enkyo. *Most Intimate: A Zen Approach to Life's Challenges*. Shambhala, 2014.
- Ostaseski, Frank. *The Five Invitations: Discovering What Death Can Teach Us About Living Fully.* Flatiron Books, 2017.
- Real, Terrence. *How Can I Get Through to You? Reconnecting Men and Women.* Scribner, 2002.
- Rilke, Rainer Maria. *Letters to a Young Poet.* Translated by M. D. Herter Norton. W. W. Norton, 1993.
- Rinpoche, Tenzin Wangyal. *The Tibetan Yogas of Dream and Sleep: Practices for Awakening.* Shambhala, 2022.
- Rinpoche, Tsoknyi, and Eric Swanson. *Open Heart, Open Mind: Awakening the Power of Essence Love.* Harmony/Rodale, 2012.
- Siegel, MD, Dan. *The Neurobiology of Trauma,* NICABM Treating Trauma Master Series.
- Trungpa, Chögyam. *Cutting Through Spiritual Materialism*. Shambhala, 2002.
- Vaughan-Lee, Llewellyn. *The Return of the Feminine and the World Soul.* Golden Sufi Center, 2009.
- Vernick, Leslie. *The Emotionally Destructive Relationship: Seeing It, Stopping It, Surviving It.* Harvest House Publishers, 2007.
- Wallace, David Foster. *The Last Interview Expanded with New Introduction: And Other Conversations.* Melville House, 2018.

We are

Monkfish Book Publishing

...an independent press publishing spiritual and literary books from a diverse range of perspectives. Genres include memoirs, wisdom literature, fiction, and scholarly works of thought. Monkfish books appeal to the seasoned or novice seeker as well as to the general public looking for reliable sources on spirituality. The readers we had in mind when we began Monkfish in 2002 were devoted spiritual seekers, the type whose passion for the spiritual quest would lead them to read across a dazzling array of traditions: Buddhist, Hindu, Jewish, Christian, Muslim, Native American and more. It has always been our intent to publish works of spiritual authenticity for the general public as well as the specialist and scholar.

Our books are available from booksellers everywhere.

Use this QR code to see recently published books:

Use this one to sign-up for our monthly newsletter:

www.ingramcontent.com/pod-product-compliance
Lightning Source LLC
Jackson TN
JSHW020855080925
89953JS00003B/2